Reader's Guide
to
G.G. LORD BYRON

Reader's Guide
to
G.G. LORD BYRON

W. Cormier

CENTRUM PRESS
NEW DELHI-110002 (INDIA)

CENTRUM PRESS
H.O.: 4360/4, Ansari Road, Daryaganj,
New Delhi-110 002 (India)
Ph.: 23278000, 23261597

B.O.: No. 1015, Ist Main Road, BSK IIIrd Stage
IIIrd Phase, IIIrd Block,
Bangalore - 560 085 (India)
Tel.: 080-41723429
Visit us at: www.centrumpress.com

Reader's Guide to G.G. Lord Byron

First Edition, 2009

ISBN 978-93-80106-61-8

PRINTED IN INDIA

Printed at Salasar Imaging Systems, Delhi-110035 (India)

Contents

Preface

George Gordon Byron came of an ancient line who traced descent from a long line of soldiers back to the Conquest; and in 1643 had obtained a peerage for services in the civil war. During the 18th century the Byrons were distinguished as seamen, as spendthrifts, and debauchees. Suffice to say that it is the story of splendid genius and a truly noble nature, stained though not ruined by vice, egoism, and some paltry desires. But a spirit capable of such intense and enduring love, of such passion for great causes and high endeavours, of so much courage, generosity, and sympathy, and a life flung with such stormy energy into an ideal world of mighty and passionate beings—wipe out the memory of the sensualities which scandalise many and the meanness and affectation which have exercised so many over-busy pens.

Byron's first poems were published at the age of 19; his travels began at the age of 21; he left England forever at the age of 28; the next eight years of his life were memorable for their prodigious poetic activity, and within them almost all his main work was done; he died during the war of Greek Independence at Missolonghi, April 1824, aged 36. His ashes lie with his ancestors in Hucknall-Torkard Church, Nottinghamshire. He never seems to have realised the art of poetry as a mysterious alembic of musical language; but he poured out a torrent of impetuous thoughts in verse with the same reckless profusion as did Scott in prose. And both, we are now told, gave us rank commonplace, because they spoke in hot haste, using the first phrase that rose to the lip.

Author

Chapter 1

Introduction

George Gordon Byron, later Noel, 6th Baron Byron FRS (22 January 1788 – 19 April 1824) was a British poet and a leading figure in Romanticism. Amongst Byron's best-known works are the brief poems *When We Two Parted, She Walks in Beauty,* and *So, we'll go no more a roving,* in addition to the narrative poems *Childe Harold's Pilgrimage* and *Don Juan*. He is regarded as one of the greatest European poets and remains widely read and influential, both in the English-speaking world and beyond.

Byron's fame rests not only on his writings but also on his life, which featured extravagant living, numerous love affairs, debts, separation, and marital exploits. He was famously described by Lady Caroline Lamb as "mad, bad, and dangerous to know". Byron served as a regional leader of Italy's revolutionary organization, the Carbonari, in its struggle against Austria. He later traveled to fight against the Ottoman Empire in the Greek War of Independence, for which Greeks revere him as a national hero. He died from a fever in Messolonghi in Greece.

EARLY LIFE

Byron was born in a house on Hollis Street in London, the son of Captain John "Mad Jack" Byron and his second wife, the former Catherine Gordon, heiress of Gight in Aberdeenshire, Scotland. Byron's paternal grandparents were Vice-Admiral John "Foulweather Jack" Byron and Sophia Trevanion. Vice Admiral John Byron had circumnavigated the globe and was the younger brother of the 5th Baron Byron, known as "the Wicked Lord". He was christened George Gordon at St Marylebone Parish Church, after his maternal grandfather, George Gordon of Gight, a descendant of King James I. This grandfather committed suicide in 1779. Byron's mother Catherine had to sell her land and title to pay her husband's debts. John Byron may have married Catherine for her money and, after squandering it, deserted her. Catherine regularly experienced mood swings and bouts of melancholy.

Catherine moved back to Scotland shortly afterward, where she raised her son in Aberdeen. On 21 May 1798, the death of Byron's great-uncle, the "wicked" Lord Byron, made the 10-year-old the 6th Baron Byron, inheriting the title and estate, Newstead Abbey, in Nottinghamshire, England. His mother proudly took him to England.

Byron only lived at his estate infrequently as the Abbey was rented to Lord Grey de Ruthyn, among others, during Byron's adolescence. In August 1799, Byron entered the school of William Glennie, an Aberdonian in Dulwich. Byron would later say that around this time and beginning when he still lived in Scotland, his governess, May Gray, would come to bed with him at night and "play tricks with his person".

According to Byron, this "caused the anticipated melancholy of my thoughts—having anticipated life". Gray was dismissed for allegedly beating Byron when he was 11. Byron received his early formal education at Aberdeen Grammar School. In 1801 he was sent to Harrow, where he remained until July 1805. He represented Harrow during the very first Eton v Harrow cricket match at Lord's in 1805.[8] After school he went on to Trinity College, Cambridge.

Byron's names changed throughout his life. He was christened "George Gordon Byron" in London. "Gordon" was a baptismal name, not a surname, honouring his maternal grandfather. In order to claim his wife's estate in Scotland, Byron's father took the additional surname "Gordon", becoming "John Byron Gordon", and he was occasionally styled "John Byron Gordon of Gight". Byron himself used this surname for a time and was registered at school in Aberdeen as "George Byron Gordon". At the age of 10, he inherited the

English Barony of Byron, becoming "Lord Byron", and eventually dropped the double surname (though after this point his surname was hidden by his peerage in any event).

When Byron's mother-in-law died, her will required that he change his surname to "Noel" in order to inherit half her estate, and so he obtained a Royal Warrant allowing him to "take and use the surname of Noel only". Very unusually, the Royal Warrant also allowed him to "subscribe the said surname of Noel before all titles of honour", and from that point he signed himself "Noel Byron" (the usual signature of a peer being merely the peerage, in this case simply "Byron").

He was also sometimes referred to as "Lord Noel Byron", as if "Noel" were part of his title, and likewise his wife was sometimes called "Lady Noel Byron". Lady Byron eventually succeeded to the Barony of Wentworth, becoming "Lady Wentworth"; her surname before marriage had been "Milbanke".

EARLY CAREER

While not at school or college, Byron lived with his mother at Burgage Manor in Southwell, Nottinghamshire in some antagonism. While there, he cultivated friendships with Elizabeth Pigot and her brother, John, with whom he staged two plays for the entertainment of the community.

During this time, with the help of Elizabeth Pigot, who copied many of his rough drafts, he was encouraged to write his first volumes of poetry. *Fugitive Pieces* was the first, printed by Ridge of Newark, which contained poems written when Byron was only 14.

However, it was promptly recalled and burned on the advice of his friend, the Reverend Thomas Beecher, on account of its more amorous verses, particularly the poem *To Mary*. *Pieces on Various Occasions*, a "miraculously chaste" revision according to Byron, was published after this.

Hours of Idleness, which collected many of the previous poems, along with more recent compositions, was the culminating book. The savage, anonymous criticism this received (now known to be the work of Henry Peter

Brougham) in the *Edinburgh Review* prompted his first major satire, *English Bards and Scotch Reviewers* (1809).

The work so upset some of these critics they challenged Byron to a duel; over time, in subsequent editions, it became a mark of prestige to be the target of Byron's pen. After his return from his travels, the first two cantos of Childe Harold's Pilgrimage were published in 1812, and were received with acclaim.

In his own words, "I awoke one morning and found myself famous". He followed up his success with the poem's last two cantos, as well as four equally celebrated Oriental Tales, The Giaour, The Bride of Abydos, The Corsair, and Lara, which established the Byronic hero. About the same time, he began his intimacy with his future biographer, Thomas Moore.

PERSONAL LIFE

A more complete picture of Byron's personal life has only been possible in recent years with the freeing up of the archive of John Murray, Byron's original publishers, which had formerly withheld compromising letters and instructed at least one major biographer (Leslie A. Marchand, 1957) to censor details of his bisexuality.

Byron's first loves included Mary Duff and Margaret Parker, his distant cousins, and Mary Chaworth, whom he met while at Harrow. Byron later wrote that his passion for Duff began when he was "not [yet] eight years old" and was still unforgettable in 1813.

Byron refused to return to Harrow in September 1803 due to his love for Chaworth; his mother wrote, "He has no indisposition that I know of but love, desperate love, the worst of all maladies in my opinion. In short, the boy is distractedly in love with Miss Chaworth." In Byron's later memoirs, "Mary Chaworth is portrayed as the first object of his adult sexual feelings." He returned to Harrow in January 1804 to a more settled period which saw the formation of a circle of emotional involvements with other Harrow boys recalled with great vividness: 'My School friendships were with *me passions* (for I was always violent).'

The most enduring of those was with the John FitzGibbon, 2nd Earl of Clare — four years Byron's junior — whom he was to meet unexpectedly many years later in Italy (1821), to great intensity of feeling. His nostalgic poems about his Harrow friendships, 'Childish Recollections' (1806), express a sense of melancholy at the passing of youthful freedoms, even a prescient 'consciousness of sexual differences that may in the end make England untenable to him.'

"Ah! Sure some stronger impulse vibrates here,
Which whispers friendship will be doubly dear
To one, who thus for kindred hearts must roam,
And seek abroad, the love denied at home."

While at Trinity, he met and formed a close friendship with a fifteen year old choirboy by the name of John Edleston. About his "protégé" he wrote, "He has been my almost constant associate since October, 1805, when I entered Trinity College. His voice first attracted my attention, his countenance fixed it, and his manners attached me to him for ever." In his memory Byron composed *Thyrza,* a series of elegies. Byron wore a ring of Edleston's for the 13 years until he died. In later years he described the affair as 'a violent, though *pure* love and passion'.

This however has to be read in the context of hardening public attitudes to homosexuality in England and the severe sanctions (including public hanging) against convicted or suspected offenders. The liaison on the other hand may well have been 'pure' out of respect for Edleston's innocence, in contrast to the (probably) more sexually overt relations experienced at Harrow School.

AFFAIRS AND SCANDALS

In an early scandal, Byron embarked in 1812 on a well-publicized affair with the married Lady Caroline Lamb that shocked the British public. Byron eventually broke off the relationship, but Lamb never entirely recovered, pursuing him even after he tired of her. She was emotionally disturbed and lost so much weight that Byron cruelly commented to her mother-in-law, his friend Lady Melbourne, that he was "haunted by a skeleton". She began to call on him at home, sometimes dressed in disguise as a page boy, at a time when such an act could ruin both of them socially. One day, during such a visit, she wrote on a book at his desk, "Remember me!" As a retort, Byron wrote a poem entitled Remember Thee!

Remember Thee! which concludes with the line "Thou false to him, thou fiend to me". As a child, Byron had seen little of his half-sister Augusta Leigh; in adulthood, he formed a close relationship with her that has been interpreted by some as incestuous and by others as innocent. Augusta (who was married) gave birth on 15 April 1814 to her third daughter, Elizabeth Medora Leigh. Eventually Byron began to court Lady Caroline's cousin Anne Isabella Milbanke ("Annabella"), who refused his first proposal of marriage but later accepted. They married at Seaham Hall, County Durham, on 2 January 1815. The marriage proved unhappy.

He treated her poorly and showed disappointment at the birth of a daughter (Augusta Ada) rather than a son. On 16 January 1816, Lady Byron left him, taking Ada with her. On 21 April, Byron signed the Deed of Separation. Rumours of marital violence, adultery with actresses, incest with Augusta Leigh, and sodomy were circulated, assisted by a jealous Lady Caroline. In a letter, Augusta quoted him as saying: "Even to have such a thing said is utter destruction & ruin to a man from which he can never recover."

FIRST TRAVELS TO THE EAST

Byron racked up numerous debts as a young adult due to what his mother termed a reckless disregard for money. She lived at Newstead during this time, in fear of her son's creditors. From 1809 to 1811, Byron went on the Grand Tour then customary for a young nobleman. The Napoleonic Wars forced him to avoid most of Europe, and he instead turned to the Mediterranean. Correspondence among his circle of Cambridge friends also suggests that a key motive was the hope of homosexual experience, and other theories saying that he was worried about a possible dalliance with the married Mary Chatsworth, his former love (the subject of his poem from this time, "To a Lady: On Being Asked My Reason for Quitting England in the Spring"). He travelled from England over Spain to Albania and spent time at the court of Ali Pasha of Ioannina, and in Athens. For most of the trip, he had a traveling companion in his friend John Cam Hobhouse.

While in Athens, Byron met Nicolò Giraud, who became quite close and taught him Italian. Byron sent Giraud to school at a monastery in Malta and bequeathed him a sizable sum of seven thousand pounds sterling. The will, however, was later cancelled.

LATER LOVE LIFE

After this break-up of his domestic life Byron again left England, forever as it turned out. He passed through Belgium and continued up the Rhine River. In the summer of 1816 he settled at the Villa Diodati by Lake Geneva, Switzerland with his personal physician, John William Polidori. There Byron befriended the poet Percy Bysshe Shelley, and Shelley's future wife Mary Godwin.

He was also joined by Mary's stepsister, Claire Clairmont, with whom he had had an affair in London. Byron initially refused to have anything to do with Claire, and would only agree to remain in her presence with the Shelleys, who eventually persuaded Byron to accept and provide for Allegra, the child she bore him in January 1817.

Kept indoors at the Villa Diodati by the "incessant rain" of "that wet, ungenial summer" over three days in June, the five turned to reading fantastical stories, including *Fantasmagoriana*, and then devising their own tales. Mary Shelley produced what would become *Frankenstein, or The Modern Prometheus* and Polidori was inspired by a fragmentary story of Byron's to produce *The Vampyre*, the progenitor of the romantic vampire genre. Byron's story fragment was published as a postscript to *Mazeppa;* he also wrote the third canto of *Childe Harold*. Byron wintered in Venice, pausing his travels when he fell in love with Marianna Segati, in whose Venice house he was lodging, and who was soon replaced by 22-year-old Margarita Cogni; both women were married.

Cogni could not read or write, and she left her husband to move into Byron's Venice house. Their fighting often caused Byron to spend the night in his gondola; when he asked her to leave the house, she threw herself into the Venetian canal.

In 1817, he journeyed to Rome. On returning to Venice, he wrote the fourth canto of *Childe Harold*. About the same time, he sold Newstead and published *Manfred, Cain,* and *The Deformed Transformed*.

The first five cantos of *Don Juan* were written between 1818 and 1820, during which period he made the acquaintance of the young Countess Guiccioli, who found her first love in Byron, who in turn asked her to elope with him. It was about this time that he received a visit from Thomas Moore, to whom he confided his autobiography or "life and adventures", which Moore, Hobhouse and Byron's publisher, John Murray, burned in 1824, a month after Byron's death.

CHILDREN

Byron had a child, The Hon. Ada Augusta Byron (later Countess of Lovelace), in 1815 with Augusta Ada Byron, Lady Byron (*née* Anne Isabella Milbanke, or "Annabella"), later Lady Wentworth.

Ada Lovelace, notable in her own right, collaborated with Charles Babbage on the analytical engine, a predecessor to modern computers. He also had an illegitimate child in 1817, Clara Allegra Noel-Byron, with Claire Clairmont, stepsister of Mary Shelley and stepdaughter of *Political Justice* and *Caleb Williams* writer, William Godwin:

Allegra is not entitled to the style "The Hon." as is usually given to the daughter of barons since she was illegitimate. Born in Switzerland in 1817, Allegra lived with Byron for a few months in Venice; he refused to allow an Englishwoman caring for the girl to adopt her, nor for her to be raised in the Shelleys' household. He wished for her to be brought up Catholic and not marry an Englishman.

He made arrangements for her to inherit 5,000 lira upon marriage or reaching age 21, provided she did not marry a native of Britain. However, the girl died at five years old of a fever in Bagna Cavallo, Italy while Byron was in Pisa; he was deeply upset by the news. He had Allegra's body sent back to England to be buried at his old school, Harrow, because Protestants could not be buried in consecrated ground in Catholic countries. At one time he himself had wanted to be buried at Harrow. Byron was indifferent towards Allegra's mother, Claire Clairmont.

POLITICAL CAREER

Byron eventually took his seat in the House of Lords in 1811, shortly after his return from the Levant, and made his first speech there on 27 February 1812. A strong advocate of social reform, he received particular praise as one of the few Parliamentary defenders of the Luddites: specifically, he was against a death penalty for Luddite "frame breakers" in Nottinghamshire, who destroyed textile machines that were putting them out of work.

His first speech before the Lords was loaded with sarcastic references to the "benefits" of automation, which he saw as producing inferior material as well as putting people out of work. He said later that he "spoke very violent sentences with a sort of modest impudence" and thought he came across as "a bit theatrical".

In another Parliamentary speech he expressed opposition to the established religion because it was unfair to people of other faiths. These experiences inspired Byron to write political poems such as *Song for the Luddites* (1816) and *The Landlords' Interest*, Canto XIV of *The Age of Bronze*. Examples of poems in which he attacked his political opponents include *Wellington: The Best of the Cut-Throats* (1819) and *The Intellectual Eunuch Castlereagh* (1818).

LIFE ABROAD

Reasons for Byron's Departure

Ultimately, Byron resolved to escape the censure of British society (due to allegations of sodomy and incest) by living abroad, thereby freeing himself of the need to conceal his sexual interests. Byron left England in 1816 and did not return for the last eight years of his life, even to bury his daughter.

Byron and the Armenians in Venice

In 1816, Byron visited Saint Lazarus Island in Venice where he acquainted himself with Armenian culture through the Mekhitarist Order. He learned the Armenian language from Fr. H. Avgerian and attended many seminars about language and history. He wrote *English grammar and the Armenian* in 1817, and *Armenian grammar and the English* (1819) in which he quoted samples from classical and modern Armenian.

He participated in the compilation of the *English Armenian dictionary* (1821) and wrote the preface where he explained the relationship of the Armenians with and the oppression of the Turkish "pashas" and the Persian satraps, and their struggle of liberation. His two main translations are the *Epistle of Paul to the Corinthians*, several chapters of Khorenatsi's *Armenian History* and sections of Lambronatsi's *Orations*.

When in Polis he discovered discrepancies in the Armenian vs. the English version of the Bible and translated some passages that were either missing or deficient in the English version. His fascination was so great that he even considered a replacement of Cain story of the Bible with that of the legend of Armenian patriarch Haik. He may be credited with the birth of Armenology and its propagation. His profound lyricism and ideological courage has inspired many Armenian poets, the likes of Fr. Ghevond Alishan, Smbat Shahaziz, Hovhannes Tumanyan, Ruben Vorberian and others. Byron had a bust sculpted of him by Bertel Thorvaldsen at this time.

BYRON IN ITALY AND GREECE

From 1821 to 1822, he finished Cantos 6–12 of *Don Juan* at Pisa, and in the same year he joined with Leigh Hunt and Percy Bysshe Shelley in starting a short-lived newspaper, *The Liberal*, in the first number of which appeared *The Vision of Judgment*.

His last Italian home was Genoa, where he was still accompanied by the Countess Guiccioli, and where he met Charles John Gardiner, 1st Earl of Blessington and Marguerite, Countess of Blessington and provided the material for her work *Conversations with Lord Byron,* an important text in the reception of Byron in the period immediately after his death.

Byron lived in Genoa until 1823 when, growing bored with his life there and with the Countess, he accepted overtures for his support from representatives of the movement for Greek independence from the Ottoman Empire. On 16 July, Byron left Genoa on the *Hercules,* arriving at Kefalonia in the Ionian Islands on 4 August.

He spent £4000 of his own money to refit the Greek fleet, then sailed for Messolonghi in western Greece, arriving on 29 December to join Alexandros Mavrokordatos, a Greek politician with military power. During this time, Byron pursued his Greek page, Lukas Chalandritsanos, but the affections went unrequited. When the famous Danish sculptor Thorvaldsen heard about Byron's heroics in Greece, he voluntarily resculpted his earlier bust of Byron in Greek marble.

DEATH

Mavrokordatos and Byron planned to attack the Turkish-held fortress of Lepanto, at the mouth of the Gulf of Corinth. Byron employed a fire-master to prepare artillery and took part of the rebel army under his own command and pay, despite his lack of military experience, but before the expedition could sail, on 15 February 1824, he fell ill, and the usual remedy of bleeding weakened him further.

He made a partial recovery, but in early April he caught a violent cold which therapeutic bleeding, insisted on by his doctors, aggravated.

It is suspected this treatment, carried out with unsterilized medical instrumentation may have caused him to develop sepsis.

He developed a violent fever, and died on 19 April. It has

been said that had Byron lived, he might have been declared King of Greece.

POST MORTEM

Alfred, Lord Tennyson would later recall the shocked reaction in Britain when word was received of Byron's death. The Greeks mourned Lord Byron deeply, and he became a hero. The national poet of Greece, Dionysios Solomos, wrote a poem about his unexpected loss, named *To the Death of Lord Byron*. Âýñùí ("Vyron"), the Greek form of "Byron", continues in popularity as a masculine name in Greece, and a suburb of Athens is called Vyronas in his honour.

Byron's body was embalmed, but the Greeks wanted some part of their hero to stay with them. According to some sources, his heart remained at Messolonghi. According to others, it was his lungs, which were placed in an urn that was later lost when the city was sacked. His other remains were sent to England for burial in Westminster Abbey, but the Abbey refused for reason of "questionable morality".

Huge crowds viewed his body as he lay in state for two days in London. He is buried at the Church of St. Mary Magdalene in Hucknall, Nottingham. At her request, Ada Lovelace, the child he never knew, was buried next to him. In later years, the Abbey allowed a duplicate of a marble slab given by the King of Greece, which is laid directly above Byron's grave.

Byron's friends raised the sum of 1,000 pounds to commission a statue of the writer; Thorvaldsen offered to sculpt it for that amount. However, for 10 years after the statue was completed in 1834, most British institutions turned it down while it remained in storage: the British Museum, St. Paul's Cathedral, Westminster Abbey and the National Gallery. Trinity College, Cambridge finally placed the statue of Byron in its library.

In 1969, 145 years after Byron's death, a memorial to him was finally placed in Westminster Abbey. Robert Ripley had drawn a picture of Boatswain's grave with the caption "Lord Byron's dog has a magnificent tomb while Lord Byron himself has none". This came as a shock to the English, particularly schoolchildren, who, Ripley said, raised funds of their own accord to provide the poet with a suitable memorial.

The memorial had been lobbied for since 1907; *The New York Times* wrote, "People are beginning to ask whether this ignoring of Byron is not a thing of which England should be ashamed... a bust or a tablet might put in the Poets' Corner and England be relieved of ingratitude toward one of her really great sons." Upon his death, the barony passed to Byron's cousin George Anson Byron, a career military officer and his polar opposite in temperament and lifestyle.

POETIC WORKS

Byron wrote prolifically. In 1833 his publisher, John Murray, released the complete works in 17 duodecimo volumes, including a life by Thomas Moore. Although Byron falls chronologically into the period most commonly associated with Romantic poetry, much of his work looks back to the satiric tradition of Alexander Pope and John Dryden.

DON JUAN

Byron's magnum opus, *Don Juan,* a poem spanning 17 cantos, ranks as one of the most important long poems published in England since Milton's *Paradise Lost.* The masterpiece, often called the epic of its time, has roots deep in literary tradition and, although regarded by early Victorians as somewhat shocking, equally involves itself with its own contemporary world at all levels—social, political, literary and ideological.

Byron published the first two cantos anonymously in 1819 after disputes with his regular publisher. over the shocking nature of the poetry; by this time, he had been a famous poet for seven years and when he self-published the beginning cantos, they were well-received in some quarters. It was then released volume by volume through his regular publishing house. By 1822, cautious acceptance by the public had turned to outrage, and Byron's publisher refused to continue to publish the works. In Canto III of *Don Juan,* Byron expresses his detestation for poets such as William Wordsworth and Samuel Taylor Coleridge.

Byronic Hero

The figure of the Byronic hero pervades much of his work, and Byron himself is considered to epitomize many of the characteristics of this literary figure. Scholars have traced the literary history of the Byronic hero from John Milton, and many authors and artists of the Romantic Movement show Byron's influence during the 19th century and beyond, including Charlotte and Emily Bronte.

The Byronic hero presents an idealised but flawed character whose attributes include: having great talent, exhibiting great passion, having a distaste for society and social institutions, expressing a lack of respect for rank and privilege, thwarted in love by social constraint or death, rebelling, suffering exile, hiding an unsavoury past, arrogance, overconfidence or lack of foresight, and ultimately, acting in a self-destructive manner.

Parthenon Marbles

Byron was a bitter opponent of Lord Elgin's removal of the Parthenon marbles from Greece, and "reacted with fury" when Elgin's agent gave him a tour of the Parthenon in which he saw the missing friezes and metopes. He penned a poem, *The Curse of Minerva,* to denounce Elgin's actions.

Character and Description

Lord Byron obtained a reputation as being extravagant, melancholy, courageous, unconventional, eccentric, flamboyant and controversial. He was independent and given to extremes of temper; on at least one trip, his traveling companions were so puzzled by his mood swings they thought he was mentally ill. He enjoyed adventure, especially relating to the sea.

He believed his depression was inherited, and he wrote in 1821, "I am not sure that long life is desirable for one of my temper & constitutional depression of Spirits." Byron was noted even during his time for the extreme loyalty he inspired in his friends. Hobhouse said, "No man lived who had such devoted friends."

Physical Description

Byron's adult height was about 5 feet 10 inches (1.78 m), his weight fluctuating between 9.5 stone (133 lb, 60 kg) and 14 stone (200 lb, 89 kg). He was renowned for his personal beauty, which he enhanced by wearing curl-papers in his hair at night. He was athletic, being a competent boxer and an excellent swimmer.

At Harrow, he played cricket despite his lameness. From birth, Byron suffered from an unknown deformity of his right foot, causing a limp that resulted in lifelong misery for him, aggravated by the suspicion that with proper care it might have been cured. However, he refused to wear any type of mechanical device that could improve the limp, although he often wore specially made shoes that would hide the deformed foot.

Byron and other writers such as his friend John Cam Hobhouse left detailed descriptions of his eating habits. From the time that he entered Cambridge he went on a strict diet to control his weight. He also exercised a great deal and at that time wore a great number of clothes to cause himself to perspire.

For most of his life he was a vegetarian and often lived for days on dry biscuits and white wine. Occasionally he would eat large helpings of meat and desserts, after which he would purge himself. His friend Hobhouse claimed that when he became overweight, the pain of his deformed foot made it difficult for him to exercise.

Celebrity

Byron is considered to be the first modern-style celebrity. His image as his own Byronic hero personified fascinated the public, and his wife Annabella coined the term "Byromania" to refer to the mania surrounding him. His self-awareness and personal promotion are seen as a beginning to what would become the modern rock star; he would instruct artists painting portraits of him not to paint him with pen or book in hand, but as a "man of action". While Byron first welcomed fame, he later turned away from it by going into voluntary exile from Britain.

Fondness for animals

Byron had a great fondness for animals, most famously for a Newfoundland dog named Boatswain; when Boatswain contracted rabies, Byron reportedly nursed him without any fear of becoming bitten and infected. Boatswain lies buried at Newstead Abbey and has a monument larger than his master's. Byron at one point expressed interest in being buried next to Boatswain. The inscription, Byron's *Epitaph to a Dog,* has become one of his best-known works, reading in part:

Near this Spot
are deposited the Remains of one
who possessed Beauty without Vanity,
Strength without Insolence,
Courage without Ferosity,
and all the Virtues of Man without his Vices.
This praise, which would be unmeaning Flattery
if inscribed over human Ashes,
is but a just tribute to the Memory of
BOATSWAIN, a DOG,
who was born in Newfoundland May 1803,
and died at Newstead Nov.ʳ 18th, 1808.

Byron also kept a bear while he was a student at Trinity College, Cambridge (reputedly out of resentment of Trinity rules forbidding pet dogs — he later suggested that the bear apply for a college fellowship). At other times in his life, Byron kept a fox, monkeys, a parrot, cats, an eagle, a crow, a crocodile, a falcon, peacocks, guinea hens, an Egyptian crane, a badger, geese, a heron, and a bear.

Lasting influence

The re-founding of the Byron Society in 1971 reflects the

fascination that many people have for Byron and his work. This society has become very active, publishing a learned annual journal. Today some 36 Byron Societies function throughout the world, and an International Conference takes place annually. Hardly a year passes without a new book about the poet appearing. In the last 20 years, two new feature films about him have screened, and a television play has been broadcast.

Byron exercised a marked influence on Continental literature and art, and his reputation as a poet is higher in many European countries than in Britain or America, although not as high as in his time, when he was widely thought to be the greatest poet in the world. Byron has inspired the works of Franz Liszt and Giuseppe Verdi.

Fictional depictions

Byron first appeared as a thinly disguised fictional character in his ex-love Lady Caroline Lamb's book *Glenarvon,* published in 1816. Byron is the main character of the film *Byron* by the Greek film maker Nikos Koundouros. Byron's spirit is one of the title characters of the *Ghosts of Albion* books by Amber Benson and Christopher Golden, published by Del Rey in 2005 and 2006.

Byron is an immortal still alive in modern times in the hit television show Highlander: The Series in the fifth season episode The Modern Prometheus, living as a decadent rock star. John Crowley's novel Lord Byron's Novel: The Evening Land At Night (2005) involves the rediscovery of a lost manuscript by Lord Byron, as does Frederic Prokosch's The Missolonghi *Manuscript* (1968).

Tom Holland, in his 1995 novel *The Vampyre,* romantically describes how Lord Byron became a vampire during his first visit to Greece — a fictional transformation that explains much of his subsequent behaviour towards family and friends, and finds support in quotes from Byron poems and the diaries of John Cam Hobhouse.

It is written as though Byron is retelling part of his life to his great great-great-great-granddaughter. He describes traveling in Greece, Italy, Switzerland, meeting Percy Bysshe Shelley, Shelley's death and many other events in life around that time. The Byron as vampire character returns in the 1996 sequel *Supping with Panthers*.

Byron appears as a character in Tim Powers's *The Stress of Her Regard* (1989) and Walter Jon Williams's novella *Wall, Stone Craft* (1994), and also in Susanna Clarke's *Jonathan Strange & Mr Norrell* (2004). Byron and Percy and Mary Shelley are portrayed in Roger Corman's final film *Frankenstein Unbound*, where the time traveler Dr. Buchanan (played by John Hurt) meets them as well as Victor von Frankenstein (played by Raul Julia).

The Black Drama by Manly Wade Wellman, originally published in Weird Tales, involves the rediscovery and production of a lost play by Byron (from which Polidori's *The Vampyre* was plagiarised) by a man who purports to be a descendant of the poet. Tom Stoppard's play *Arcadia* revolves around a modern researcher's attempts to find out what made Byron leave the country.

Television portrayals include a major 2003 BBC drama on Byron's life, and minor appearances in *Highlander: The Series* (as well as the Shelleys), *Blackadder the Third, The Grim Adventures of Billy and Mandy*, and episode 60 (Darkling) of *Star Trek: Voyager*. He makes an appearance in the alternative history novel *The Difference Engine* by William Gibson and Bruce Sterling. In a Britain powered by the massive, steam-driven, mechanical computers invented by Charles Babbage, he is leader of the *Industrial Radical Party*, eventually becoming Prime Minister.

The events featuring the Shelleys' and Byron's relationship at the house beside Lake Geneva in 1816 have been fictionalized in film at least three times.

- A 1986 British production, *Gothic*, directed by Ken Russell, and starring Gabriel Byrne as Byron.
- A 1988 Spanish production, *Rowing with the Wind* (*Remando al viento*), starring Hugh Grant as Byron.
- A 1988 U.S.A. production *Haunted Summer*. Adapted by Lewis John Carlino from the speculative novel by Anne Edwards, staring Philip Anglim as Lord Byron.

The brief prologue to *Bride of Frankenstein* includes Gavin Gordon as Byron, begging Mary Shelley to tell the rest of her Frankenstein story. The writer and novelist, Benjamin Markovits, is in the process of producing a fictional trilogy about the life of Byron. *Imposture* (2007) looked at the poet via his friend and doctor,

John Polidori. *A Quiet Adjustment,* which came out in January 2008, is an account of Byron's marriage more sympathetic to his wife, Annabella, than many of its predecessors. He is currently writing the third installment. Byron is portrayed as an immortal in the book, *Divine Fire,* by Melanie Jackson.

In Episode 50 *Ecto Cooler* (Season 5) of *The Grim Adventures Of Billy And Mandy* the ghost of Lord Byron appears from Billy's mouth and teaches him to be cool, with disastrous results. Byron is depicted in the book *Edward Trencom's Nose* by Giles Milton. Byron is depicted in Tennessee William's play *Camino Real.*

The biographies of literary men are not usually very interesting, except to those who are interested in the record and analysis of their works; they are mostly uneventful. But in some cases men combine action with contemplation. And in certain instances it is difficult to separate the man from his work; he puts so much of himself into it; it is so identified with his own experience. His contemporaries feel as much fascination in his personality as in what he writes. Then is there difficulty in following the counsel of Tennyson to keep silence about a poet's life:—

"No public life was his on earth, No blazon'd statesman he, nor king.

He gave the people of his best; His worst he kept, his best he gave. My Shakespeare's curse on clown and knave Who will not let his ashes rest! "

But neither Shakspeare, Dante, Tasso, Milton, nor

Spenser lived recluse student lives like Wordsworth. And for my own part I wish we knew a great deal more of Shakespeare's private history than we do. We should probably find a great deal of human nature in him, seeing that we find it in his work—in the sonnets, for instance. But ought we therefore to be very much shocked, and desire to hush all the falls and errors up? "No one is a hero to his valet, but that's the fault of the valet."

There is no use in feigning that the hero of your biography was a bloodless, featureless monster of abstract perfection. I am disposed to think indeed that, in *every case,* the life and work of a considerable writer are capable of throwing light mutually upon one another. In certain salient instances there can be no doubt at all that it is so. Who would wish to consider the Rowley poems apart from Chatterton, "the marvellous boy"?

And Burns, can we sever his character and career from his poetry? But no doubt the personality of some artists is recognized for something more than their art—I do not say greater, but more— while that of others (usually the "impeccable" artists perhaps) appears less.

Mere thinking-machines—philosophers, mathematicians — are not usually picturesque. But Byron, like Rousseau, was one who wished us to know a good deal about him, and took care that we should: he put himself forward. Emotion, imagination, the roving Berserker nature, Bohemianism, give colour. And he was possessed of a fascinating, arresting personality, of what Goethe called a "demonic personality." Here was more than an author; here was a man; whereas "mere artists are often man kins."

One must look generously, and with human sympathy, at the errors, not denying that they were such, or covering them up, but admitting fully the virtues also, and discerning that the specific quality, or idiosyncrasy, of such a man's creation is vitally related to his errors and weaknesses, even as also to whatsoever of strength and goodness belong to him. To deal thus with a great man's faults and vices is not to " disturb his ashes " in the spirit of "clown or knave," nor to cater (except accidentally) for the "many-headed beast's" unhealthy appetite for gossip and scandal; it is rather to try and understand a man who has done great things for his country and for Europe.

Whether the influence of this poet has been for good or evil will always be a debated point. But on Eckermann's doubting whether there is "a gain for pure culture" in Byron's work, Goethe replies:

"There I must contradict you. The audacity and grandeur of Byron must certainly tend towards culture. We should take care not to be always looking for it in the decidedly pure and moral. Everything that is great promotes cultivation, as soon as you are aware of it." And again he says profoundly: "Greatness is always formative"; or, to *adapt* a happy phrase of John Nichol: Byron "keeps the soul alive, if he does not save it."

But death is the dreadful thing, not life; while there is life there is hope. He is, like Burns, the poet of youth and passion, of enjoyment, of intense, vivid, physical life; that is one main element in his immense popularity. He tells simple tales in verse, before the epoch of novels.

He also clearly, and with unequalled vigour, expresses the *average* thought and feeling of his time, setting them to facile music; he does not soar over people's heads into some astral ether, like Shelley, nor dive into calm profundities beyond their cognizance, like Wordsworth. And then nothing succeeds like success. The bookseller, the editor, the *Brummagem* critic, and the general public are in love, not with the popular man, but with his popularity, that is, with the echoes of their own "sweet voices."

It then becomes a question of fashion only, and birthday presents to lie on drawing-room tables. But such a degraded view of Byron as Leigh Hunt took is manifestly absurd, because it fails to account for the *poetry, i.e.,* for the main product and staple of the man's own inmost self.

No true poet is a mere mechanical medium for inspiration from without. He *co-operates* with it, and is at his highest in producing. Lady Byron never showed her essential incompatibility with her husband more than when she said he "feigned enthusiasm." Nor could Trelawny penetrate behind his persiflage, which his own tone drew from Byron, little as he suspected it.When the Guiccioli (after becoming

Madame de Boissy) wrote to prove him a sheer seraph and saint, we need to put the hostile representations of his wife and others together with this, and those of his friends, to get an adequate portrait. "

Angel or demon?" Lamartine asked. I answer, a little of both. For seven years he must have turned the angel side of him toward Theresa Guiccioli; and we ought to give weight to what she tells us of his many virtues, *while allowing for the partiality of love.*

There is, undoubtedly, nourishment for the lower, as well as for the higher, faculties and desires of human nature, in this poetry. But that coinage is the more adapted for general circulation whose gold is tempered with alloy. Byron, indeed, is one of the poets whom Plato might have banished from his ideal republic. For Pride, Resentment, Anger, Lawless Pleasure have their niches in that temple, and serve to strengthen the dominion of earthly impulse over us. But then there is so much more.

There is the joy in all that is strong, energetic, brave, and determined—delight in "life, the mere living," joy in all beautiful and sublime things, pathos, and reverent love for external nature; hatred of and battle with the tyrant; pity for his victim, for the feeble, the outcast, and oppressed; scorn of hollow conventions, cant, and mere seeming propriety; withering satire, winged Apollonian shafts for the lay-figure virtues of our cruel English respectability.

But here the warrior and troubadour are one as of old, singer and doer. If this man sings to you of Greece and her woes, he also takes up arms in her cause, he dies in her defence; and so the active function harmonizes with, and adds fresh lustre to the contemplative.

There is the same turbid, troubled, impure element also in the poetry as in the life. The cynic, the man of the world, are appealed to by a writer who was a little of both, and derived strength from contact with his mother earth. The epigrams, the witty couplets and stinging sarcasms of one who could not always, I fear, appropriate to himself that noble boast of a yet greater poet,

"J'ai fait peur aux petits hommes, Jamais aux petits enfants!"

Have fascinated and amused cynical men and women of the world; and these were sometimes literary echoes from certain baser traits of his own character, certain muddy passages of his own experience. Young people, too, were taken by the romantic guise of the poet, by the mystery he affected, as also by his beauty, high birth, and becoming sadness. The young can be sad for very wantonness.

Nothing so dainty sweet as lovely melancholy! Byron "posed" charmingly in his stories; he obtruded sentimentally his private wrongs, and angled with alluring baits to secure public sympathy. But much of all this popularity was essentially factitious and illegitimate; and much was accidentally begotten of the poet's circumstances, and fashionable personality as peer and *parti*, put *en evidence*. This has faded with the man, and the hour. Newer, and flimsier literary fashions are now in vogue.

It was, on the whole, a credit to our anti-poetical English race that it took to Byron; though most of us perchance have been graciously pleased to condone his merits for the sake of his faults. Assuredly certain "lewd fellows of the baser sort," foul-feeders, feed upon the offal he provides "for the general" along with caviare for the few. How refreshing to the clumsy speculative intellect of the average Anglo-Saxon, which is all thumbs, that joke of Byron's about philosophic idealism:—

"When Bishop Berkeley said there was no matter, 'Twas no matter what he said."

"That's just what every fellow has always thought, don't you know, put so pat ! What clever fellows we are after all, and Byron quite agrees with us! *"Don Juan "*has been belittled by the foolish praise of little men. Yet a great proportion of the work was sincere and enduring.

Much of the scathing satire is legitimate, destructive to mean and evil things; much of the serious verse is elevating, ennobling, making for truth and justice, enlarging our outlook, quickening sensibility, intensifying, deepening, widening experience, bracing and nerving men to noble endeavour; while the book also provides them with abundant humour, with inexhaustible stores of wit and buffoonery—no despicable boon this in our heavy spleenful atmosphere of suicide-provoking fogs, for men treading their dull treadmill of daily work wearying rounds !

"No genuine good thought," says Carlyle, "was ever revealed by him to mankind." Yet Goethe observed to Eckermann, "A character of such eminence has never existed before, and probably will never come again; I did right to present him with that monument of love in Helena " (he is *Euphorion* in the second part of " Faust ") —" I could not make use of any man as the representative of the modern poetic era except him, who is undoubtedly to be regarded as the greatest talent of our century." But then Goethe also remarked, "He is a child when he begins to reflect."

Doubtless it is this very absence of profound original thought which suffers him to be carried along so lightly and freely, like a thistle-down, over extensive plains of the average mind, which is not a soil congenial to the germination of ideas—the average mind, which neither forgives, nor comprehends original thought.

But we must observe that Byron was the most eminent representative and mouthpiece of his age, which was an age of scepticism, denial, unrest, uprooting of established beliefs and institutions, as also of what the Germans call "world-sorrow," despair with oneself, and with the world around, in the absence of that faith which had heretofore afforded men film foothold amid overwhelming waves.

All things were questioned by the all-dissolving human reason, and such a general mood needed—needs even now—expression; the more powerful the better. Questioning and denial are the inevitable condition of future synthesis, of larger comprehension, more pregnant reaffirmation of what had been denied. Byron is a great iconoclastic voice breaking upon contented and comfortable slumbers, as with the sound of a sea bursting barriers; shattering cherished idols—troubled and turbulent as the sea—the poet of revolt. From a child he loved to breathe the breath of battle.

And Carlyle ignores that Byron, with Rousseau and

Chateaubriand, sent us to the contemplation of Nature, was the chief hierophant for Europe of that sacred cult, which is distinctive of modern times. As I have said elsewhere, "his burning words of passionate admiration kindled our boyhood to behold and worship; his magnificent music, sonorous with storm and ocean, with all that is free, illimitable, and enduring, thrilled to the very heart of Europe, compelling it, as at a god's command, to bow down once more, when the angels of Faith and Hope seemed to be deserting for ever the desecrated shrines of mankind.

In a time when all secrets were at length supposed to be laid bare before man's microscopic understanding, all superstitions exploded, all mysteries explained; when the universe, emptied of ancient awe, seemed no longer venerable, but a hideous lazar-house rather, made visible to all human eyes in every ghastly corner of it; before the Circe-wand of materialism, love metamorphosed into a sensation, and man shrivelled to a handful of dust; when the body of God's own breathing world was laid with familiar irreverence upon the board of a near sighted professor to be dissected—then the prophet poets,

Rousseau and Byron, pointed men to the World-Soul, commanding men once more to veil their faces before the swift, subtle splendour of Divine Life in nature." Yet, indeed, Wordsworth was purer, profounder, more subtle and delicate in his appreciation of nature, as well as Byron's precursor in the same cult.

Before telling briefly the story of his life, I shall quote testimony of another kind, coming from a source which every good and true man should respect. "The day will come," says Mazzini, "when Democracy will remember all that it owes to Byron.

England, too, will, I hope, one day remember the mission—so entirely English, yet hitherto overlooked by her—which Byron fulfilled on the Continent; the European *rôle* given by him to English literature, and the appreciation and sympathy for England which he awakened among us." (For he was, in fact, European rather than English in his own sympathy.) "He led," adds Mazzini, "the genius of Britain on a pilgrimage through Europe." "I know no more beautiful symbol of the future destiny and mission of art than the death of Byron in Greece. The holy alliance of poetry with the cause of the people—the union, still so rare, of thought and action—the grand solidarity of all nations in the conquest of the rights ordained by God for all his children—all that is now the religion and the hope of the party of progress in Europe is gloriously typified in this image."

All which cannot be set aside by any pedantic, intemperate, microscopic cavils about the occasional shortcomings of this swift, spontaneous, full-blooded, long-and-strong-flighted eagle in rhythm and rhyme, too often slovenly, over colloquial, and aristocratically careless in the use of his native tongue. But they who prefer the clothes to the man may say *ditto* to such foolish depreciation. His words are "open to criticism," and they are also "above" it. " The magic still works," as Mr. Morley says.

There are worse faults—coarseness, commonplace, ribaldry, occasional want of subtlety and distinction in thought and phrase, as well as in music; above all, monotony of subject and treatment—a tendency to theatrical "pose," and enthronement of the anti-social, aggressive, insatiable, impatient individual. Yet the measures are often sonorous and masterly, the sentiment rouses to high moods, like a clarion, in language, vigorous, limpid, terse, memorable—though to the *voces, et praeterea nihil* of our day, Byron will never commend himself.

Where there is such weight and originality of substance, combined with so much effective expression, minute verbal criticism of technical details is impertinent when offered as a sufficient reason for refusing the biys, or for dethroning a great poet, upon whose claim Europe and posterity have pronounced their verdict.

" He was," says the eloquent Spaniard, Castelar, in his splendid eulogy, " like one of those Greek heroes— youthful, resplendent, as skilful with the sword as with the lyre—beloved by a beautiful woman, conqueror alike in sports as in battles; and yet condemned from the cradle by a cruel destiny to the infernal deities. Byron never gained a heart without afflicting it, or himself. All the sweetness of his rich fancy turned to bitterness at the presence of reality." "Men know not that all extraordinary virtue, all surpassing merit, is born of a disproportion between human faculties." "Demand of the Creator why the eagle sings not like the nightingale.

All supernatural genius is an internal infirmity. Genius is a Divine infirmity, a martyrdom. The poet cannot go into the fire without being burned; cannot enter the thundercloud without receiving the shock of electricity. They feed the splendour, burning in the lamp of their own brain, with tears from their eyes, and with blood from their hearts," "The sea falls like a drop of gall, and the earth like an atom of powder, into the unfathomable abyss of desire.

Every poet feels that which is called in common language home-sickness—the sorrow of exile, the longing after things higher and holier. Every great poet is like an exiled angel." "In Virgil, Petrarch, Raphael, it is a gentle melancholy; in Michael Angelo, Dante, Byron, an abandonment of grief, which borders on despair, like the roaring of a hurricane above the foam of the ocean.

Many men of genius console themselves by unfolding their souls in their works. Michael Angelo secluded himself, and peopled the roof of the Sistine with prophets, sibyls, sublime Titans, that cost him the most profound emotion. All of them are the produce of his soul's agony." "This great genius lived to repeat the aspirations of all peoples." "We enter on the truth by scepticism, by despair, as we enter into life by sorrow, with tears in our eyes, and sobs in our bosoms. The age which doubts not is an age which asks not; and we should importune the truth with questions, as we should come to God with supplications."

The poet was very proud of his descent both on the father's and mother's side. The Byrons are an old Norman family, whose ancestors came over with the Conqueror. Some of their number fought at Cressy; others at the siege of Calais and at Bosworth. Henry VIII. granted Newstead Abbey, on the dissolution of the monasteries, to one known as " Little Sir John of the great beard." The Sir John of Elizabeth's reign was illegitimate. At Edgehill there were seven Byrons in the field. For his services at Newbury another was created Baron of Rochdale in 1643.

Of the rest, Admiral Byron, called "Foul-weather Jack" for his misfortunes by sea, and the "wicked Lord Byron," who married a daughter of Lord Berkeley, grand-uncle of the poet, who succeeded this "wicked lord" in the peerage, are the best known. Admiral the Hon. John Byron wrote a spirited account of his own adventures by sea, which were many, alluded to in "*Don Juan*," whose hardships were "Comparative To those related in my granddad's narrative."

"He had no rest on sea, nor I on shore," says the grandson. The "wicked lord" is celebrated for his irregular and savage duel with his neighbour and kinsman, Mr. Chaworth—fought in the room of an inn by the light of a tallow candle.

Chaworth was run through the body, and Byron was tried for his life, a verdict of manslaughter being returned; and though he was afterwards set free, he is said to have lived a solitary, spectre-haunted kind of a life at Newstead, generally avoided. All sorts of false stories were told about him, but he seems to have been a bad man, and half cracked.

It is alleged that the crickets, whom he fed and chastised with straws, left the abbey in a body when he died. He hated his sons, and cut down the trees in the park to spite them. This man surely must, in part, have suggested Lara, and the poet's other gloomy heroes. "Mad Jack Byron," the poet's father, was a handsome rake, who seduced the Marquis of Carmarthen's wife (Lady Conyers in her own right), and married her after a divorce had been obtained. She was mother of Augusta, the poet's half-sister, who married Colonel Leigh, and had a numerous family.

After his first wife's death he married Catherine Gordon, of Gight, an heiress, whose fortune he soon ran through. She was very proud of her descent from James I., through his daughter Annabella and the second Earl of Huntley. Shortly after the poet's birth in Holles Street, January 22, 1788, the father, being pressed by his creditors, abandoned mother and child, leaving them with only £150 a year, and died at Valenciennes in August, 1791.

Mrs. Byron, early in 1790, settled with her child in a small house in Aberdeen. There her husband rejoined her for a while; but their incompatible tempers soon compelled a definite separation. Yet when the wife heard of his death in France, her shrieks of despair are said to have disturbed the neighbourhood.

(Sir Walter Scott relates that, *before* her marriage, she was carried out of the theatre, when Mrs. Siddons was personating Isabella in Southerne's "Fatal Marriage," screaming, "O my Biron, my Biron!") Byron told Harness that his father died insane and by his own hand; but this has been generally assumed to have been a fib. There is no further evidence that it was true.

The poet remembered the father lovingly, who used to waylay the child at Aberdeen, and play with him; for Mad Jack took lodgings for awhile, apart from his wife, in the same town, before the final separation. And the father once took him home to spend a night with him there. He was only three then, yet remembered this. [i] In his early poems he says:

"Stern death forbade my orphan youth to share The tender guidance of a father's care."

And in "Lara":

" Left by his sire, too young such loss to know,
Lord of himself, that heritage of woe,
That fearful empire, which the human breast
But holds to rob the heart within of rest,
With none to check, and few to point in time
The thousand paths that slope the way to crime."

What an utter incapacity in the man, even had he lived long enough, to guide a son's inexperienced footsteps, and such a son's! The mother !—sometimes a mother may almost make up by her affectionate and gentle wisdom for the absence of firm kindness and judiciously applied experience in a father. But here there was no such mother. What an irreparable loss! not to have learned to reverence woman in the celestial light shed upon her out of one's own sacred experience of Motherhood! Poor Mrs. Byron was a warm-hearted person indeed, truly fond of her son in her own strange way; but as one of the poet's schoolboy friends too candidly observed to him, "Byron, your mother is a fool;"—to which he could only reply, "I know it !"

She was vehement, undisciplined, subject to fits of fury, hysterical, and, on the whole, would seem to have been appointed in irony to train this volcanic child of abnormal sensibility and genius. And her extraordinary conduct to him is sufficient to account for a trait, which would, had we not known the facts, have appeared very unamiable—his comparative want of affection for the poor lady, as shown in his letters to her, and otherwise. Now she would lavish caresses on him, and now blows, with little other justification than her own arbitrary whims and moods.

The image of him as a child defending himself with the chairs from her, trying to fling the poker at him, remains in the memory of all who have read Lord Beaconsfield's "Venetia." On one occasion, after violent abuse, she finished by calling him "a lame brat!" His lips quivered, his face whitened, a fearful light came into his eyes, as he replied, "I was born so, mother!" The scene was in his mind when he wrote the "Deformed Transformed" at Pisa.

Such was the inheritance, and such the education provided for this poet. His own disposition as a child prophesied what he would be in after-life—" passionate, sullen, defiant of authority, but singularly amenable to kindness." On being scolded by his first nurse for soiling a dress, he tore it from top to bottom, as he had seen his mother tear her caps and gowns. But to his next nurse, Mary Gray, he remained always attached.

To her is attributed his considerable knowledge of the Bible; he was, she said later, fond of putting puzzling questions about religion even as a child. To her he owed that profound tincture of Calvinism which he retained to the end. But there is one high and noble characteristic which he owed to his mother. While, on the one hand, overweeningly proud of her descent, and teaching her son to be so of his—Mrs. Byron yet avowed herself "a democrat," which implied at that time in England no small courage. She taught the poet to abhor tyrants, to pity the poor, the weak, the oppressed.

I ought not to proceed without mention of his lameness. For beautiful in person as he was, save for this one deformity, he was so vain, self-conscious, and morbidly sensitive, that it embittered his life from childhood forward. As has been remarked, a clubfoot was incapable of disturbing the serene nature of Walter Scott. But then, after all, Byron's seems to have been a particularly painful, perturbing, and injurious kind of lameness.

The right *Achilles tendon* was so contracted that he could never put the foot flat on the ground, wearing for it a boot made with a high heel, and a padding inside under the heel of the foot; indeed the tendons of both feet were contracted; he had to walk on the balls and toes of his feet; but the right foot is said to have been so distorted as to turn inwards; yet this probably was owing to the unskilful surgical treatment of some one who operated on the foot. He used to "hop about like a bird," Leigh Hunt assures us rather spitefully.

This affliction prevented Byron from taking a healthy and normal amount of exercise, aggravating thereby his predisposition to corpulency. No wonder that he adopted all sorts of plans, more or less injurious to his health in other ways, to keep himself thin. Why he should be sneered at for not wishing to look clumsy and unwieldy, having been born with natural advantages of face, figure, and complexion, I could never understand, the contempt for bodily beauty appearing to me no virtue, but an indication either of defective sensibility, or of an immoral ascetic theory.

Besides, corpulency is itself a painful disease, to be combated on the score of health. So he starved, and took frequent doses of Epsom salts—a very weakening habit. But his adoption of a low and meagre diet, though persisted in for long periods together, was somewhat fitful and irregular, and he would make up for his enforced abstinence now and again by orgies of eating and drinking. Although, like Scott, Byron had a very insensitive palate, and was no gourmet to distinguish delicate flavours, it can have been no easy task for him to go so perpetually hungry "clapping," as he says, "the muzzle on his own jaws.

But by starving his body he thought he subdued his animal nature, and kept his brains clear. No man had brighter eyes, or a clearer voice. A child called him "the gentleman with the beautiful voice." He lived for days together on biscuits and soda water; then, half famished, would swallow a huge mess of potatoes, rice, and fish, drenched with vinegar. Such a regimen, in concert with the immense draughts of brain-work made on his nervous energy, rendered his digestion in later life a torment to him.

He would roll on the ground in agony with it, and could not sleep. As a rule, he was very moderate in drinking; but occasionally went in for a drinking bout with Moore, or some other friend. "Why should I make myself more stupid than God made me?" the boy Chatterton once observed, excusing himself for not eating; but needing, alas! soon little excuse enough. In 1816, and at Venice, Byron took brandy to excess, and was for some time a laudunam drinker, chewing tobacco also to mitigate the craving for food. But this was more or less exceptional with him.

As for exercise, swimming and riding were about the only forms of it possible to him; boxing and fencing also, however, in some measure, and even cricket. Yet of running he could have done little, and his power of "roving over the hills "as "a young highlander," of which he speaks in his early poems, must ever have been limited. This at least was usually done on pony-back.

" In early life," says Trelawny, " whilst his frame was light and elastic, he might have tottered along for a mile or two; but after he had waxed heavier, he seldom attempted to walk more than a few hundred yards, without squatting or leaning against the first wall, bank, tree, or rock at hand, never sitting on the ground, as it would have been difficult for him to get up again.""He won several fights at Harrow," says Jeaffreson, "but in every case he won them by rushing at his adversary with the *élan* of a French foot-soldier, and making a short business of each round by putting in quickly two or three blows with his singularly muscular arms.

When he could not snatch success in this manner he was beaten," on account of his weak feet. He boxed with Jackson the pugilist, and his pupils, in the same manner. He used to enter London drawing-rooms, in the height of his popularity, running rather than walking, and stopped himself suddenly by planting his left foot on the ground, and resting upon it.

"What a pretty boy George is !" said a friend, to his nurse, when he was a child; " what a pity he has such a leg ! "On which he, cutting after him with a baby's whip, cried out, "Dinna speak of it!" He hated Harrow till he got high up in the school; the brutal, big bullies there would put his lame foot into a bucket of water by way of a joke.

He used, later in life, to fancy that the beggars and street-sweepers in London were mocking his gait—though Lady Blessington says that his lameness was not particularly noticeable till he referred to it. In his verses called "The Waltz" he satirized dancing; and in *"Lara"* one recalls that picture of the stern melancholy man, leaning against a pillar, while the gay dancers footed it round him.

At Matlock the poet had, indeed, watched his own love, Mary Chaworth, in the arms of other partners, while he himself could only look on. His lameness! ought he not to have minded it ? Why even Mary Chaworth, the lady of his love, struck the last cruel blow upon his boyish passion in the contemptuous reproach he overheard when she said to her maid, not knowing he was near, " Do you think I could care for that lame boy ? " Upon which he rushed out of the house that held her, and flew to Newstead.

On his death-bed he refused to let mustard be applied to his feet, according to the doctor's order; though at last he allowed Fletcher, his trusty servant, to do it, after ordering every one else out of the room. This makes the indelicacy of Trelawny's *post-mortem* examination of, and report upon, his feet, to my mind considerable; for, according to his own account, he did not uncover the feet, which Fletcher had religiously covered, before sending the poor valet away to fetch him a glass of water! Still Trelawny's is a book to rank with Boswell's "*Johnson*," and the better for not being written by a professed bookman, in spite of its *animus* against Byron.

After passing through the hands of certain preparatory tutors, the poet was sent to the Aberdeen Grammar School, in 1794. There he showed no particular aptitude for learning the common tasks inflicted at our schools upon all boys, without any discrimination of their particular bents; and he arrived at the top of his form in a singular manner; for it was the custom there to invert the proper order of the classes at the beginning of the lesson, so that the most ignorant were for the moment placed first; and more than once the master said, bantering him, " Now, George, man, let me see how soon you'll be at the foot !"

But even then he was a reader of books, and educated himself, while refusing the kind of education provided for him by his adult inferiors. He gives a surprising list of books read by him before he was ten. About this time, when he was in his ninth year, he "fell in love" with his cousin Mary Duff, a little older than himself. He says that he used to coax a maid to write letters from him to her, and that when he was sixteen, on being informed by his mother that his cousin was married, he nearly fell into convulsions.

This reminds one of Dante's passion for Beatrice in his tenth year. He tells us also of his "silent rages and sullen fits "—which Lady Byron found so unpleasant later on. In 1796, after an attack of scarlet fever at Aberdeen, he was taken by his mother to Ballater, and from this period he informs us he dates his love of mountainous countries. "After I returned to Cheltenham I used to watch the Malvern Hills every afternoon at sunset with a sensation which I cannot describe." In the "Island" he says:—

"The infant rapture still survived the boy,
And Loch-na-gair with Ida looked o'er Troy,
Mix'd Celtic memories with the Phrygian mount,
And Highland linns with Castalie's clear fount."

His nurse denied that he ever did "climb the steep summit

of Morven," as he boasts, but at any rate he wandered about the mountain in imagination as he gazed. In May, 1798, on the death of his grand-uncle, the fifth and so called "wicked lord," George Gordon, in his eleventh year, succeeded to the family title, having become the next heir when his cousin, the fifth lord's grandson, died in Corsica. And in the autumn of the same year, Mrs. Byron (having sold her household effects for about £75) set out for England with her son, who never re-visited Scotland.

On passing the toll bar of Newstead in a post-chaise, Moore tells us that Mrs. Byron asked the woman in charge to whom the Abbey belonged, and on her replying that the late lord had died some time since, Mrs. Byron further inquired who was the next heir, to which the woman answered, " They say it is a little boy who lives in Aberdeen."

Whereupon the nurse, Mary Gray, who was in the carriage with the boy, ejaculated: "And this is he; bless him!" But Mrs. Byron could not afford to live there, and took up her abode at Nottingham. The house, moreover, had been left in a very ruined and dilapidated condition by the late owner. The estate was already in Chancery, and the Earl of Carlisle— George Gordon's first cousin (once removed), son of Isabella Byron, sister of the fifth lord—was appointed his guardian.

Mrs. Byron lived about twelve months at Nottingham, where she found for her son a certain tutor named Rogers, whom he regarded with affection. He suffered much here from a bonesetter called Lavender, who maltreated his foot, and put him to useless torture. On him Byron played a childish trick—arranging the letters of the alphabet in gibberish words he asked Lavender what language that was, upon which the man replied, *"Italian,"* to the boy's huge delight.

When the poor little fellow was sitting, doing his lessons in much pain from his foot one day, the kind tutor said how it troubled him to see his pupil suffering. "Never mind, Mr. Rogers," answered the brave lad, "you sha'n't see any signs of it again."

It is said also that here an old lady he disliked was the occasion of Byron's first verses—satirical ones. She believed that our souls would live in the moon after death, and having offended him one day, he suddenly exclaimed to his nurse that " he couldn't bear the sight of the old witch," and broke out into the following doggerel:—

"In Nottingham County there lives at Swan Green
As curst an old lady as ever was seen;
And when she does die, which I hope will be soon,
She firmly believes she will go to the moon."

The following year, Mrs. Byron moved to Sloane Terrace, in London, having received a pension of £300 a year from the Civil List, and at Lord Carlisle's suggestion the boy was taken to Dr. Baillie (a brother of Joanna), who directed that a particular kind of shoe should be made for him, on the lines originally suggested by John Hunter, the well-known surgeon.

Mary Gray, the nurse, now returned to Scotland. The child parted from her with affectionate sorrow, giving her the first watch he had ever possessed, which on her death-bed passed to Dr. Ewing, of Aberdeen, who also received from her some memoranda about the poet's early years, and the child gave her a miniature of himself by Ray.

He was now sent to a school at Dulwich, kept by a Dr. Glennie. Sleeping in the doctor's library, he was encouraged by him to read the books there, and these he eagerly devoured. "In my study," says Dr. Glennie, "he found, among others, a set of our poets from Chaucer to Churchill, which I am almost tempted to say he had more than once perused from beginning to end." One of the books was the *"Narrative of the Shipwreck of the Juno,"* from which, almost word for word, the picture of the two fathers in the shipwreck of *"Don Juan"* is taken.

Mrs. Byron would have her son with her from Saturday to Monday, and interrupted his education in various ways. Lord Carlisle, on Dr. Glennie's appealing to him, exerted his authority against these interruptions; but Mrs. Byron exhibited so much temper on his remonstrating, that he said to the master: "I can have nothing more to do with Mrs. Byron; you must now manage her as you can."

Dr. Glennie, though fond of the son, has given a very unfavourable account of the mother. After two years, she requested Lord Carlisle to remove the poet to Harrow, where he accordingly went (1801) in his fourteenth year.

In his twelfth year (1800), the boy fell in love with his cousin, Margaret Parker—a girl of an exquisitely delicate complexion. "My passion," he says, "had its usual effects upon me. I could not sleep—I could not eat—I could not rest; and although I had reason to know that she loved me, it was the texture of my life to think of the time which must elapse before we could meet again, being usually about twelve hours of separation.

But I was a fool then, and am not much wiser now! My sister told me that when she went to see her shortly before her death, upon accidentally mentioning my name, Margaret coloured through the paleness of mortality to the eyes, to her great astonishment, she knowing nothing of the attachment."

It was at Cheltenham that his mother was much moved by the prediction of a fortune-teller that her son should be in danger from poison before he was of age, and should be twice married—the second time to a foreign lady. Margaret Parker died of consumption about two years after the poet fell in love with her. On her he wrote his first serious verses, and later the lines:

"Hush'd are the winds, and still the evening gloom;
Not e'en a zephyr wanders through the grove,
Whilst I return to view my Margaret's tomb,
And scatter flowers on the dust I love."

Was this girl "*Thyrza,*" as Mr. Jeaffreson thinks? I believe not. Moore says that Thyrza was a creation of the poet's imagination, and that the poems addressed to her were "the essence, the abstract spirit as it were, of many griefs," *sorrow for the loss of Eddlestone, his young chorister friend at Cambridge,* being one of them.

The verses seem to commemorate "a violent, though pure love and passion," whose object is unknown, which he mentions in his journal as having possessed him in the summer of 1806, his first year at Cambridge, contemporaneously with his friendship for Edward Noel Long, who was drowned on his voyage to Lisbon with his regiment, in 1809.

He writes of this to Mr. Dallas, on the exact date of some of the lines to Thyrza, October II, 1811, saying, " I have been shocked with a death, and have lost one very dear to me in happier times, but 'I have almost forgot the taste of grief,' and supped full of horrors till I have become callous; nor have I a tear left for an event which five years ago would have bowed my head to the earth." Several years after, Lord Byron, being asked to whom the poems referred, refused to answer, with marks of painful agitation.

At any rate, the lines commencing, *"And thou art dead, as young and fair,"* are probably as beautiful and tender as any in our language. It is very possible that "Thyrza" was the chorister friend—not only partly, as Moore believes—probably because Byron had avowed thus much—but solely;—only to avoid banter, and even possible misconception, he gave his lost boy-friend a female name, and to the language of the poems a turn appropriate to the disguise adopted. If justification were needed, one might refer to the Sonnets of Shakespeare, or even to "In Memoriam."

Byron was a Harrow boy from the summer of 1801 to that of 1805, and for some time he was under Dr. Drury, of whom he was fond, and whom he never ceased to respect, while the head-master was fond of his pupil, and predicted his future greatness.

He said to Lord Carlisle, who was inquiring about his abilities, "He has talents, my lord, which will add lustre to his rank." And Dr. Drury, in his story of this episode, adds that the guardian's only reply was the monosyllable *"Indeed!"* pronounced with an accent of surprise, which did not express all the satisfaction the good Doctor had expected.

"We are left in doubt," says Nichol," whether the indifference proceeded from the jealousy that clings to poetasters," (for the Earl had written indifferent verses, which his ward unkindly calls " the paralytic pulings of Carlisle,") "from incredulity, or a feeling that no talent *could* add lustre to rank." Of Dr. Drury Byron says:

"He was the best, the kindest (and yet strict too) friend I ever had, and I look on him still as a father, whose warnings I have remembered but too well, though too late, when I have erred, and whose counsel I have but followed when I have done well or wisely."

Yet till the last year and a half he hated Harrow—that is till he was high up in the school, and could lead. He was very unpopular at first, but though he was bullied when very young, he remained long enough to show the native energy and determination of his character, and become respected among his schoolfellows; yet he never did much schoolwork there.

In 1805, Dr. Drury retired, and was succeeded by Dr. Butler, an appointment unpopular with the boys, who would have preferred Henry Drury, son of the former master. Byron, always famous for rows, was a ringleader of the boy rebels. He tore down the window-gratings before some of the Master's windows, "because they darkened the hall."

He also set limits to the rebellion, however, when some of the wilder spirits would have burned one of the class-rooms, preventing this outrage by reminding them that so they would destroy the old desks, upon which their own fathers and grandfathers had carved their names when they were boys.

One of Byron's schoolfellows told Moore that when Dr. Butler sent him an invitation to dinner as an upper boy, he refused to go, and on being asked for a reason, replied, "Why, Dr. Butler, if you should happen to come into my neighbourhood when I am staying at Newstead, I certainly should not ask you to dine with me, so therefore I feel that I ought not to dine with you." But Dr. Butler assured Moore that there was very little foundation in fact for the story; it is evident, however, from the terms of this disclaimer, that there was some.

Byron apologized later for his rudeness; yet in "Hours of Idleness" he published some offensive verses about the Master, calling him "Pomposus of the narrow brain." "I soon found," says Dr. Drury, "that a wild mountain colt had been committed to my care. But there was mind in his eye.... A degree of shyness hung about him," (which indeed clung to him through life). "His manner and temper soon convinced me that he might be led by a silken string to a point, rather than by a cable—on that principle I acted."

The master also relates that when the boy recited a written declamation, in common with some of his schoolfellows, he diverged with much fire and animation from what was written, bringing his oration to a successful conclusion, and coming back to the written theme, though unconscious that he had so diverged; and that his manner and delivery were excellent. Drury thought he would turn out a great orator.

While Sir George Sinclair used frequently to do his exercises for Byron, the latter more than once fought Sinclair's battles for him with his fists. "He was pacific, and I savage; so I fought for him; thrashed others for him, or thrashed himself to make him thrash others, when it was necessary as a point of honour and stature that he should so chastise.... I fought my way very fairly; I think I lost but one battle out of seven: my most memorable combats were with Morgan, Rice, Rainsford, and Lord Jocelyn, but we were always friendly afterwards." And here I may remark that I was told by my grandfather (the same Lord Jocelyn, afterwards Earl of Roden) about this "mill" with Byron.

So far as Lord Roden could remember, it was a drawn battle (and therefore Byron cannot be said to have *"lost"* it!) My grandfather was not intimate with his celebrated schoolfellow, but recollected him as rather a rowdy, not particularly attractive boy, who amused himself, at any rate on one occasion, by wringing the neck of a duck (presumably one of those swimming upon the water, called "duck puddle," at Harrow!) This reminds one that the poet, who afterwards became beautiful in face and figure, and was himself but too conscious of a fact which the women did not allow him to forget, appears as a schoolboy to have possessed few personal attractions.

He was described by Miss Pigot of Southwell—a partial acquaintance—as "a fat, bashful boy, with hair combed straight over his forehead, and looking a perfect gaby." Moore learnt from several quarters that he was by no means popular among girls of his own age.

Moreover, he was conceited, shy, and awkward, with rough and odd manners. Yet thoughtful moods must have characterized him even then, for we hear of him reclining by the hour on the well-known tombstone under the elm in the churchyard, from which there is so beautiful a view, and near to which now rests little Allegra, his beloved illegitimate daughter. Later, he became so tender to animals that he repudiated field sports and fishing.

The list of books he read, moreover, drawn up by him in 1809, is a remarkably long one—so that he must have done a fair amount of reading even at Harrow, including much history, biography, and some divinity. Dr. Glennie says he was greatly interested in talking over *religious* questions with him at Dulwich.

"I read eating, read in bed, read when no one else reads," he writes—and he had a most retentive memory. But his note on the passage in " *Childe Harold* " on " *Soracte and the Latian Echoes* " is worth transcribing here, as bearing on the system of education which then prevailed, and has been modified only to some degree since:—

"I wish to express that we become tired of the task before we can comprehend the beauty; that we learn by rote before we get by heart; that the freshness is worn away, and the future pleasure and advantage deadened and destroyed at an age when we can neither feel, nor understand the power, of composition; which it requires an acquaintance with life, as well as Latin and Greek, to relish or to reason upon.... In some parts of the Continent young persons are taught from common authors, and do not read the best classics till their maturity."

"My school friendships," he says, in one of his journals, "were with me passions, for I was always violent; but I do not know that there is one which has endured (to be sure, some have been cut short by death) till now. That with Lord Clare began one of the earliest, and lasted longest—being only interrupted by distance." "I never hear the word ' Clare ' without a beating of the heart even now, and I write it with the feelings of 1803-4-5-*ad infinitum." From Pisa {November 5, 1821) he writes about a chance meeting with this friend:*

"I met him on the road between Imola and Bologna, after not having met for seven or eight years.... This meeting annihilated for a moment all the years between the present time and the days of Harrow. It was a new and inexplicable feeling, like rising from the grave to me. Clare, too, was much agitated—more in appearance even than myself, for I could feel his heart beat to his fingers' ends, unless indeed it was the pulse of my own that made me think so.... We were but five minutes together, and on the public road, but I hardly recollect an hour of my existence which could be weighed against them."

And this is the man whom his enemies represent to have had no feeling, to have been capable only of acting and simulating feeling! One may laugh at it as " sentiment "; but he was so sensitive and affectionate that, as a Harrow boy, he wrote a letter to a friend, complaining that this friend had addressed him as "my dear " instead of " my dearest " Byron.

Mr. Harness, with whom he was intimate, says " of his attachment to his friends no one can read ' Moore's Life,' and entertain a doubt. He required a great deal from them—not more perhaps than he, from the abundance of his love, freely and fully gave—but more than they had to return."

Whatever evils might be incidental to this passionate and loving comradeship, it could hardly be otherwise than ennobling, especially among the formal, cold, calculating denizens of our northern clime, and Byron seems to have been a sort of apostle of friendship in his later Harrow career.

It is certainly true that, made up as he was ever of strange, perplexing contradictions, he was at Harrow a curious combination of shyness, and meditative, almost feminine sensibility, with pluck, energy, and activity, even roughness and occasional brutality. His favourites were the Duke of Dorset, Lord Clare (whom he calls " Lycus "), Lord Delawarr ("Euryalus " — " Shall fair Euryalus pass by unsung?"), the Honourable John Wingfield, brother of Lord Powerscourt, whose early death by fever in Portugal he commemorates in a stanza of "Childe Harold " (" Alonzo "), Cecil Tattersall (" Davus"), Edward Noel Long ("Cleon "), Wildman, who bought

Newstead, and Sir Robert Peel. The latter, afterwards so distinguished as a statesman, was born in the same year. A big bully claiming the right to fag little Peel, and the latter resisting, the big boy determined to punish him for his refractoriness; so twisting one of his arms round, he beat the little fellow on it severely.

Byron was looking on with tears in his eyes, and though he knew he was too weak and small to fight the bully with success, he came forward, and asked in a voice trembling with indignation how many stripes the tyrant meant to inflict? "Why, you little rascal," returned he, "what is that to you?"

"Because, if you please," said Byron, holding out his arm, "I would take half." When people with the modern detestation of class distinctions rail at him for his rather comical plea in favour of Lord Delawarr, whom Wildman was going to thrash, on the ground that he was a "brother peer" (which failed of course, as it deserved to do !),

They might remember the foregoing incident, as also the following:—Young Harness, still lame from an accident in his childhood, and just recovering from severe illness, was rescued from another hulking bully by Byron; and the next day, as he was standing alone, Byron came up to him saying, " Harness, if any one bullies you, tell me, and I'll thrash him, if I can." They had not been friends till then, but afterwards became the warmest. "The child is father of the man," and this generosity of spirit showed itself later in Italy and Greece.

He thrashed other bullies there. The cynic may sneer that Byron liked to lead and to protect now, as later, from vanity; and so also he may sneer that Nelson wished for "a peerage, or Westminster Abbey." But human nature is made up of selfish and unselfish elements, difficult to disentangle, and thus the rough work of the world gets done. Byron's pride of rank was no doubt excessive.

]Since Thackeray (who owned himself a "snob") we have agreed that rank may be made an idol, to worship which is "snobbish." Yet there miy be more ignoble idols even than blood, or caste. At Dulwich, Byron's ostentation of rank had procured for him the nickname of the "Old English Baron."

And on his accession to the peerage, when his name was first read out in school with *Dominus* before it, he burst into tears from emotion. Byron cared much for beauty in his friends, as is well known.

Thus he mentions the beauty of his friend, Delawarr. His own hair was auburn, his complexion very fair, his eyes large, blue grey, and luminous, his lips voluptuous and well formed. Coleridge and Scott both agreed about the wonderful beauty of his face, and Trelawny, who often swam with him, mentions that, save for the defect in his foot, his body and limbs were of Apollonian symmetry and fairness—the delicate shapeliness of his hands being noticed by many, men as well as women.

But he was not nearly so handsome at fifteen as he afterwards became, and his serious love affair at that age shows sufficiently that Mary Chaworth was insensible to whatever personal attractions he may then have possessed.

In the summer of 1803, Mrs. Byron was in lodgings at Nottingham, where her son came to spend the holidays with her. Lord Grey de Ruthven, the tenant under Chancery, and occupier of Newstead, made acquaintance with the young peer, and put a room at his disposal in the Abbey, which was to be his future home.

The Chaworths, who lived near, at Annesley, also invited him to sleep there. At first he would not, but went back to Newstead in the evening, alleging that the ancestral Chaworths would come down from their picture-frames and take revenge on him for his grand-uncle's fatal and irregular duel with one of their race.

But he afterwards consented to stay, and Annesley became his head quarters during a part of the summer holidays. So he fell in love with the heiress—" the bright morning star of Annesley." Had she returned his love, the result would have been a union which, he said, "would have joined broad lands, healed an old feud, and satisfied at least one heart." They went together to Matlock and Castleton; at the former took place those dances to which I have referred as making the lame boy jealous and miserable; and at Castleton, let him describe what occurred in his own words:—

"When I was fifteen years of age, it happened that in a cavern in Derbyshire, I had to cross in a boat, in which two people only could lie down—a stream which flows under a rock, with the rock so close upon the water as to admit the boat only to be pushed on by a ferryman (a sort of Charon), who wades at the stern, stooping all the time.

The companion of my transit was M. A. C., with whom I had long been in love, and never told it, though she had discovered it. I recollect my sensations, but cannot describe them, and it is as well."

He was fifteen, but she two years older, and what a difference this makes! To her he was a mere school boy—to him what was she not? He rode with her on his pony about the broad lands of their fathers, he listened to her playing and singing in the summer evenings; but the Montagues and the Capulets were not to be so united.

Mary was a lively and pleasant girl of some beauty, who preferred her pale, commonplace, fox-hunting squire, whom she soon afterwards married; for her cousin was lame, and shy, and awkward, and had not yet proved himself one of the master minds of England; and who was she that she should divine his greatness ? or value it, even if divined ? Nobody had told her. Moreover, it was a greatness that burned rather than warmed any on whom its beams might chance to fall.

I have already related the manner in which the cup of happiness he had dared raise to his lips was dashed from them. A year later they met again on the "hill of Annesley "—

"the hill
Crowned with a peculiar diadem
Of trees in circular array, so fixed
Not by the sport of nature, but of man."

That interview stands immortal in "*The Dream*," a beautiful poem, written in 1816, at Diodati, "amid a flood of tears." "I suppose," he said," the next time I see you, you will be Mrs. Chaworth (her betrothed, Mr. Musters, was to assume her family name). "I hope so," she had replied.

She only laughed when the boycoxcomb showed her a locket given him by an old love, in order to kindle her own love to him! The announcement of her marriage (August, 1805) was made to him by his mother, with the remark, "I have some news for you. Take out your handkerchief—you will require it." When he heard what she had to say, he became pale, but assuming an air of forced calm, answered, "Is that all?" and turned the conversation.

Yet the wound had pierced deep. How strange and how sad it seems, to look back from this distance of time on it all! She was unhappy in her marriage, was separated from her husband, and her mind passed under a cloud. She died in 1832, of a fright caused by a Nottingham riot.

"I have taken," said Byron, "all my fables about the celestial nature of women from the perfection my imagination created in her. I say created,... for," he added cynically, " I found her anything but perfect." In the following year he accepted an invitation to dine at Annesley, and was much affected by the sight of the infant daughter of the woman he had loved. He sent her the lines beginning,

"O had my fate been joined with thine!"

And shortly after, when about to leave England for the first time, he addressed her in the verses:

"'Tis done, and shivering in the gale, The bark unfurls her snowy sail."

It was in one of these Harrow vacations also that he first learned to know, and love his half-sister Augusta, with a love never after to be dimmed by time or distance— a purifying and ennobling love—that inspired some of his tenderest poetry. It was the best and most abiding influence of his life, let Calumny lay harpy hands on it as she may. The children had been separated till 1802, for Augusta had lived with old Lady Holdernesse, her grandmother, but on the latter's death they came together.

Augusta was four years older than her brother, and called him "Baby Byron," even after he had become a famous man, perceiving, with a kindly sense of humour, certain childish traits in him, which, methinks, were not the least amiable features of a complex character. This meeting took place at Brighton. His sister was rather plain than beautiful, but amiable, pious, and excellent in all the relations of life. From Nottingham Mrs. Byron moved with her son to Southwell, a small country town with a fine old church, not far from Newstead. There occurred here many furious hurricanes of wrath on the part of the mother, which provoked her son's "sullen rages"; and such was the estimate formed by each of the other's violence, that mother and son went one evening separately to the apothecary, and cautioned him against selling poison to the other, should it be asked for.

The poker or tongs having just missed him on one occasion, he sought refuge in the house of a friend, and decided on escaping to London, where he remained for some time in Piccadilly. Mrs. Byron pursued him, but they separated eventually, and he went to Worthing for awhile, rejoining her in August of the same year.

In the novel *"Venetia,"* Lord Beaconsfield has imitated these rows in the encounters he describes between young Lord Cadurcis and his mother. But in one of his own graphic letters to Mr. Pigot, a Southwell acquaintance, Byron himself gives what, to some of us who know all a mother may be, and has been more than once, to an only son, must appear a very grievous, though amusing account of these scenes; with comments upon them. Byron was a delightful letter-writer, lively, graphic, nervous, vigorous, and homely in style, never writing as if "for publication";— but letter-writing is a lost art.

"His journal," says Beyle, "his familiar letters, all his unstudied prose is, as it were, trembling with wit, anger, and enthusiasm; since St. Simon we have seen no more life-like confidences. All styles appear dull, and all souls sluggish by the side of his." To me the absence of bookishness, formal pedantry, airs of professional authorship, is one of Byron's most distinguished charms.

He is no sapless, dry abstraction from humanity, and no literary *petit maître,* but a man; hence he will ever be distasteful to the academic prig, and to the mere *littérateur,* who holds that his own ability to turn a sentence prettily places him at the centre and summit of creation, while any other kind of human function might so very easily be dispensed with altogether. But he will always be dear to the men and women of Europe. He says in "Beppo":—

"One hates an author that's all author, fellows
In foolscap uniforms turned up with ink,
So very anxious, clever, fine, and jealous,
One don't know what to say to them, or think."

And he went to Greece partly to show the world that he could, as he expressed it, "do something better than write verses." He died dreaming in his fever heats that he was leading the Greeks to assault Lepanto.

He cared as much for his fourteen-feet dives with Matthews into the Cam, to pick up coins and trinkets; for his amorous adventures with the ladies in England, and darker orgies at Venice; his sea-rovings in the *Bolivar,* and long swims with Trelawny or Ekenhead; his travels with Hobhouse, and solitary communings with nature; for his pleasant hours with young Eddlestone, the sweet chorister of Cambridge; and the home-life with Augusta; for Ada, and Allegra—cared as much for these as for the composition of *"Childe Harold"* or " *Don Juan."*

There was the rather vulgar ostentation of rank to set off against these keen interests in life, the whim, or affectation, of wishing rather to be treated as a lord than as a poet, which may have made him too careless, or less conscientious than it behoves every true artist to be in the technical finish of his art, which ought to be sacred with him, the ideal wife, the queen of all mistresses.

Still it was, I think, pure gain for Byron to be no mere bookman, hide-bound in calf, instead of human skin, and treating the universe as so much docile material for such as he to make pretty little things out of. He was a Berserker, whose wild spirit found vent in song, and his was a bleeding human heart, even though he made of it "a pageant." What he does has the salt breath of impetuously moving sea, the thrill of warm-blooded life; his fervid voice has the living accent.

It was not in order to write poems that he conversed much with sea and mountain, or humanity; though these inspired him with the irresistible impulse to write. He mixed with men and women, helped them or marred, eat, drank, and caroused with them.

But nature and men were as much to him as the creations they inspired, which, having taken their own resplendent shapes in the high and solitary places of reflection and imagination, issued therefrom, transformed and immortal. It is mainly this rare and memorable combination of interest alike in action and contemplation which gives Byron the eminent personality attributed to him by Goethe.

But, at the same time, it must be added that he lived under a "plague of microscopes." Every lesser person who could gain a little reflected lustre by describing him, noted down every least significant word, mood, look, whim, gesture; passing it, moreover, through the sometimes distorting medium of his own understanding, and too often also through that of his own rancour or prejudice, heightening this trait, diminishing or ignoring the other; so that we are left with a series of indifferent photographs, which hardly enable us to do the man justice. Who could come scathless out of such an ordeal?

And then, as Miss Blind says, in her excellent introduction to his "*Letters*," he was all things to all men, reflected chameonlike the character of his companions, or correspondents; he was many characters in turn. So while all the sketches have a one-sided truth, they need to be combined and modified into a portrait.

Chapter 2

Milton and Byron

I am too happy in being coupled in any way with Milton, and shall be glad if they find any points of comparison between him and me.

-Byron to Thomas Medwin

When we think of Milton's influence upon English Romanticism the poets who first come to mind are Blake, Wordsworth, Keats, and perhaps Shelley. As for Byron, Milton rightly seems an altogether less dominating forebear since we remember only too well his distaste for blank verse, even Milton's blank verse:

Blank verse, ... [except] in the drama, no one except Milton ever wrote who could rhyme ... I am aware that Johnson has said, after some hesitation, that he could not "prevail upon himself to wish that Milton had been a rhymer" ...; but, with all humility, I am not persuaded that the *Paradise Lost* would not have been more nobly conveyed to posterity ... in the Stanza of Spenser or of Tasso, or in the terza rima of Dante, which the powers of Milton could easily have grafted on our language.

Byron had a number of other criticisms of Milton's poetic crafts/ manship, so one is not surprised that Milton did not haunt his work. Nevertheless, Milton's importance for Byron, both in his art and his life, was by no means insignificant.

To speak of Milton's influence upon Byron is, I believe, immediately to close the discussion under two principal headings. The first of these is well known and has to do with Byron's Satanism and the poetic tradition of the criminal hero. Though fairly and frequently treated, the matter has still to be properly elucidated, and the first part of this essay will deal with certain areas of the subject which have not been explained. The second way in which Milton was an important influence upon Byron involves Byron's interpretation and imaginative use of Milton's life. This aspect of Milton's influence did not appear until Byron exiled himself from England in 1816.

At this time he began to elaborate an autobiographical myth which was shaped in no small way by his interpretation of Milton's personal and political history. To my knowledge, no scholar has yet seen fit to go into this curious matter. Since the subject is rather complex and little known, I will leave it until after we have looked into the more familiar problem of Byron's Satanism.

Though Milton's influence upon Byron's gloomy and problematic heroes begins at least as early as 1812, the subject has always (and properly) been studied from the vantage of 1821 –1822, when *Cain* was published and the famous discussion of the play was begun. Byron defended *Cain* against the charge of blasphemy by calling Milton to his defense:

> If "Cain" be blasphemous, "Paradise Lost" is blasphemous; and the words ... "Evil, be thou my good!" are from that very poem, from the mouth of Satan, – and is there anything more in that of Lucifer, in the Mystery? "Cain" is nothing more than a drama, not a piece of argument.
>
> I could not make Lucifer expound the Thirty-nine Articles, nor talk as the Divines do: that would never have suited his purpose, – nor, one would think, theirs. They ought to be grateful to him for giving them a subject to write about. What would they do without evil in the Prince of Evil? Othello's occupation would be gone. I have made Lucifer say no more in his defence than was absolutely necessary, – not half so much as Milton makes his Satan do.
>
> I was forced to keep up his dramatic character. *Au reste,* I have adhered closely to the Old Testament, and I defy any one to question my moral. Johnson, who would have been glad of an opportunity of throwing another stone at Milton, redeems him from any censure for putting impiety and even blasphemy into the mouths of his infernal spirits. By what rule,

then, am I to have all the blame? When Leigh Hunt commented upon Byron's arguments later in *Lord Byron and some of his Contemporaries*, he cut through Byron's deliberately "mystifying" remarks. Byron's defence, Hunt says:

> is not sincere. "Cain" was undoubtedly meant as an attack upon the crude notions of the Jews respecting evil and its origin. Lord Byron might not have thought much about the matter, when he undertook to write it; but such was his feeling. He was conscious of it; and if he had not been, Mr. Shelley would not have suffered him to be otherwise. But the case is clear from internal evidence. Milton, in his "Paradise Lost," *intended* nothing against the religious opinions of his time; Lord Byron did.
>
> The reader of the two poems feels certain of this; and he is right. It is true, the argumentative part of the theology of Milton was so bad, that a suspicion has crossed the minds of some in these latter times, whether he was not purposely arguing against himself; but a moment's recollection of his genuine character and history does it away.
>
> Milton was as decidedly a Calvinist at the time he wrote "Paradise Lost," and subject to all the gloomy and degrading sophistries of his sect, as he certainly altered his opinions afterwards, and subsided in a more *Christian* Christianity. [4]

Hunt's criticisms make it plain that Byron's remarks were not so much lies as obfuscations. Byron's careful prose leaves unsaid everything that is truly germane to the issue, for the fact is that Milton's poem is fundamentally fideistic whereas *Cain* is just as radically skeptical.

This does not mean that Byron saw Lucifer as his play's moral exemplar; on the contrary, Byron clearly (and sincerely) represented Lucifer in a critical light. But if he gave his diabolic prince certain negative qualities, he also created for him a number of sympathetic contexts, as well as several powerful speeches. Lucifer's parting words to Cain are a stirring rhetorical plea for one of Byron's deepest convictions: intellectual freedom.

The mixed character of Byron's Lucifer makes him a fitting inheritor of that line of post-Miltonic criticism which liked to sympathize with the demon's grandeur or power or suffering. Most of Byron's ideas about Milton, and *Paradise Lost* in particular, have little to do with that odd fragment of literary history, for Byron's Miltonic preoccupations were often of a technical nature.

But when Byron did comment upon the character of Milton's Satan, he clearly echoed those eighteenth-century critics who had done so much to establish the ground for the Romantic idea that Satan was the hero of *Paradise Lost*.

I must remark from *Aristotle* and *Rymer*, that the *hero* of tragedy and (I add *meo periculo*) a tragic poem must *be guilty*, to excite *"terror and pity,"* the end of tragic poetry. But hear not *me*, but my betters. "The pity which the poet is to labour for is *for* the criminal. The terror is likewise in the punishment of the said criminal, who, if he be represented too great an offender, will *not be pitied*; if altogether *innocent* his punishment will be unjust" ... Who is the hero of *Paradise Lost?* Why Satan – and Macbeth, and Richard, and Othello, and Pierre, and Lothario, and Zanga?

Byron does not idealize Satan any more than he idealizes his own Lucifer. Rather, Byron's argument depends upon a humanized interpretation of the fallen angel. In this respect, Byron's view is the direct inheritor of that eighteenth-century critical tradition which, by attempting to defend the probability of Milton's rebel angel, developed an elaborate exegesis of his human qualities and reactions.

Unlike his remarks on *Cain* and Milton, Byron's commentary on Satan as the hero of *Paradise Lost* is completely sincere. Byron believed that the devil was equivocally represented in Milton's epic, and if Leigh Hunt was able to discern the assured fideistic character of *Paradise Lost*, Byron was equally certain that the poem was basically non-dogmatic. "Cain," Byron said, "is not a piece of argument".

It represented neither the devil's party nor God's, for Byron had no intention (nor any inclination) to choose forms of worship with his poetic tales. In this matter Byron felt himself to be following Milton's lead precisely, for he could not see an unequivocal theology in *Paradise Lost*. Milton's epics, for Byron, mirrored the open mind of their creator. According to Byron, they "prove nothing".

His great epics ... prove nothing ... He certainly excites compassion for Satan, and endeavours to make him out an injured personage – he gives him human passions too, makes him pity Adam and Eve, and justify himself much as Prometheus does ... I should be very curious to know what his real belief was.

The "Paradise Lost" and "Regained" do not satisfy me on this point. This text is the crucial one for understanding Milton's influence upon Byron's Satanism. It not only contains the germ of his attitude toward Milton the thinker, it explains why Milton's influence upon the Byronic hero took the peculiar form it did.

Byron's gloomy heroes have long been recognized as the descendants of Milton's Satan through the intermediacy of such famous hero-villains as Karl Moor, Ambrosio, and Schedoni. Indeed, when Byron made his notorious remark that Satan was the hero of *Paradise Lost* he was not commenting directly on *Paradise Lost* at all.

His letter was a reply to his friend Francis Hodgson, who had made some severe criticisms of Gothic hero-villains, that "long series of depraved ... profligates adorned with courage, and rendered interesting by all the warmth and tenderness of love ... [They] cannot but have had the worst effect upon the minds of the young."

Byron's answer to Hodgson justifies (to a certain extent) his repeated assertions that his tragic heroes were never meant to be taken as models for behaviour. The histories of the Giaour, Conrad, Manfred, Lucifer, Cain, Christian, *et al.* are records of guilt and suffering, and for this reason Byron was right to object when critics accused him of immorality. Byron defended *Cain,* his own many dark heroes, as well as the fascinating villains of Gothic literature, on the same principle which guided his reading of *Paradise Lost.*

Milton's poem was intellectually problematic for Byron because all of Milton's characters seemed humanized. Following Pope and others, Byron criticized Milton's portrayal of God because He seemed altogether too mundane, and hence sounded ridiculous while delivering His long theological disquisitions. According to Byron, He never should have appeared in the epic at all. Similarly, Satan's character had been wrought with the greatest art, but the psychological result was the portrait of a criminal-hero. Guilty he most certainly was, but a pure principle of evil he was not.

This humanistic reading of *Paradise Lost* helped Byron to create his own famous portraits of the criminal-hero. If Byron wondered what Milton's true beliefs might have been, his own lifelong uncertainty and skepticism about ultimate philosophical and theological questions were continually represented in his Gothic and oriental tales and his meta/physical dramas.

These poems were Byron's means not for asserting his philosophical convictions, but for exploring the intellectual questions which never ceased to bother him. Moreover, the crucial vehicles for his intellectual questionings were his notorious and deeply problematical heroes, all of whom, as we know, trace their heritage back to Milton's Satan.

Byron told his wife that he believed himself the avatar of a fallen angel. This bizarre conviction explains, among other things, his fascination with the Satan of *Paradise Lost*. Byron's early heroes are frequently associated in more or less explicit ways with Milton's fallen angel.

He stood a stranger in this breathing world, An erring spirit from another hurl'd;

(Lara, I, 315–316)

Enough—no foreign foe could quell Thy soul, till from itself it fell.

(The Giaour, 138–139)

His soul was changed, before his deeds had driven Him forth to war with man and forfeit heaven.

(The Corsair, I, 251 –252)

All such figures are, for Byron, guilty but fascinating beings. They are Satanic, and the measure of his judgment upon them is taken in his lyric "Prometheus." Like Shelley, Byron distinguished between the divine rebellions of Satan on the one hand and Prometheus on the other. His Satanic heroes, all "errant on dark ways diverse," are properly self/ destroyed. But Prometheus is the innocent victim of an arbitrary external power. Far from making war on man, as Byron's Satanic heroes do, Prometheus is marvellously humanitarian. In Byron's terms he is not a tragic figure at all.

But while this distinction between the Promethean and the Satanic in Byron is necessary, the poems quite clearly represent even the most reprobate of Byron's heroes in a sympathetic way. The following remarks of Byron to Lady Blessington explain the reason for his sympathetic portraits of bad men.

It is my *respect for morals that makes me so indignant against its vile substitute cant, with which I wage war,* and this the good-natured world chooses to consider as a sign of my *wickedness.*

We are all the creatures of circumstance, the greater part of our errors are caused, if not excused, by events and situations over which we have had little control; the world see the faults, but they see not what led to them: therefore I am always lenient to crimes that have *brought their own punishment,* while I am a little disposed to pity those who think they atone for their own sins by exposing those of others, and add cant *and hypocrisy to the catalogue of their vices.*

Thus speaks Byron the genteel reformer. His famous tales of guilty adventurers are all exercises in which sympathy is evoked for the hero by forcing the reader to consider all the circumstances of the case. The reader is asked not to excuse but to seek understanding.

There was in him a vital scorn of all; As if the worst had fall'n which could befall, He stood a stranger in this breathing world, An erring spirit from another hurl'd; A thing of dark imaginings, that shaped By choice the perils he by chance escaped; But 'scaped in vain, for in their memory yet His mind would half exult and half regret.

With more capacity for love than earth Bestows on most of mortal mould and birth, His early dreams of good outstripp'd the truth, And troubled manhood follow'd baffled youth; with thought of years in phantom chase misspent, And wasted powers for better purpose lent; And fiery passions that had pour'd their wrath.

In hurried desolation o'er his path, And left the better feelings all at strife In wild reflection o'er his stormy life; But haughty still and loth himself to blame, He call'd on Nature's self to share the shame, And charged all faults upon the fleshly form She gave to clog the soul, and feast the worm; Till he at last confounded good and ill, And half mistook for fate the acts of will.

Such men are vital because they are so problematic. The verse runs us through a series of paradoxes and contradictory circumstances. Indeed, the rushing movement of these portraits is essential to their effect, for the read erismeant to best ruck with a sense that, thoug hone may understand the nature and causes of the detailed situation, one must always remain behindhand with solutions.

Too many factors are inevitably involved in human affairs, something crucial is always beyond one's control. Just as the Byronic hero's life is confounded equally in his will and in his fate, so the reader's schemes for moral order – whatever they may be – are confounded by Byron's presentation.

Our sympathy for such a man is the melancholy sign of human ineffectuality. Indeed, the Byronic hero illustrates in his life what the reader, meeting him, discovers in himself. They "prove nothing"; rather, they raise questions.

To instill in the reader a dislocated and melancholy intelligence is the primary function of the Byronic hero, who is, therefore, another of Byron's devices for making war on "cant." All Byronic heroes are almost hypnotically fascinating. The monks in *The Giaour* fear to look upon the hero of that tale because his very appearance troubles their consciences. The effect he produces is typical of the whole species.

With all that chilling mystery of mien, And seeming gladness to remain unseen, He sad (if 'twere not nature's boon) an art Of fixing memory on another's heart: It was not love perchance, nor hate, nor aught That words can image to express the thought; But they who saw him did not see in vain, And once beheld, would ask of him again: And those to whom he spake remember'd well, And on the words, however light, would dwell: None knew, nor how, nor why, but he entwined Himself perforce around the hearer's mind; There he was stamp'd, in liking, or in hate, If greeted once; however brief the date That friendship, pity, or aversion knew, Still there within the inmost thought he grew.

You could not penetrate his soul, but found, Despite your wonder, to your own he wound; His presence haunted still; and from the breast He forced an all unwilling interest: Vain was the struggle in that mental net, His spirit seem'd to dare you to forget!

One dares not forget the sight of such a man because he is a living challenge to the comforts of undemanding and conventional ethics. To have known the Byronic hero is to have discovered a new and terrifying problematics of morality. For infinite as boundless space The thought that Conscience must embrace, Which in itself can comprehend Woe without name, or hope, or end.

Sorrows and disasters hunt the Byronic hero because he remains, in some radical way, unprotected. Ordinary men *are* ordinary not merely because they do not suffer in the nets of circumstance which have trapped these heroes, but even more because they do not see the true complexities of good and evil. Ordinary men are protected by their ordinary mortalities, by cant. He knew himself a villain, but he deem'd The rest no better than the thing he seem'd; And scorn'd the best as hypocrites who hid Those deeds the bolder spirit plainly did.

As Marino Faliero observes: "I am not innocent – but are these guiltless?" (V, iii, 40). His question illustrates the reflexive purpose of the Byronic hero's life. Meditating on the obscure complexities of this figure, the reader is thrown back on himself. The Corsair is a fearful object of scrutiny not because of what he reveals about himself but because he threatens to expose to the observer his *own* hidden heart.

Though smooth his voice, and calm his general mien, Still seems there something he would not have seen: His features' deepening lines and varying hue At times attracted, yet perplex'd the view, As if within that murkiness of mind

Word'd feelings fearful and yet undefin'd; Such might it be—that none could truly tell— Too close inquiry his stern glance would quell.

There breathe but few whose aspect might defy The full encounter of his searching eye: He had the skill, when Cunning's gaze would seek To probe his heart and watch his changing cheek, At once the observer's purpose to espy, And on himself roll back his scrutiny, Lest he to Conrad rather should betray Some secret thought, than drag that chief 's to day. The inscrutable appearance of Conrad is a mirror in which the observer sees his own life in a clarified extreme. To the reader the Byronic hero whispers, threatens a self-revelation.

This special quality of the Byronic hero sets him apart from most Gothic villains, who served, however, as Byron's immediate inspiration. For the typical Gothic villain does not set out to promote a radical critique of established moral issues. Circumstances have indeed warped Ambrosio's character, as they have warped Karl Moor, but in both cases we never doubt the rightness of an essential, and discoverable, code of values. A sense of prevenient order is always present in the pre-Byronic treatment of the hero-villain.

But Byron's tales and plays achieved their enormous influence, and sometimes bad reputation, because their heroes forced the reader to a more searching inquiry into norms for order and value.

We say that they are skeptical, and problematic, for they do not allow things to come out right in the end. We are always left wondering about the events and puzzling over their significance.

This quality in, for example, *The Giaour,* or *Lara,* or *Cain,* is the necessary consequence of Byron's "existential" reading of Aristotle on tragic effect. The "end" of tragedy, Byron remarked, is pity and fear, but he says nothing about the purgation of these emotions and the restoration of a final sense of order.

Byron's reading of Aristotle stays *in medias res* just as his tales and plays characteristically refuse to set the problems they raise within a context of comfort, understanding, and government.

Pre-Byronic hero-villains are sentimental figures because they finally set aside the intellectual issues which they themselves have raised for us. But the Byronic hero carries out his skeptical programs. This is why Byron's tales and plays are actively intellectual works, whereas *The Monk* and *The Italian* and *Die Räuber* at some point rein in their questionings and set the reader's consciousness at rest.

Byron seems to have sensed this moderating quality in most Gothic treatments of the hero-villain. Milton, however, the unwitting father of these figures, he specifically excepted. Milton's mind, Byron says, is as searching and unsettled as his own. Indeed, Milton's mind is not only not made up, it positively avoids "argument" on a system or "proof" for a set of fixed ideas.

He too provokes one to wonder about the issues involved in his epics by his non-dogmatic handling of certain very dogmatically conditioned materials. Most modern scholars would agree with Leigh Hunt, and disagree with Byron, about the belief structure of Milton's epics. That is another scholarly issue altogether.

What is certain is that Milton was a signal influence not only upon the details which make up a portrait of the Byronic hero, but upon Byron's peculiarly skeptical treatment of that hero and his milieu. The intellectual freedom which Milton championed assumed a new and wilder form when it rose again, under Milton's own influence, in Byron. One is probably safe in assuming that Milton would not have approved – would probably have disavowed – his wayward offspring. But then fathers from at least the time of Jahweh have always fallen out with those children most fashioned in their own image and likeness.

In April 1814 – less than a year before his marriage and just two years before he was to leave England for good – Byron composed a poem on one of his greatest heroes. The *Ode to Napoleon Buonaparte,* at once a lament and a denunciation, was soon to acquire a weirdly self-reflexive dimension. Of the fallen

Emperor Byron writes: Since he, miscall'd the Morning Star, Nor man nor fiend hath fallen so far. (Stanza 1)

Byron's own fall from society, via his falling out with his wife, was a descent of similar notoriety, and – so it came to seem for Byron – of equal significance and magnitude. Of the Giaour Byron had written, in remembrance of Milton, that nothing "could quell / Thy soul, till from itself it fell." Napoleon too, the Ode tells us, is another hero fallen from himself. Byron was quick to see in his own life this pattern of eminence and degradation when the appropriate time came. In exile in Switzerland he writes to his sister:

The fault was mine—nor do I seek to screen My errors with defensive paradox— I have been cunning in mine overthrow The careful pilot of my proper woe.

The last two lines draw Byron into the Miltonic company of the self/ fallen and self-condemned. But the first two lines of the passage, though not themselves Miltonic, distinctly echo an important Miltonic passage in *Manfred.*

There is a power upon me which withholds, And makes it my fatality to live; If it be life to wear within myself This barrenness of spirit, and to be My own soul's sepulchre, for I have ceased To justify my deeds unto myself— The last infirmity of evil.

The allusion to "Lycidas" ("Fame is the spur ... That last infirmity of noble minds") occurs in a passage full of significance for Byron. *Manfred* is a nakedly autobiographical piece in which Byron tries to represent what sort of life can remain for a man once he knows not only that his soul is a sepulchre, but that he himself has made it so. In the "[Epistle to Augusta]," where he says that "The world is all before me," the way he finally takes is at least as solitary and problematic as Adam and Eve's.

But in *Manfred,* if the circumstances are equivocal and lonely throughout, the hero comes not only to accept his own barrenness of spirit, but even to find in such desolation an unexpected gift (see the pun on "desert" in *Manfred,* III, iv, 136, quoted below). Echoing Milton once again, Byron establishes Satan as Manfred's ancestor: "on his brow / The thunder/ scars are graven" (III, iv, 76–77). But Byron's Satanic hero takes the famous dictum of Milton's fallen angel

The mind is its own place, and in itself Can make a Heaven of Hell, a Hell of Heaven.

and alters its significance as radically as he had altered the significance of the "Lycidas" passage. Twice Byron echoes Satan's famous remark (III, i, 70ff., and III, iv, 129ff.) and in each case we are given a glimpse of the state of mind of a man who has freed himself of the last infirmity of his own confessed evil. Gone is the possibility of any "defensive paradox" or self-justification; if Manfred is to be born again, it will have to be from the knowledge of his own desert. And so it is.

The mind which is immortal makes itself Requital for its good or evil thoughts, Is its own origin of ill and end, And its own place and time; its innate sense, When stripp'd of this mortality, derives No colour from the fleeting things without, But is absorb'd in sufferance or in joy, Born from the knowledge of its own desert.

In *Manfred* and several other poems of 1816–1817, Milton helped Byron to explore the nature and extent of his downfall. But as Byron let his mind turn more and more on Milton (the process began in 1816 about the time he took up residence in the Villa Diodati – of Miltonic memory), he began to see a broad but clear parallel between the trials, betrayals, and goals of Milton's life and the similar circumstances of his own. The result of this was a noticeable shift in Byron's Miltonic echoes and borrowings whenever he wrote within the context of his own life's drama.

Manfred (like Byron's Dante) learns to avoid the last infirmity of his own evil nature not only by recalling "Lycidas" but even more by invoking the history of Milton Agonistes. When Byron tells us that he had been the cause of his own "proper woe, " and when Manfred wonders, just before the "Lycidas" allusion, "If it be life to wear within myself / This barrenness of spirit, and to be / My own soul's sepulchre, " we are, in both cases, being asked to recall passages in *Samson Agonistes:*

Nothing of all these evils hath befallen me But justly; I

myself have brought them on, Sole author I, sole cause. To live a life half dead, a living death, And buried; but O yet more miserable! Myself, my sepulchre, a moving grave.

Immediately and for some time after the separation, Byron seems to have been obsessed with the parallels between his own situation and that of Samson/Milton. Canto III of *Childe Harold* concludes with a general parallel between Samson and Byron (stanza 103). Even more particularly, the famous line near the end of "Stanzas to Augusta" – "In the desert a fountain is springing" – echoes the divine act which, in Samson's need, "caused a fountain at thy prayer / From the dry ground to spring" (581 –582).

In the fourth canto of *Childe Harold* Byron drastically extended the range of his willed identifications with "fallen ... and buried greatness." Prowling through the museums and libraries of history, Byron found that he was not only the avatar of numerous Western heroes, real and mythological, but that a remarkable number of dead poetic spirits found their second selves in George Gordon.

This inclination to seek his own image throughout history produced those bizarre autobiographical ex/ ercises *The Lament of Tasso* and *The Prophecy of Dante*. But while many Italian spirits march across the stanzas of *Childe Harold IV*, itisan English poet, Milton, who stands as Byron's unnamed but clearly invoked precursor.

Childe Harold IV has two subjects, one personal (involving the disastrous history of Lord Byron) and one political (involving the present state of Italian degradation). As the poem develops, it becomes clear that the two subjects depend upon each other.

Briefly, Byron hopes to reacquire a vital personal control upon life through his poetry, which he gives over to the service of Italian *risorgimento*. But in setting about this task, Byron invokes England's other traduced republican genius. Milton too spoke out for freedom in another time of trouble, and Byron returns to him for a present guidance and a present strength.

Yet, Italy! through every other land Thy wrongs should

ring, and shall, from side to side; Mother of Arts, as once of arms; thy hand Was then our guardian, and is still our guide; Parent of our Religion, whom the wide Nations have knelt to for the keys of heaven! Europe, repentant of her parricide, Shall yet redeem thee, and, all backward driven, Roll the barbarian tide, and sue to be forgiven. (Stanza 47)

A pivotal stanza in *Childe Harold IV,* it looks forward to the so-called "Forgiveness-curse" stanzas (stanzas, 130–137) and backward to Milton's proud sonnet "Cyriak, this three years day" (Sonnet 22). The allusion to Milton is brilliantly apt, for with it Byron reminds us that his political career is as related to his more intimate history as Milton's political involvements were to *his* personal life:

What supports me dost thou ask? The conscience, friend, to have lost [my sight] overplied In Liberty's defence, my noble task, Of which all Europe talks from side to side.

Later in the canto Byron extends the Milton parallels. The "immedicable wound" suffered by England at the death of the politically liberal (it was believed) Princess Charlotte recalls the "immedicable soul" of all those whose lives seem to be "not in / The harmony of things." Both phrases reach back to recover a pertinent series of verses in *Samson Agonistes.*

My griefs not only pain me As a lingering disease, But finding no redress, ferment and rage, Nor less than wounds immedicable Rankle, and fester.

As it ensues, Byron takes at least the formal pattern for his behaviour in Canto IV from Samson's. Though confessing his responsibility for the disasters of his life, Byron denounces the treachery of his unnamed familial connection. Samson does the same. Both Samson and Byron leave the execution of revenge to other lords (*SA,* 506–508; *CHP IV,* 130–133), both offer a fury of forgiveness, both speak to their consorts "At distance" (*SA,* 954), both represent their wives in recurrent ophidian metaphors.

Furthermore, the image of an independent and powerful hero imprisoned in darkness and chains flits through Byron's poem, as it does through a number of other works of Byron's exilic period, most obviously *The Prisoner of Chillon* and *The*

Lament of Tasso (both of which contain Milton echoes). In *Childe Harold IV,* this Samson-like image is given its most powerfully Miltonic turn immediately after Byron's allusive reference to man's "immedicable soul."

Yet let us ponder boldly; 'tis a base Abandonment of reason to resign Our right of thought, our last and only place Of refugee ... Though from our birth the faculty divine Is chain'd and tortured ... And bred in darkness, lest the truth should shine Too brightly for the unpreparéd mind, The beam pours in, for time and skill will couch the blind. But not until *Don Juan* does Byron explicitly draw out the parallels he felt between his own life and Milton's.

The only two that in my recollection Have sung of heaven and hell, or marriage, are Dante and Milton, and of both the affection Was hapless in their nuptials, for some bar Of fault or temper ruin'd the connection (Such things, in fact, it don't ask much to mar): But Dante's Beatrice and Milton's Eve Were not drawn from their spouses, you conceive.

In the very act of writing such a stanza Byron establishes his equality with these two poets. Like *Childe Harold IV,* the verses enact Byron's achievement of his place among the community of the world's poetic geniuses, only in this case Byron stands with them not because of his tragic history, but because of his urbanity and great wit. He does not meet them because of likenesses in personal history, but because of the verse skills he displays in the handling of those likenesses.

Earlier in his masterpiece – in fact, at the outset – Byron reached for an identification with Milton in a mood more severe, if no less witty.

X If, fallen in evil days on evil tongues, Milton appealed to the Avenger, Time, If Time, the Avenger, execrates his wrongs, And makes the word "Miltonic" mean "*sublime,*" *He* deign'd not to belie his soul in songs, Nor turn his very talent to a crime; *He* did not loathe the Sire to laud the Son, But closed the tyrant-hater he begun.

XI Think'st thou, could he—the blind Old Man—arise, Like Samuel from the grave, to freeze once more The blood of monarchs with his prophecies, Or be alive again—again all hoar With time and trials, and those helpless eyes, And heartless daughters—worn—and pale—and poor; Would *he* adore a sultan? *he* obey The intellectual eunuch Castlereagh?

("Dedication" to *Don Juan*)

Be recalling stanzas 130–133 of *Childe Harold IV* Byron underlines the Miltonic character of that poem's most intimately autobiographical pas/ sages, and reminds us that we were not wrong to hear in them the undersong of *Samson Agonistes.*

Further, Byron also makes explicit the political and poetic inheritance to which, in his mind, he was the true heir. As the whole of the "Dedication" shows, Byron set out in *Don Juan* to dispute with those Miltonists, Southey and Wordsworth, the right to take Milton as their forebear. Wordsworth and Southey may affect the Miltonic style, may wear the trappings of his Muse, but it is Byron in whom Milton's living spirit survives.

"Though fall'n on evil dayes, " like Milton, Byron wittily recalls the invocation to Urania in Book VII of *Paradise Lost* in order to justify the ways of his "pedestrian Muses" to men. Southey and Wordsworth may be off and flying on their time-serving and pompous steeds just as they are free to seek their fortunes in the world of Lord Castlereagh, Poet-Laureateships, and places "in the Excise." To let them have their way is to let them condemn themselves.

For me, who, wandering with pedestrian Muses, Contend not with you on the winged steed, I wish your fate may yield ye, when she chooses, The fame you envy, and the skill you need; And recollect a poet nothing loses In giving to his brethren their full meed Of merit, and complaint of present days Is not the certain path to future praise.

("Dedication" to *Don Juan* stanza VIII)

Meantime, while these bastard children of Milton soar in their illusory poetic heavens, Byron will gather himself back to his father and begin *Don Juan* under the aegis of the human books of *Paradise Lost.*

Return me to my Native Element: Least from this flying Steed enrein'd (as once *Bellerophon,* though from a lower Clime)

Dismounted, on th' *Aleian* Field I fall Erroneus there to wander and forlorne.

Half yet remaines unsung, but narrower bound Within the visible Diurnal Spheare; Standing on Earth, not rapt above the Pole More safe I Sing with mortal voice, unchang'd To hoarce or mute, though fall'n on evil dayes, On evil dayes though fall'n and evil tongues; In darkness, and with dangers compast round, And solitude; yet not alone, while thou Visit'st my slumbers Nightly, or when Morn Purples the East: still govern thou my Song, *Urania,* and fit audience find, though few.

Chapter 3

Byron, Mobility, and the Poetics of Historical Ventriloquism

Byron's popularity – the fact that he was a bestseller and "famous in [his] time" – has always focused certain literary problems, not least of all, at the outset, for Byron himself. "Lord Byron cuts a figure – but he is not figurative", Keats waspishly observed in a letter to the George Keatses. This is an envious and illuminating remark which reveals as much about Keats and his ambitions for a successful career as it does about the character of Byron's verse, the phenomenon of Byronism, and the changing structure of the institution of letters at the beginning of the nineteenth century.

Later writers have sometimes condescended to Byron, particularly to the Byron of the pre-exilic period, as a factitious writer who had merely seized the main chance during the Years of Fame. Of course it is true that he was himself largely responsible for creating the enormous popularity of the Oriental and Byronic Tales.

Nevertheless – so the story goes – he cranked out verse between 1812 and 1815 to various formulas and audience expectations. In this activity he was not so much a poet as he was a pander and whore to public tastes. It passes without saying that those tastes were corrupt. (The non/ malicious version of this general view is that Byron invented the myth of himself as The Romantic Poet, thereby creating a new structure of authorship which answered to the changing conditions that were rapidly transforming the English literary institution.)

Byron himself was well aware of these events and social formations. His letters and his poetry alike reflect on these matters often. In May 1813, for example, at the peak of his London years, Byron writes to Thomas Moore about projects in poetry:

Stick to the East; – the oracle, Staël, told me it was the only poetical policy. The little I have done in that way is merely a "voice in the wilderness" for you; and, if it has had any success, that also will prove that the public are orientalizing, and pave the path for you. (*Byron's Letters and Journals*. Ed. Leslie Marchand (hereafter *BLJ*), III, 101)

Later, of course, he came to speak more critically, even disparagingly, of this kind of careerist calculation. In January 1822 he tells Douglas Kinnaird that "*my* object is not *immediate* popularity in my present productions which are written on a different system from the rage of the day"; and in another letter three days later:

"Now once and for all about publication – I *[n]ever courted the* public – and I will never yield to it. – As long as I can find a *single* reader I will publish my Mind ... and write while I feel the impetus" (*BLJ*, IX, 92, 94).

Byron arrived at this changed position largely because of the Separation Controversy and its aftermath, which exposed to critical analysis a whole train of Byron's most cherished ideas and illusions. The idea which dominates his "[Epistle to Augusta]" – that "I have been cunning in mine overthrow, / The careful pilot of my proper woe" (lines 23–24) – has its deepest filiations with Byron's public life and poetical career between 1807 and 1816, as a later passage of the same poem testifies:

With false Ambition what had I to do? Little with Love, and least of all with Fame; And yet they came unsought; and with me grew; And made me all which they can make—a Name. Yet this was not the end I did pursue; Surely I once beheld a nobler aim. This critical examination of himself, his public life, and his poetical/ moral goals will dominate most of his later years and will affect all aspects of his work in the most profound ways.

I have sketched this brief history in order to recollect two salient aspects of Byron's work, especially his later work. The first has to do with the historical/biographical dimensions of his poetry.

To speak only of *Don Juan,* we are always aware when reading the poem that its most persistent subtext is the myth (or plot) of Byron's public life, which *Don Juan* reflects upon as an exemplary history – a tale which sums up, in an English perspective, the meaning of the entire European epoch stretching from the late 1780sto 1818 and the six following years (the period of *Don Juan*'s composition and publication). More particularly, Byron's work will, as a matter of course, generate itself by echoing and reflecting his own earlier poetical works. The most dramatic example of this outside of *Don Juan* is, I suppose, stanzas 51 –52 of *Beppo.*

Oh! that I had the art of easy writing, What should be easy reading! could I scale Parnassus, where the Muses sit inditing Those pretty poems never known to fail, How quickly would I print (the World delighting) A Grecian, Syrian, or *Assyrian* tale; And sell you, mixed with western Sentimentalism, Some samples of the *finest Orientalism.* But I am but a nameless sort of person, (A broken Dandy lately on my travels).

Part of the genius of this passage is that it manages to be at once critical and sympathetic toward Byron's career, his own earlier work, and the audience which found (and which continues to find) an interest and profit in such things. This poetry institutes a benevolent critique of itself and its world, on the one hand, and, on the other, of the verse which fashion will cultivate at various times – as well as the very concept and event of fashionableness itself.

Often, however – as we have already noticed in the passages from Byron quoted above – Byron's reflective thoughts about these matters conclude on a much more problematic, even a more severe, note. This fact reveals the second important aspect of Byron's poetry: its preoccupation with the social structure of its rhetoric. This preoccupation appears frequently as a problem in Byron's verse which can be phrased, in simple terms, in the following way: a writer must have an audience and hence must operate with certain specific sets of audience expectation, need, and desire (which will be more or less explicit or inchoate); at the same time, the writer cannot merely attend upon and serve audience. Rather, the audience's social character must be reflected back to itself so that it can "reflect upon" that reflection in a critical and illuminating way.

Byron's famous discussion of "Mobility" in Canto XVI on *Don Juan* constitutes a structural analysis of this set of relations, but one that is carried out in non-literary social terms. The passage specifically calls attention to the relation of mobility to the structure of the artist's life:

This makes your actors, artists, and romancers, Heroes sometimes, though seldom—sages never; But speakers, bards, diplomatists, and dancers, Little that's great, but much of what is clever; Most orators, but very few financiers ... (98: 1 –5 – are people, in other words, whose work or life demands that they treat with others in a broadly public or spectacular field.

In a note to this passage Byron defines *mobility* as follows: "an excessive susceptibility of immediate impressions – at the same time without *losing* the past; and is, though sometimes apparently useful to the possessor, a most painful and unhappy attribute." Lady Adeline Amundeville shows that she possesses this equivocal virtue when she is observed dealing with her guests at Norman Abbey.

But Adeline was occupied by fame This day; and watching, witching, condescending To the consumers of fish, fowl and game, And dignity with courtesy so blending, As all must blend whose part it is to aim (Especially as the sixth year is ending) At their lord's, son's, or similar connection's Safe conduct through the rocks of re-elections.

Though this was most expedient on the whole, And usual—Juan, when he cast a glance On Adeline while playing her grand role, Which she went through as though it were a dance, (Betraying only now and then her soul By a look scarce perceptibly askance Of weariness or scorn) began to feel Some doubt how much of Adeline was *real*;

So well she acted, all and every part By turns—with that

vivacious versatility, Which many people take for want of heart. They err—'tis merely what is called mobility, A thing of temperament and not of art, Though seeming so, from its supposed facility; And false—though true; for surely they're sincerest, Who are strongly acted on by what is nearest.

(XVI. 95–97)

These lines deserve some attention. If mobility is "an excessive susceptibility to immediate impressions," the passage also suggests that it is not *simply* a psychological attribute. Lady Adeline is at home in this social world; indeed, her entire life in the poem shows that she is governed by a *social* "susceptibility" to this kind of structure.

She has at once a taste and a gift for managing social affairs of these kinds with brilliance. In the end, however, the passage shows that the psychological attribute and the social formation call out to each other, that they are, indeed, symbiotic and inter-dependent.

We will understand what Byron means when he says that such mobility is "a most painful and unhappy attribute" if we meditate on Lady Adeline's barely perceptible "look ... / Of weariness or scorn." Juan glimpses an important aspect of her character and its social determinants when he observes her "now and then" – in the very midst of her social brilliance – "Betraying ... her soul" in those looks of scorn and weariness. "Playing her grand role" involves, within a Romantic Ideology, a reciprocal danger: lack of authenticity. Thus Lady Adeline "betrays" her soul in at least two senses when she inadvertently reveals her mobility to Juan and to us.

What is crucial to see in all this is that mobility involves a structure of social relations and not simply a psychological characteristic. Byron *interprets* mobility in psychological terms, but his verse exposes this interpretation as a special (ultimately, a Romantic) view of what is clearly a much more complex state of affairs.

Scarcely less important is an interesting paradox which Byron calls attention to: *mobility* appears as a set of social graces, a capacity to charm and to be all things to all men, but it arises, apparently, from a ground of "sincerity" in those kinds of people "Who are strongly acted on by what is nearest." Yet it *appears* the very height of insincerity and calculation. Which is it: "a thing of" one's spontaneous "temperament," or of one's role-playing and "art"? Is it "false" or is it "true"?

This set of paradoxes and contradictions gets registered for us in Lady Adeline's looks of weariness and scorn, and in Byron's remark that mobility is painful and a source of unhappiness. Lady Adeline's "soul" is rent by these paradoxes which her situation reflects but which her consciousness does not appear to understand (or even try to understand).

When Byron reflects upon her situation he gains a clearer knowledge of the contradictions, but he too remains incapable of producing anything more than a demonstrative and aesthetic explanation (which is itself supplemented by the psychological explanation of his note). Reading Byron's verse, we *see* it all much more clearly than Lady Adeline does, for we are provided with a much more comprehensive vantage of the field of relations being played out.

The connection of social mobility to the Romantic artist's ideal of spontaneity and sincerity has often been noted by scholars, most trenchantly, perhaps, by George Ridenour. Thus we now commonly equate the "conversational facility" of *Don Juan* (XV, 20, 3), or what H.J.C. Grierson terms the "strain of passionate improvisation" in Byron's High Romantic mode ("Lord Byron: Arnold and Swinburne,"), with the mobility of Lady Adeline and the "actors, artists, and romancers" who are her equivalents.

What is less often noted is the negative dimension which Byron sees in the artist of mobility. It is mildly shocking, but quite necessary, to understand that the dark shadow cast by the mobility of the spontaneous Romantic poet is called (in *Don Juan* Robert Southey, and sometimes William Wordsworth.

Byron calls Southey an "Epic Renegade" at the very outset of the poem, in the "Dedication", and he links the recent Laureate with Wordsworth as instances of poets who apostasized their early republican principles in their later years. Southey's "conversion" "has lately been a common case", Byron says, but if such "Apostasy's ... fashionable" now, it was not always so. Milton rises up in Byron's "Dedication" as one who "deigned not to belie his soul in songs" which swerved from his initial ground and principles. Byron, of course, justifies himself with such an ideal of poetic and ideological behaviour: "And, if in flattering strains I do not predicate, / 'Tis that I still retain my 'buff and blue'".

In Byron's "Vision of Judgment" Southey's political apostasy is elaborated into a general "literary character, " a GrubStreet avatar formed in the image of his own time.

He said—(I only give the heads)—he said, He meant no harm in scribbling; 'twas his way Upon all topics; 'twas, besides, his bread, Of which he buttered both sides; 'twould delay Too long the assembly (he was pleased to dread), And take up rather more time than a day, To name his works—he would but cite a few— "Wat Tyler"—"Rhymes on Blenheim"—"Waterloo."

He had written praises of a Regicide; He had written praises of all kings whatever; He had written for republics far and wide, And then against them bitterer than ever; For pantisocracy he once had cried Aloud, a scheme less moral than 'twas clever; Then grew a hearty anti-jacobin— Had turned his coat—and would have turned his skin.

He had sung against all battles, and again In their high praise and glory; he had called Reviewing "the ungentle craft," and then Became as base a critic as e'er crawled— Fed, paid, and pampered by the very men By whom his muse and morals had been mauled: He had written much blank verse, and blanker prose, And more of both than any body knows.

He had written Wesley's life:—here turning round To Satan, "Sir, I'm ready to write yours, In two octavo volumes, nicely bound, With notes and preface, all that most allures The pious purchaser; and there's no ground For fear, for I can choose my own reviewers: So let me have the proper documents, That I may add you to my other saints." (Stanzas 96–99) Like Lady Adeline when she is "occupied by fame" (*DJ* XVI, 95, 1), Southey too is ever "watching, witching, condescending" with those who might advance his literary career and projects. He will write on any topic, from any point of view, in any style or medium.

He is, besides, keenly aware of all that is most current, and anxious to be borne along by that current. Finally, he understands how the institutions of literary production operate in his day. In his own summing up, Southey's is "a pen of all work" ("Vision" 100, 5) and he is a poet of skill and industry, without malice (or conscience), good-natured (and culpably unscrupulous).

He has all of Lady Adeline's (and by extension Byron's) gifts, and would be an exact literary reflection but for one thing: his looks never betray the telltale glance "Of weariness or scorn." His mobility is complete but, in the end, un-Byronic, for Byron's Southey does not feel it as a "most painful and unhappy attribute."

Byron's most profound presentation of his idea of Romantic mobility comes, as we might expect, when he draws himself and his own practice into the analysis. "Changeable too – yet somehow *'idem semper'*" (*DJ* XVII, 11, 3): thus Byron sought to describe both himself and his poem in his last, fragmentary canto.

The characterization intersects with the entire constellation of ideas related to the concept of mobility, and thereby also gestures toward the similarities and differences which link Byron to his dark double, Robert Southey. In Canto III these similarities and differences are fully elaborated in the figure of the poet who comes to sing at Juan and Haidée's lavish banquet and festival.

Byron's introductory stanzas describe the character of this poet as "a sad trimmer". This passage distinctly recalls what Byron had said earlier about Southey in the (abandoned) "Preface" to *Don Juan* and the (reluctantly cancelled) "Dedication." There the tone is much more savage, however, resembling in this respect the satiric passage cited earlier from "Vision of Judgment." All the (by now) familiar charges are brought forward – for example, in stanzas 80 and 85:

He was a man who had seen many changes, And always

changed as true as any needle, His polar star being one which rather ranges, And not the fix'd—he knew the way to wheedle: So vile he 'scaped the doom which oft avenges; And being fluent (save indeed when fee'd ill), He lied with such a fervour of intention— There was no doubt he earn'd his laureate pension. ...

Thus, usually, when he was ask'd to sing, He gave the different nations something national; 'Twas all the same to him—"God save the king," Or "*Ca ira,*" according to the fashion all; His muse made increment of any thing, From the high lyric down to the low rational:

If Pindar sang horse-races, what should hinder Himself from being as pliable as Pindar? These stanzas epitomize Byron's usual critique of the poet as renegade and unscrupulous time-server, and they sum up the general tone of Byron's presentation in the passage as a whole. But two other stanzas in the sequence disturbthe proprieties which customarily govern Byron's satire in these situations.

In stanza 84 Byron tells us that this poet had travell'd 'mongst the Arabs, Turks, and Franks, And knew the self-loves of the different nations; And having lived with people of all ranks, Had something ready upon most occasions— Which got him a few presents and some thanks. He varied with some skill his adulations; To "do at Rome as Romans do," a piece Of conduct was which he observed in Greece.

These lines recall nothing so much as Byron himself: first, as the Levantine cruiser of 1809–1811, and second, as the poet and social lion of 1812–1814. Byron had fun at Southey's Laureate expense, and while he sometimes protested that he never courted his immense popularity or flattered his adulators, he knew that he had in fact "filed [his] mind" (*Childe Harold* III, 113, 9) during his Years of Fame. For Byron himself, those years were far from innocent of the "adulations" for which he denounced Southey.

Of himself he could say, with far more certainty than he could of Southey, that he had written verse to foster his image and advance his career. Like Lady Adeline, however, such work was produced side by side with those self-revelatory looks (or poems) "Of weariness or scorn" which reflected critically on the "adulations." Indeed, the "adulations" themselves frequently displayed their own internal self-contradictions. In the "sad trimmer" poet, then, we glimpse the face of Robert Southey, and this is no great surprise; but in the allusion to Southey the outlines of another, unexpected face are also glimpsed. This palimpsest produces an unstable and apparently self-contradicted text whose true biographical subject – Byron himself – emerges from beneath the layers of his own normal satiric displacements:

But now being lifted into high society, And having picked up several odds and ends Of free thoughts in his travels, for variety, He deem'd, being in a lone isle, among friends, That without any danger of a riot, he Might for long lying make himself amends; And singing as he sung in his warm youth, Agree to a short armistice with truth.

This could be, and is in part, an oblique thrust at Southey's renegado turn from his youthful republicanism to his later apostasy. It is also, however, an even more oblique glimpse of Byron's political and poetical career up to 1816, which was marked by its own definite, if much less apparent, forms of ideological backsliding and dishonesty.

Byron was much more "cunning in [his] own overthrow" than Southey was, but that he had pursued "False Ambition" and betrayed his soul's "nobler aim" he could not, and would not, deny (see "[Epistle to Augusta], "). And so "for long lying" he aimed, in this passage, to "make himself amends" in the form of an imitation revolutionary Greek ballad, the famous "Isles of Greece."

The poem is at once an admonishment, or call, and a fulfillment of his highest poetical ideals. And the fulfillment lies precisely in this: that when he *now* sings "as he sung in his warm youth" he reveals, self-consciously and deliberately, both his utopian goals (to which he rededicates himself) and his understanding that he has been the worst betrayer of those goals. He is the worst because he appeared, to himself and to others, as one of the staunchest supporters of such goals.

The ballad's subtle mastery emerges when this network

of allusions, intertexts, and subtexts is fully comprehended. In general, Byron's fiction is that the ballad is sung by a Romaic poet in the late 1780s to an audience of his fellows who live quiescently under Turkish rule. It calls them from their lives of pleasure and political degeneracy to take up a more strenuous and principled course of action.

At this level, it is a poem determined to raise the Greek national consciousness. Consequently, though its fictive date is the late 1780s, and though it recalls the Greek patriotic songs of the late eighteenth century (like Rhiga's "War Song"), its 1820 context is equally operative. In fact, the Greek war for independence was to commence in 1821, and Byron's early attachment to that cause would draw him in 1823 from Italy to western Greece and his famous death in 1824.

Don Juan's fictive level – that is, the plot of Juan's career in the poem's imagined time scheme stretching from about 1787 to its (unreached) conclusion in 1793 – is always calling attention to its narrative (or "real") level: that is, to the poem as a continuing historical event which unfolds before its European audience between 1818 and 1824, and which makes that context part of its subject.

This interplay between a fictive and a narrative time scheme throws into relief a dominant fact about *Don Juan:* that it is fundamentally an autobiographical poem which comments upon and interprets the course of European history between 1787 and 1824. In the case of "The Isles of Greece, "

Byron's fictional Greek poet masks, only to reveal more clearly, the poem's true author. As always in *Don Juan,* Byron reveals and thereby manipulates his poetical machinery in a self-conscious drama of his own mind.

We therefore observe this ballad as a vehicle for satirizing Southey and all other republican turn/ coats, for satirizing generally those who have betrayed the cause of the European political ideal of liberty which had its origin in ancient Greece and which appeared once again in various revolutionary movements during the late eighteenth and early nineteenth centuries (paradigmatically in America and France).

So, when we read "The Isles in Greece" we are also to *see*

Lord Byron satirizing Robert Southey in 1820. At the poem's most complex level, we also *see through* Byron's satire of Southey into the innermost drama of his own mind. Consider the ballad's fifth stanza. And where are they? and where art thou, My country? On thy voiceless shore The heroic lay is tuneless now— The heroic bosom beats no more! And must thy lyre, so long divine, Degenerate into hands like mine?

An act of poetic ventriloquism multiplies the pronominal references in these lines. The Romaic poet sings here of himself and of Greece, but the English poet sings of England and Lord Byron. The ideal of Greece calls out to Byron's, and England's, identification with that ideal, just as the degeneracy of present-day Greece (whether conceived in the context of 1787 or of 1820) reflects upon England's, and Byron's, betrayals of their most cherished, and Greek-derived, ideals.

Two fictive voices sing "The Isles of Greece": the imaginary Romaic poet of 1787 and the imagined Robert Southey of 1820 and they sing of the ideals and betrayals of themselves and their respective countries. In the end, however, the two voices are incorporated as the poetically "actual" voice of Lord Byron, who sings of his own immediate psychic and political situation and the context in which it had developed. 'Tis something, in the dearth of fame, Though link'd among a fetter'd race, To feel at least a patriot's shame, Even as I sing, suffuse my face; For what is left the poet here? For Greeks a blush, for Greece a tear.

A passage like this dramatically reveals the complex voicing techniques of the ballad, along with the related and equally complex network of references and levels of statement. In these lines the "Fame" is Greece's, England's, and Byron's; the "fetter'd race" is Greek, but also Italian (Byron is writing his poem in the Italian dominions of the Austrian Empire), and – even more generally – European ("There is *no* freedom – even for *Masters* – in the midst of slaves" [*BLJ*, IX, 41]). Thus, when Byron gestures to "the poet here," his words resonate in the widest European context of 1787–1824.

The ballad plays itself out as a contest between the rival claims of "The Scian and the Teian muse, / The hero's harp, the lover's lute" (2, 1 –2). Representing a poetical career and its goals as a dialectic between the shifting claims of heroic and amatory verse (here, specifically, between Homer and Anacreon) is a pre-eminently Byronic structure of thought. His entire life's work as a poet develops as a self-lacerating experience of their rival claims.

Whenever Byron moves too definitively toward one of these poetical and political ideals he will call upon the other to limit, criticize, and judge its illusions and appeals. Byron's great lyric "On This Day I Complete My Thirty-Sixth Year" culminates this conflict by representing it as (by itself) a hopeless one. "On This Day" calls for its cessation by invoking the option of suicide. Such is also the option toward which "The Isles of Greece" makes its final gesture.

Place me on Sunium's marbled steep, Where nothing, save the waves and I, May hear our mutual murmurs sweep; There, swan-like, let me sing and die: A land of slaves shall ne'er be mine— Dash down you cup of Samian wine.

As in the later lyric, when the poet here chooses death to break the impasse of his life, his choice involves a decision for the claims of heroism. What is important to see is that this is an historical choice, one demanded by time, place, and circumstance. The voice of the Scian muse plays through "The Isles of Greece" to remind us of the essential virtues of a truly civilized life, which would not include war and violence. But no such life is possible when the social structure is degenerate at its ground. Fill high the bowl with Samian wine! Our virgins dance beneath the shade— I see their glorious black eyes shine; But gazing on each glowing maid, My own the burning tear-drop laves, To think such breasts must suckle slaves.

In such times the image of love itself becomes an occasion for swerving toward heroic values. Nevertheless, we have to see that the move toward the heroic is now regarded as deeply equivocal, a fate or doom embraced by those who are willing to sacrifice themselves by choosing an heroic life in order to secure, at some future date, the restoration of a civilized order.

Thus the ideological structures of "On This Day" and "The Isles of Greece" are all but exact equivalents. However, "On This Day" is a much more interiorized poem, and that difference is crucial. The fact that Byron's voice in "The Isles of Greece" is explicitly mixed with the voices of Southey and the modern Greek patriot, and implicitly with the entire Anacreontic and Homeric traditions, socializes the lyric in a number of important and specific ways. The history imbedded in "On This Day" is Byron's personal history and the drama is fundamentally psychic.

In "The Isles of Greece," on the other hand, the complex voicing extends the world of which and for which the poem is speaking. "On This Day" is set in 1824, in Greece, and in Byron's mind – finally, in the relations which the poem establishes between these three *loci* and all that each implicitly involves. The layered voices in "The Isles of Greece" dramatically enlarge the poem's network of references, forcing the reader to consider the complex *relations* of those references. In the end – like *Don Juan* itself – the lyric implies that European history between 1787 and 1820 is all of a piece, and that the condition of Greece during the period is the very symbol of the condition of Europe.

At the end of the eighteenth century Greece looked for freedom from Turkish rule as Europe looked for a revolutionary emancipation from inherited and archaic political order; in 1820, despite the intervening years of turmoil and promise, the *status quo* has been (at least formally and materially) preserved. Even more telling, however, is the poem's revelation of all of Europe's – including England's – complicity in this state of affairs. In 1809–1811 Byron began to fear the truth of such complicity and he expressed his fears in *Childe Harold's Pilgrimage I–II.* In 1820 his fears have been fully realized. "The Isles of Greece" exposes, analyzes, and judges this complicity.

The English Lord speaks as and for the failed Greek patriot and the turncoat Jacobin Southey. In *Don Juan*'s "Dedication" and elsewhere Byron will separate himself from Southey, Castlereagh, Matternich, and the forgers of Europe's spiritual slavery. Here, by contrast, he speaks with their voices and says, of himself and for all those who have judged themselves innocent: *"Hypocrite lecteur, mon semblable, mon frère."*

Chapter 4

The Attack on Lady Byron

In proving what I asserted in the first chapter, I make four points: 1st. A concerted attack upon Lady Byron's reputation, begun by Lord Byron in self-defence. 2d. That he transmitted his story to friends to be continued after his death. 3d. That they did so continue it. 4th. That the accusations reached their climax over Lady Byron's grave in Blackwood of 1869, and the Guiccioli book, and that this reopening of the controversy was my reason for speaking.

And first I shall adduce my proofs that Lady Bryon's reputation was, during the whole course of her husband's life, the subject of a concentrated, artfully planned attack, commencing at the time of the separation and continuing during his life. By various documents carefully prepared, and used publicly or secretly as suited the case, he made converts of many honest men, some of whom were writers and men of letters, who put their talents at his service during his lifetime in exciting sympathy for him, and who, by his own request, felt bound to continue their defence of him after he was dead.

In order to consider the force and significance of the documents I shall cite, we are to bring to our view just the issues Lord Byron had to meet, both at the time of the separation and for a long time after.

In Byron *Memoirs*, Vol. IV. Letter 350, under date December 10, 1819, nearly four years after the separation, he writes to Murray in a state of great excitement on account of an article in Blackwood, in which his conduct towards his wife had been sternly and justly commented on, and which he supposed to have been written by Wilson, of the Noctes

Ambrosianæ. He says in this letter: "I like and admire W——n, and he should not have indulged himself in such outrageous license..... When he talks of Lady Byron's business he talks of what he knows nothing about; and you may tell him *no man can desire a public investigation of that affair more than I do.*" (italics added by Stowe)

He shortly after wrote and sent to Murray a pamphlet for publication, which was printed, but not generally circulated till some time afterwards. Though more than three years had elapsed since the separation, the current against him at this time was so strong in England that his friends thought it best, at first, to use this article of Lord Byron's discreetly with influential persons rather than to give it to the public.

The writer in Blackwood and the indignation of the English public, of which that writer was the voice, were now particularly stirred up by the appearance of the first two cantos of "Don Juan," in which the indecent caricature of Lady Byron was placed in vicinity with other indecencies, the publication of which was justly considered an insult to a Christian community.

It must here be mentioned, for the honor of Old England, that at first she did her duty quite respectably in regard to "Don Juan." One can still read, in Murray's standard edition of the poems, how every respectable press thundered reprobations, which it would be well enough to print and circulate as tracts for our days.

Byron, it seems, had thought of returning to England, but he says, in the letter we have quoted, that he has changed his mind, and shall not go back, adding: "I have finished the Third Canto of 'Don Juan,' but the things I have heard and read discourage all future publication. You may try the copy question, but you'll lose it; the cry is up, and the cant is up. I should have no objection to return the price of the copyright, and have written to Mr. Kinnaird on this subject."

One sentence quoted by Lord Byron from the Blackwood article will show the modern readers what the respectable world of that day were thinking and saying of him:—

"It appears, in short, as if this miserable man, having

exhausted *every species* of sensual gratification, -having drained the cup of sin even to its bitterest dregs, — were resolved to show us that he is no longer a human being even in his frailties, but a cool, unconcerned fiend, laughing with detestable glee over the whole of the better and worse elements of which human life is composed."

The defence which Lord Byron makes, in his reply to that paper, is of a man cornered and fighting for his life. He speaks thus of the state of feeling at the time of his separation from his wife: —

"I was accused of every monstrous vice by public rumor and private rancor; my name, which had been a knightly or a noble one since my fathers helped to conquer the kingdom for William the Norman, was tainted. I felt that, if what was whispered and muttered and murmured was true, I was unfit for England; if false, England was unfit for me. I withdrew; but this was not enough. In other countries — in Switzerland, in the shadow of the Alps, and by the blue depth of the lakes, — I was pursued and breathed upon by the same blight. I crossed the mountains, but it was the same; so I went a little farther, and settled myself by the waves of the Adriatic, like the stag at bay, who betakes him to the waters.

"If I may judge by the statements of the few friends who gathered round me, the outcry of the period to which I allude was beyond all precedent, all parallel, even in those cases where political motives have sharpened slander and doubled enmity. I was advised not to go to the theatres lest I should be hissed, nor to my duty in Parliament, lest I should be insulted by the way; even on the day of my departure my most intimate friend told me afterwards that he was under the apprehension of violence from the people who might be assembled at the door of the carriage."

Now Lord Byron's charge against his wife was that SHE was directly responsible for getting up and keeping up this persecution, which drove him from England, — that she did it in a deceitful, treacherous manner, which left him no chance of defending himself.

He charged against her that, taking advantage of a time

when his affairs were in confusion, and an execution in the house, she left him suddenly, with treacherous professions of kindness, which were repeated by letters on the road, and that soon after her arrival at her home her parents sent him word that she would never return to him, and she confirmed the message; that when he asked the reason why, she refused to state any; and that when this step gave rise to a host of slanders against him she silently encouraged and confirmed the slanders. His claim was that he was denied from that time forth even the justice of any tangible accusation against himself which he might meet and refute.

He observes, in the same article from which we have quoted:—

"When one tells me that I cannot 'in any way *justify* my own behaviour in that affair,' I acquiesce, because no man can '*justify*' himself until he knows of what he is accused; and I have never had — and, God knows, my whole desire has ever been to obtain it — any specific charge, in a tangible shape, submitted to me by the adversary, nor by others, unless the atrocities of public rumor and the mysterious silence of the lady's legal advisers may be deemed such."

Lord Byron, his publishers, friends, and biographers, thus agree in representing his wife as the secret author and abettor of that persecution, which it is claimed broke up his life, and was the source of all his subsequent crimes and excesses.

Lord Byron wrote a poem in September, 1816, in Switzerland, just after the separation, in which he stated, in so many words, these accusations against his wife. Shortly after the poet's death Murray published this poem, together with the "Fare thee well," and the lines to his sister, under the title of "Domestic Pieces," in his standard edition of Byron's poetry. It is to be remarked, then, that this was for some time a private document, shown to confidential friends, and made use of judiciously, as readers or listeners to his story were able to bear it. Lady Byron then had a strong party in England. Sir Samuel Romilly and Dr.

Lushington were her counsel. Lady Byron's parents were living, and the appearance in the public prints of such a piece as this would have brought down an aggravated storm of public indignation. For the general public such documents as the "Fare thee well" were circulating in England, and he frankly confessed his wife's virtues and his own sins to Madame de Staäl and others in Switzerland, declaring himself in the wrong, sensible of his errors, and longing to cast himself at the feet of that serene perfection,

"Which wanted one sweet weakness, — to forgive."

But a little later he drew for his private partisans this bitter poetical indictment against her, which, as we have said, was used discreetly during his life, and published after his death.

Before we proceed to lay that poem before the reader we will refresh his memory with some particulars of the tragedy of Æschylus, which Lord Byron selected as the exact parallel and proper illustration of his wife's treatment of himself. In his letters and journals he often alludes to her as Clytemnestra, and the allusion has run the round of a thousand American papers lately, and been read by a thousand good honest people, who had no very clear idea who Clytemnestra was, and what she did which was like the proceedings of Lady Byron. According to the tragedy,

Clytemnestra secretly hates her husband Agamemnon, whom she professes to love, and wishes to put him out of the way that she may marry her lover, Ægistheus. When her husband returns from the Trojan war she receives him with pretended kindness, and officiously offers to serve him at the bath. Inducing him to put on a garment, of which she had adroitly sewed up the sleeves and neck so as to hamper the use of his arms, she gives the signal to a concealed band of assassins, who rush upon him and stab him. Clytemnestra is represented by Æschylus as grimly triumphing in her success, which leaves her free to marry an adulterous paramour.

"I did it, too, in such a cunning wise,
That he could neither scape nor ward off doom.
I staked around his steps an endless net,
As for the fishes."

In the piece entitled *"Lines on hearing Lady Byron is ill,"* Lord Byron charges on his wife a similar treachery and cruelty.

The whole poem is in Murray's English edition, Vol. IV. p. 207. Of it we quote the following. The reader will bear in mind that it is addressed to Lady Byron on a sick-bed.

"I am too well avenged, but 't was my right;
Whate'er my sins might be, thou wert not sent
To be the Nemesis that should requite,
Nor did Heaven choose so near an instrument.
Mercy is for the merciful! If thou
Hast been of such, 't will be accorded now.
Thy nights are banished from the realms of sleep,
For thou art pillowed on a curse too deep;
Yes! they may flatter thee, but thou shalt feel
A hollow agony that will not heal.
Thou hast sown in my sorrow, and must reap
The bitter harvest in a woe as real.
I have had many foes, but none like thee;
For 'gainst the rest myself I could defend,
And be avenged, or turn them into friend;
But thou, in safe implacability,
Hast naught to dread, — in thy own weakness shielded,
And in my love, which hath but too much yielded,
And spared, for thy sake, some I should not spare.
And thus upon the world, trust in thy truth,
And the wild fame of my ungoverned youth, —
On things that were not and on things that are, —
Even upon such a basis thou hast built
A monument whose cement hath been guilt!
The moral Clytemnestra of thy lord,
And hewed down with an unsuspected sword
Fame, peace, and hope, and all that better life
Which, but for this cold treason of thy heart,
Might yet have risen from the grave of strife
And found a nobler duty than to part.
But of thy virtues thou didst make a vice,
Trafficking in them with a purpose cold,
And buying others' woes at any price,
For present anger and for future gold;
And thus, once entered into crooked ways,

The early truth, that was thy proper praise,
Did not still walk beside thee, but at times,
And with a breast unknowing its own crimes,
Deceits, averments incompatible,
Equivocations, and the thoughts that dwell
In Janus spirits, the significant eye
That learns to lie with silence, the pretext
Of prudence with advantages annexed,
The acquiescence in all things that tend,
No matter how, to the desired end, —
All found a place in thy philosophy.
The means were worthy and the end is won.
I would not do to thee as thou hast done." (italics were added by Stowe)

Now, if this language means anything, it means, in plain terms, that, whereas, in her early days, Lady Byron was peculiarly characterized by truthfulness, she has in her recent dealings with him acted the part of a liar, — that she is not only a liar, but that she lies for cruel, mean, and malignant purposes, — that she is a moral assassin, and her treatment of her husband has been like that of the most detestable murderess and adulteress of ancient history, -that she has learned to lie skilfully and artfully, that she equivocates, says incompatible things, and crosses her own tracks, — that she is doublefaced, and has the art to lie even by silence, and that she has become wholly unscrupulous, and acquiesces in *any*thing, no matter what, that tends to the desired end, and that end the destruction of her husband.

This is a brief summary of the story that Byron made it his life's business to spread through society, to propagate and make converts to during his life, and which has been in substance reasserted by Blackwood in a recent article this year.

Now, the reader will please to notice that this poem is dated in September, 1816, and that on the 29th of March, of that same year, he had thought proper to tell quite another story. At that time the deed of separation was not signed, and negotiations between Lady Byron, acting by legal counsel, and himself were still pending. At that time, therefore, he was standing in a community who knew all he had said in former days of his wife's character, who were in an aroused and excited state by the fact that so lovely and good and patient a woman had actually been forced for some unexplained cause to leave him. His policy at that time was to make large general confessions of sin, and to praise and compliment her, with a view of enlisting sympathy. Everybody feels for a handsome sinner, weeping on his knees, asking pardon for his offences against his wife in the public newspapers.

The celebrated "Fare thee well," as we are told, was written on the 17th of March, and accidentally found its way into the newspapers at this time "through the imprudence of a friend whom he allowed to take a copy." These "imprudent friends" have all along been such a marvellous convenience to Lord Byron.

But the question met him on all sides, What is the matter? This wife you have declared the brightest, sweetest, most amiable of beings, and against whose behaviour as a wife you actually never had nor can have a complaint to make, -why is she *now* all of a sudden so inflexibly set against you?

This question required an answer, and he answered by writing another poem, which also *accidentally* found its way into the public prints. It is in his "Domestic Pieces," which the reader may refer to at the end of this volume, and is called " A Sketch."

There was a most excellent, respectable, well behaved Englishwoman, a Mrs. Clermont, who had been Lady Byron's governess in her youth, and was still, in mature life, revered as her confidential friend. It appears that this person had been with Lady Byron during a part of her married life, especially the bitter hours of her lonely child-bed, when a young wife so much needs a sympathetic friend. This Mrs. Clermont was the person selected by Lord Byron at this time to be the scapegoat to bear away the difficulties of the case into the wilderness.

We are informed in Moore's Life what a noble pride of rank Lord Byron possessed, and how when the head-master of a school, against whom he had a pique, invited him to dinner, he declined, saying, "To tell you the truth, Doctor, if you should come to Newstead, I should n't think of inviting *you* to dine with *me*, and so I don't care to dine with you here." Different countries, it appears, have different standards as to good taste; Moore gives this as an amusing instance of a young lord's spirit. Accordingly, his first attack against this "lady," as we Americans should call her, consists in gross statements concerning her having been born poor and in an inferior rank. He begins by stating that she was

"Born in the garret, in the kitchen bred,
Promoted thence to deck her mistress' head;
Next — for some gracious service unexpressed
And from its wages only to be guessed —
Raised from the toilet to the table, where
Her wondering betters wait behind her chair.
With eye unmoved and forehead unabashed,
She dines from off the plate she lately washed;
Quick with the tale, and ready with the lie,
The genial confidante and general spy, —
Who could, ye gods! her next employment guess, —
An only infant's earliest governess!
What had she made the pupil of her art
None knows; but that high soul secured the heart,
And panted for the truth it could not hear
With longing soul and undeluded ear!"
(italics were added by Stowe)

The poet here recognizes as a singular trait in Lady Byron her peculiar love of truth, — a trait which must have struck every one that had any knowledge of her through life. He goes on now to give what he certainly knew to be the real character of Lady Byron: —

"Foiled was perversion by that youthful mind,
Which flattery fooled not, baseness could not blind,
Deceit infect not, nor contagion soil,
Indulgence weaken, or example spoil,
Nor mastered science tempt her to look down
On humbler talent with a pitying frown,
Nor genius swell, nor beauty render vain,
Nor envy ruffle to retaliate pain."

We are now informed that Mrs. Clermont, whom he afterwards says in his letters was a spy of Lady Byron's mother, set herself to make mischief between them. He says: —

"If early habits, — those strong links that bind
At times the loftiest to the meanest mind, —
Have given her power too deeply to instil
The angry essence of her deadly will;
If like a snake she steal within your walls,
Till the black slime betray her as she crawls;
If like a viper to the heart she wind,
And leaves the venom there she did not find, —
What marvel that this hag of hatred works
Eternal evil latent as she lurks."

The noble lord then proceeds to abuse this woman of inferior rank in the language of the upper circles. He thus describes her person and manner: —

"Skilled by a touch to deepen scandal's tints
With all the kind mendacity of hints,
While mingling truth with falsehood, sneers with smiles,
A thread of candor with a web of wiles;
A plain blunt show of briefly spoken scheming;
A lip of lies; a face formed to conceal,
And without feeling mock at all who feel;
With a vile mask the Gorgon would disown, —
A cheek of parchment and an eye of stone.
Mark how the channels of her yellow blood
Ooze to her skin and stagnate there to mud,
Cased like the centipede in saffron mail,
Or darker greenness of the scorpion's scale, —
(For drawn from reptiles only may we trace
Congenial colors in that soul or face,)
Look on her features! and behold her mind

AS IN A MIRROR OF ITSELF DEFINED

Look on the picture! deem it not o'ercharged;
There is no trait which might not be enlarged."

The poem thus ends: —

"May the strong curse of crushed affections light

Back on thy bosom with reflected blight,
And make thee in thy leprosy of mind
As loathsome to thyself as to mankind!
Till all thy self-thoughts curdle into hate,
Black — as thy will for others would create;
Till thy hard heart be calcined into dust,
And thy soul welter in its hideous crust.
O, may thy grave be sleepless as the bed,
The widowed couch of fire, that thou hast spread!
Then when thou fain wouldst weary Heaven with prayer,
Look on thy earthly victims — and despair!
Down to the dust! and as thou rott'st away,
Even worms shall perish on thy poisonous clay.
But for the love I bore and still must bear
To her thy malice from all ties would tear,
Thy name, — thy human name, — to every eye
The climax of all scorn, should hang on high,
Exalted o'er thy less abhorred compeers,
And festering in the infamy of years."
March 29, 1816.

Now, on the 29th of March, 1816, this was Lord Byron's story. He states that his wife had a truthfulness even from early girlhood that the most artful and unscrupulous governess could not pollute, — that she always *panted* for truth, — that flattery could not fool nor baseness blind her, — that though she was a genius and master of science, she was yet gentle and tolerant, and one whom no envy could ruffle to retaliate pain.

In September of the same year she is a monster of unscrupulous deceit and vindictive cruelty. Now, what had happened in the five months between the dates of these poems to produce such a change of opinion? Simply this: —

1st. The negotiation between him and his wife's lawyers had ended in his signing a deed of separation in preference to standing a suit for divorce.

2d. Madame de Staël, moved by his tears of anguish and professions of repentance, had offered to negotiate with Lady Byron on his behalf, and had failed. The failure of this application is the only apology given by Moore and Murray for this poem, which gentle Thomas Moore admits was not in quite as generous a strain as the "Fare thee well."

But Lord Byron knew perfectly well, when he suffered that application to be made, that Lady Byron had been entirely convinced that her marriage relations with him could never be renewed, and that duty both to man and God required her to separate from him.

The allowing the negotiation was, therefore, an artifice to place his wife before the public in the attitude of a hard-hearted, inflexible woman; her refusal was what he knew beforehand must inevitably be the result, and merely gave him capital in the sympathy of his friends, by which they should be brought to tolerate and accept the bitter accusations of this poem.

We have recently heard it asserted that this last-named piece of poetry was the sudden offspring of a fit of ill-temper, and was never intended to be published at all. There were certainly excellent reasons why his friends should have advised him not to publish it *at that time*. But that it was read with sympathy by the circle of his intimate friends, and believed by them, is evident from the frequency with which allusions to it occur in his confidential letters to them.

About three months after, under date March 10, 1817, he writes to Moore: "I suppose now I shall never be able to shake off my sables in public imagination, more particularly since my moral —— clove down my famé." Again to Murray in 1819, three years after, he says: "I never hear anything of Ada, the little Electra of Mycenæ."

Electra was the daughter of Clytemnestra, in the Greek poem, who lived to condemn her wicked mother, and to call on her brother to avenge the father. There was in this mention of Electra more than meets the ear. Many passages in Lord Byron's poetry show that he intended to make this daughter a future partisan against her mother, and explain the awful words he is stated in Lady Anne Barnard's diary, to have used when first he looked on his little girl, — "What an instrument of torture I have gained in you!" In a letter to Lord Blessington, April 6, 1823, he says, speaking of Dr. Parr: —

"He did me the honor once to be a patron of mine, though a great friend of the *other branch of the house of Atreus,* and the Greek teacher, I believe, of my *moral* Clytemnestra. I say *moral* because it is true, and is so useful to the virtuous, that it enables them to do anything without the aid of an Ægistheus."

If Lord Byron wrote this poem merely in a momentary fit of spleen, why were there so many persons evidently quite familiar with his allusions to it? and why was it preserved in Murray's hands? and why published after his death? That Byron was in the habit of reposing documents in the hands of Murray, to be used as occasion offered, is evident from a part of a note written by him to Murray respecting some verses so intrusted: "Pray let not these *versiculi* go forth with my name except *to the initiated.*"

Murray, in publishing this attack on his wife after Lord Byron's death, showed that he believed in it, and, so believing, deemed Lady Byron a woman whose widowed state deserved neither sympathy nor delicacy of treatment.

At a time when every sentiment in the heart of the most deeply wronged woman would forbid her appearing to justify herself from such cruel slander of a dead husband, an honest, kindhearted, worthy Englishman actually thought it right and proper to give these lines to her eyes and the eyes of all the reading world. Nothing can show more plainly what this poem was written for, and how thoroughly it did its work! Considering Byron as a wronged man, Murray thought he was contributing his mite towards doing him justice. His editor prefaced the whole set of "Domestic Pieces" with the following statements: —

They all refer to the unhappy separation, of which the precise causes are still a mystery, and which he declared to the last were never disclosed to himself. He admitted that pecuniary embarrassments, disordered health, and dislike to family restraints had aggravated his naturally violent temper and driven him to excesses. He suspected that his mother-in-law had fomented the discord, -which Lady Byron denies, — and that more was due to the malignant offices of a female dependant, who is the subject of the bitterly satirical sketch.

To these general statements can only be added the still vaguer allegations of Lady Byron, that she conceived his conduct to be the result of insanity, — that, the physician pronouncing him responsible for his actions, she could submit to them no longer, and that Dr. Lushington, her legal adviser, agreed that a reconciliation was neither proper nor possible.

No weight can be attached to the opinions of an opposing counsel upon accusations made by one party behind the back of the other, who urgently demanded and was pertinaciously refused the least opportunity of denial or defence. He rejected the proposal for an amicable separation, but consented when threatened with a suit in Doctors' Commons." (italics were added by Stowe)

Neither honest Murray nor any of Byron's partisans seem to have pondered the admission in these last words. Here, as appears, was a woman, driven to the last despair, standing with her child in her arms, asking from English laws protection for herself and child against her husband. She had appealed to the first counsel in England, and was acting under their direction.

Two of the greatest lawyers in England have pronounced that there has been such a cause of offence on his part that a return to him is neither proper nor possible, and that no alternative remains to her but separation or divorce. He asks her to state her charges against him. She, making answer under advice of her counsel, says, "That if he *insists* on the specifications, he must receive them in open court in a suit for divorce."

What, now, ought to have been the conduct of any brave, honest man, who believed that his wife was taking advantage of her reputation for virtue to turn every one against him, who saw that she had turned on her side even the lawyer he sought to retain on his*; that she was an unscrupulous woman, who acquiesced in every and any thing to gain her ends, while he stood before the public, as he says, "accused of every monstrous vice, by public rumor or private rancor"? When she, under advice of her lawyers, made the alternative legal separation or open investigation in court for divorce, what did he do? He Signed The Act Of Separation And Left England. Now, let any man who knows the legal mind of England, — let any lawyer who knows the character of Sir Samuel Romilly and Dr. Lushington, ask whether *they* were the men to take a case into court for a woman that had no *evidence* but her own statements and impressions?

Were *they* men to go to trial without proofs? Did they not know that there were artful, hysterical women in the world, and would they, of all people, be the men to take a woman's story on her own side, and advise her in the last issue to bring it into open court, without legal proof of the strongest kind? Now, as long as Sir Samuel Romilly lived, this statement of Byron's — that he was condemned unheard, and had no chance of knowing whereof he was accused — never appeared in public.

It, however, was most actively circulated in private. That Byron was in the habit of intrusting to different confidants articles of various kinds to be shown to different circles as they could bear them, we have already shown. We have recently come upon another instance of this kind. In the late eagerness to exculpate Byron, a new document has turned up, of which honest John Murray, it appears, had never heard when, after Byron's death, he published in the preface to his "Domestic Pieces" the sentence:

"He rejected the proposal for an amicable separation, but consented when threatened with a suit in Doctors' Commons."

It appears that, up to 1853, neither John Murray senior, nor the son who now fills his place, had taken any notice of this newly found document, which we are now informed "was drawn up by Lord Byron in August, 1817, while Mr. Hobhouse was staying with him at La Mira, near Venice, given to Mr. Matthew Gregory Lewis, for circulation among friends in England, found in Mr. Lewis's papers after his death, and now in the possession of Mr. Murray." Here it is: —

"It has been intimated to me that the persons understood to be the legal advisers of Lady Byron have declared 'their lips to be sealed up' on the cause of the separation between her and myself. If their lips are sealed up, they are not sealed up by me, and the greatest favour *they* can confer upon me will be to open them.

From the first hour in which I was apprised of the intentions of the Noel family to the last communication between Lady Byron and myself in the character of wife and husband (a period of some months), I called repeatedly and in vain for a statement of their or her charges, and it was chiefly in consequence of Lady Byron's claiming (in a letter still existing)

A promise on my part to consent to a separation, if such was *really* her wish, that I consented at all; this claim, and the exasperating and inexpiable manner in which their object was pursued, which rendered it next to an impossibility that two persons so divided could ever be reunited, induced me reluctantly then, and repentantly still, to sign the deed, which I shall be happy — most happy — to cancel, and go before any tribunal which may discuss the business in the most public manner.

"Mr. Hobhouse made this proposition on my part, viz. to abrogate all prior intentions — and go into court — the very day before the separation was signed, and it was declined by the other party, as also the publication of the correspondence during the previous discussion. Those propositions I beg here to repeat, and to call upon her and hers to say their worst, pledging myself to meet their allegations, — whatever they may be, -and only too happy to be informed at last of their real nature.

" BYRON."

" August 9, 1817.

"P. S. — I have been, and am now, utterly ignorant of what description her allegations, charges, or whatever name they may have assumed, are; and am as little aware for what purpose they have been kept back, — unless it was to sanction the most infamous calumnies by silence.

"BYRON.

"LA MIRA, near VENICE."

It appears the circulation of this document must have been very private, since Moore, not over-delicate towards Lady

Byron, did not think fit to print it; since John Murray neglected it, and since it has come out at this late hour for the first time.

If Lord Byron really desired Lady Byron and her legal counsel to understand the facts herein stated, and was willing at all hazards to bring on an open examination, why was this *privately* circulated? Why not issued as a card in the London papers? Is it likely that Mr. Matthew Gregory Lewis, and a chosen band of friends acting as a committee, requested an audience with Lady Byron, Sir Samuel Romilly, and Dr. Lushington, and formally presented this cartel of defiance?

We incline to think not. We incline to think that this small serpent, in company with many others of like kind, crawled secretly and privately around, and when it found a good chance, bit an honest Briton, whose blood was thenceforth poisoned by an undetected falsehood.

The reader now may turn to the letters that Mr. Moore has thought fit to give us of this stay at La Mira, beginning with Letter 286, dated July 1, 1817, where he says: "I have been working up my impressions into a *Fourth* Canto of Childe Harold," and also "Mr. Lewis is in Venice. I am going up to stay a week with him there."

Next, under date La Mira, Venice, July 10, * he says: "Monk Lewis is here; how pleasant!" Next, under date July 20, 1817, to Mr. Murray: "I write to give you notice that I have *completed the fourth and ultimate canto of Childe Harold.....* It is yet to be copied and polished, and the notes are to come."

Under date of La Mira, August 7, 1817, he records that the new canto is one hundred and thirty stanzas in length, and talks about the price for it. He is now ready to launch it on the world; and, as now appears, on August 9, 1817, two days after, he wrote the document above cited, and put it into the hands of Mr. Lewis, as we are informed, "for circulation among friends in England."

The reason of this may now be evident. Having prepared a suitable number of those whom he calls in his notes to Murray "the initiated," by private documents and statements, he is now prepared to publish his accusations against his wife, and the story of his wrongs, in a great immortal poem, which shall have a band of initiated interpreters, shall be read through the civilized world, and stand to accuse her after his death.

In the Fourth Canto of " Childe Harold," with all his own overwhelming power of language, he sets forth his cause as against the silent woman who all this time had been making no party, and telling no story, and whom the world would therefore conclude to be silent because she had no answer to make. I remember well the time when this poetry, so resounding in its music, so mournful, so apparently generous, filled my heart with a vague anguish of sorrow for the sufferer, and of indignation at the cold insensibility that had maddened him.

Thousands have felt the power of this great poem, which stands, and must stand to all time, a monument of what sacred and solemn powers God gave to this wicked man, and how vilely he abused this power as a weapon to slay the innocent.

It is among the ruins of ancient Rome that his voice breaks forth in solemn imprecation:—

"O Time, thou beautifier of the dead,
Adorner of the ruin, comforter,
And only healer when the heart hath bled!
Time, the corrector when our judgments err,
The test of truth, love,—sole philosopher,
For all besides are sophists,—from thy shrift
That never loses, though it doth defer!
Time, the avenger! unto thee I lift
My hands and heart and eyes, and claim of thee a gift.
"If thou hast ever seen me too elate,
Hear me not; but if calmly I have borne
Good, and reserved my pride against the hate
Which shall not whelm me, let me not have worn
This iron in my soul in vain,—shall THEY *not mourn?*
And thou who never yet of human wrong
Left the unbalanced scale, great Nemesis,
Here where the ancients paid their worship long,
Thou who didst call the Furies from the abyss,

And round Orestes bid them howl and hiss
For that unnatural retribution,—just
Had it but come from hands less near,—in this
Thy former realm I call thee from the dust.
Dost thou not hear my heart? awake thou shalt and must!
It is not that I may not have incurred
For my ancestral faults, and mine the wound
Wherewith I bleed withal, and had it been conferred
With a just weapon it had flowed unbound,
But now my blood shall not sink in the ground.
"But in this page a record will I seek;
Not in the air shall these my words disperse,
Though I be ashes,—a far hour shall wreak
The deep prophetic fulness of this verse,
And pile on human heads the mountain of my curse.
That curse shall be forgiveness. Have I not,—
Hear me, my Mother Earth! behold it, Heaven,—
Have I not had to wrestle with my lot?
Have I not suffered things to be forgiven?
Have I not had my brain seared, my heart riven,
Hopes sapped, name blighted, life's life lied away,
And only not to desperation driven,
Because not altogether of such clay
As rots into the soul of those whom I survey?
"From mighty wrongs to petty perfidy,
Have I not seen what human things could do,—
From the loud roar of foaming calumny,
To the small whispers of the paltry few,
And subtler venom of the reptile crew,
The Janus glance of whose significant eye,
Learning to lie with silence, would seem true,
And without utterance, save the shrug or sigh,
Deal round to happy fools its speechless obloquy?"
(italics were added by Stowe)

The reader will please notice that the lines in italics are almost, word for word, a repetition of the lines in italics in the former poem on his wife, where he speaks of a *significant eye* that has *learned to lie in silence,* and were evidently meant to apply to Lady Byron and her small circle of confidential friends.

Before this, in the Third Canto of "Childe Harold," he had claimed the sympathy of the world, as a loving father, deprived by a severe fate of the solace and society of his only child:—

"My daughter,—with this name my song began,—
My daughter,—with this name my song shall end,—
I see thee not and hear thee not, but none
Can be so wrapped in thee; thou art the friend
To whom the shadows of far years extend.
"To aid thy mind's developments, to watch
The dawn of little joys, to sit and see
Almost thy very growth, to view thee catch
Knowledge of objects,—wonders yet to thee,—
And print on thy soft cheek a parent's kiss,—
This it should seem was not reserved for me.
Yet this was in my nature,—as it is,
I know not what there is, yet something like to this.
"Yet though dull hate as duty should be taught,
I know that thou wilt love me; though my name
Should be shut out from thee as spell still fraught
With desolation and a broken claim,
Though the grave close between us,—'t were the same.
I know that thou wilt love me, though to drain
My blood from out thy being were an aim
And an attainment,—all will be in vain."

To all these charges against her, sent all over the world in verses as eloquent as the English language is capable of, the wife replied nothing. 'As a lamb before her shearers is dumb, so she opened not her mouth.'

"Assailed by slander and the tongue of strife,
Her only answer was,—a blameless life."

She had a few friends, a very few, with whom she sought solace and sympathy. One letter from her, written at this time, preserved by accident, is the only authentic record of how the matter stood with her.

We regret to say that the publication of this document was not brought forth to clear Lady Byron's name from her husband's slanders, but to shield *him* from the worst accusation against him, by showing that this crime was not included in the few private confidential revelations that friendship wrung from the young wife at this period. Lady Anne Barnard, authoress of "*Auld Robin Grey,*" a friend, whose age and experience made her a proper confidant, sent for the broken-hearted, perplexed wife, and offered her a woman's sympathy.

To her Lady Byron wrote many letters, under seal of confidence, and Lady Anne says: "I will give you a few paragraphs transcribed from one of Lady Byron's own letters to me. It is sorrowful to think that in a very little time this young and amiable creature, wise, patient, and feeling, will have her character mistaken by every one who reads Byron's works.

To rescue her from this I preserved her letters, and when she afterwards expressed a fear that anything of her writing should ever fall into hands to injure him (I suppose she meant by publication), I safely assured her that it never should. But here this letter shall be placed, a sacred record in her favour, unknown to herself."

"I am a very incompetent judge of the impression which the last Canto of 'Childe Harold' may produce on the minds of indifferent readers. "It contains the usual trace of a conscience restlessly awake, though his object has been too long to aggravate its burden, as if it could thus be oppressed into eternal stupor. I will hope, as you do, that it survives for his ultimate good.

"It was the acuteness of his remorse, impenitent in its character, which so long seemed to demand from my compassion to spare every semblance of reproach, every look of grief, which might have said to his conscience, 'You have made me wretched.' "I am decidedly of opinion that he *is* responsible. He has wished to be thought partially deranged, or on the brink of it, to perplex observers and *prevent them from tracing effects to their real causes* through all the intricacies of his conduct. I was, as I told you, at one time the dupe of his acted insanity, and clung to the former delusions in regard to the motives that concerned me personally, till the whole system was laid bare.

"He is the absolute monarch of words, and uses them, as Bonaparte did lives, for conquest, without more regard to their intrinsic value, considering them only as ciphers, which must derive all their import from the situation in which he places them, and the ends to which he adapts them, with such consummate skill.

"Why, then, you will say, does he not employ them to give a better colour to his own character? Because he is too good an actor to over-act, or to assume a moral garb, which it would be easy to strip off.

"In regard to his poetry, egotism is the vital principle of his imagination, which it is difficult for him to kindle on any subject with which his own character and interests are not identified; but by the introduction of fictitious incidents, by change of scene or time, *he has enveloped his poetical disclosures in a system impenetrable except to a very few,* and his constant desire of creating a sensation makes him not averse to be the object of wonder and curiosity, even though accompanied *by some dark and vague suspicions.*

"Nothing has contributed more to the misunderstanding of his real character than the lonely grandeur in which he shrouds it, and his affectation of being above mankind, when he exists almost in their voice. The romance of his sentiments is another feature of this mask of state. I know no one more habitually destitute of that enthusiasm he so beautifully expresses, and to which he can work up his fancy chiefly by contagion.

"I had heard he was the best of brothers, the most generous of friends, and I thought such feelings only required to be warmed and cherished into more diffusive benevolence. Though these opinions are eradicated, and could never return but with the decay of my memory, you will not wonder if there are still moments when the association of feelings which arose from them soften and sadden my thoughts.

"But I have not thanked you, dearest Lady Anne, for your

kindness in regard to a principal object,—that of rectifying false impressions. I trust you understand my wishes, which never were to injure Lord Byron in any way; for, though he would not suffer me to remain his wife, he cannot prevent me from continuing his friend; and it was from considering myself as such that I silenced the accusations by which my own conduct might have been more fully justified.

"It is not necessary to speak ill of his heart in general; it is sufficient that to me it was hard and impenetrable,—that my own must have been broken before his could have been touched. I would rather represent this as *my* misfortune than as *his* guilt; but, surely, that misfortune is not to be made my crime! Such are my feelings; you will judge how to act.

"His allusions to me in '*Childe Harold*' are cruel and cold, but with such a semblance as to make *me* appear so, and to attract all sympathy to himself. It is said in this poem that hatred of him will be taught as a lesson to his child. I might appeal to all who have ever heard me speak of him, and still more to my own heart, to witness that there has been no moment when I have remembered injury otherwise than affectionately and sorrowfully.

"It is not my duty to give way to hopeless and wholly unrequited affection; but, so long as I live, my chief struggle will probably be not to remember him too kindly. I do not seek the sympathy of the world, but I wish to be known by those whose opinion is valuable and whose kindness is dear to me. Among such, my dear Lady Anne, you will ever be remembered by your truly affectionate

"A. BYRON."

On this letter I observe Lord Lindsay remarks that it shows a noble but rather severe character, and a recent author has remarked that it seemed to be written rather in a "cold spirit of criticism." It seems to strike these gentlemen as singular that Lady Byron did not enjoy the poem! But there are two remarkable sentences in this letter which have escaped the critics hitherto. Lord Byron, in this, the Third Canto of "*Childe Harold*," expresses in most affecting words an enthusiasm of love for his sister. So long as he lived he was her faithful correspondent; he sent her his journals; and, dying, he left her and her children everything he had in the world. This certainly seems like an affectionate brother; but in what words does Lady Byron speak of this affection?

"I *had heard he was the best of brothers,* the most generous of friends. I thought these feelings only required to be warmed and cherished into more diffusive benevolence. These opinions are eradicated, and could never return but with the decay of memory."

Let me ask those who give this letter as a proof that at this time no idea such as I have stated was in Lady Byron's mind, to account for these words. Let them please answer these questions: Why had Lady Byron ceased to think him a good brother? Why does she use so strong a word as that the opinion was eradicated, torn up by the roots, and could never grow again in her except by decay of memory? And yet this is a document Lord Lindsay vouches for as authentic, and which he brings forward in *defence* of Lord Byron.

Again she says, "Though he *would not suffer me to remain his wife,* he cannot prevent me from continuing his friend." Do these words not say that in some past time, in some decided manner, Lord Byron had declared to her his rejection of her as a wife? I shall yet have occasion to explain these words. Again she says, "I silenced accusations by which my conduct might have been more fully justified."

The people in England who are so very busy in searching out evidence against my true story have searched out and given to the world an important confirmation of this assertion of Lady Byron's. It seems that the confidential waiting-maid who went with Lady Byron on her wedding journey has been sought out and interrogated, and, as appears by description, is a venerable, respectable old person, quite in possession of all her senses in general, and of that sixth sense of propriety in particular, which appears not to be a common virtue in our days.

As her testimony is important, we insert it just here, with a description of her person in full. The ardent investigators thus speak: —

"Having gained admission, we were shown into a small but neatly furnished and scrupulously clean apartment, where sat the object of our visit. Mrs. Minns is a venerable-looking old lady, of short stature, slight and active appearance, with a singularly bright and intelligent countenance. Although midway between eighty and ninety years of age, she is in full possession of her faculties, discourses freely and cheerfully, hears apparently as well as ever she did, and her sight is so good that, aided by a pair of spectacles, she reads the Chronicle every day with ease.

Some idea of her competency to contribute valuable evidence to the subject which now so much engages public attention on three continents may be found from her own narrative of her personal relations with Lady Byron. Mrs. Minns was born in the neighborhood of Seaham, and knew Lady Byron from childhood. During the long period of ten years she was Miss Milbanke's lady's-maid, and in that capacity became the close confidante of her mistress. There were circumstances which rendered their relationship peculiarly intimate.

Miss Milbanke had no sister or female friend to whom she was bound by the ties of more than a common affection; and her mother, whatever other excellent qualities she may have possessed, was too high-spirited and too hasty in temper to attract the sympathies of the young. Some months before Miss Milbanke was married to Lord Byron Mrs. Minns had quitted her service on the occasion of her own marriage with Mr. Minns, but she continued to reside in the neighborhood of Seaham, and remained on the most friendly terms with her former mistress.

As the courtship proceeded, Miss Milbanke concealed nothing from her faithful attendant, and when the wedding-day was fixed she begged Mrs. Minns to return and fulfil the duties of lady's-maid, at least during the honeymoon. Mrs. Minns at the time was nursing her first child, and it was no small sacrifice to quit her own home at such a moment, but she could not refuse her old mistress's request.

Accordingly, she returned to Seaham Hall some days

before the wedding, was present at the ceremony, and then preceded Lord and Lady Byron to Halnaby Hall, near Croft, in the North Riding of Yorkshire, one of Sir Ralph Milbanke's seats, where the newly married couple were to spend the honeymoon. Mrs. Minns remained with Lord and Lady Byron during the three weeks they spent at Halnaby Hall, and then accompanied them to Seaham, where they spent the next six weeks.

It was during the latter period that she finally quitted Lady Byron's service, but she remained in the most friendly communication with her Ladyship till the death of the latter, and for some time was living in the neighborhood of Lady Byron's residence in Leicestershire, where she had frequent opportunities of seeing her former mistress. It may be added that Lady Byron was not unmindful of the faithful services of her friend and attendant in the instructions to her executors contained in her will.

Such was the position of Mrs. Minns towards Lady Byron, and we think no one will question that it was of a nature to entitle all that Mrs. Minns may say on the subject of the relations of Lord and Lady Byron to the most respectful consideration and credit."

Such is the chronicler's account of the faithful creature, whom nothing but intense indignation and disgust at Mrs. Beecher Stowe would lead to speak on her mistress's affairs; but Mrs. Beecher Stowe feels none the less sincere respect for her, and is none the less obliged to her for having spoken. Much of Mrs. Minns's testimony will be referred to in another place; we only extract one passage, to show that while Lord Byron spent his time in setting afloat slanders against his wife, she spent hers in sealing the mouths of witnesses against him.

Of the period of the honeymoon Mrs. Minns says: —

"The happiness of Lady Byron, however, was of brief duration; even during the short three weeks they spent at Halnaby the irregularities of Lord Byron occasioned her the greatest distress, and she even contemplated returning to her father. Mrs. Minns was her constant companion and confidante through this painful period, and she does not believe that her ladyship concealed a thought from her. With laudable reticence, the old lady absolutely refuses to disclose the particulars of Lord Byron's misconduct at this time; she gave Lady Byron a solemn promise not to do so.

"So serious did Mrs. Minns consider the conduct of Lord Byron, that she recommended her mistress to confide all the circumstances to her father, Sir Ralph Milbanke, a calm, kind, and most excellent parent, and take his advice as to her future course.

At one time Mrs. Minns thinks Lady Byron had resolved to follow her counsel and impart her wrongs to Sir Ralph; but on arriving at Seaham Hall her ladyship strictly enjoined Mrs. Minns to preserve absolute silence on the subject, — a course which she followed herself, — so that when, six weeks later, she and Lord Byron left Seaham for London, not a word had escaped her to disturb her parents' tranquillity as to their daughter's domestic happiness.

As might be expected, Mrs. Minns bears the warmest testimony to the noble and lovable qualities of her departed mistress. She also declares that Lady Byron was by no means of a cold temperament, but that the affectionate impulses of her nature were checked by the unkind treatment she experienced from her husband."

We have already shown that Lord Byron had been, ever since his separation, engaged in a systematic attempt to reverse the judgment of the world against himself, by making converts of all his friends to a most odious view of his wife's character, and inspiring them with the zeal of propagandists to spread these views through society. We have seen how he prepared partisans to interpret the Fourth Canto of *Childe Harold*.

This plan of solemn and heroic accusation was the first public attack on his wife. Next we see him commencing a scurrilous attempt to turn her to ridicule in the First Canto of *Don Juan*.

It is to our point now to show how carefully and cautiously this Don Juan campaign was planned.

Vol. IV. p. 138, we find *Letter 325 to Mr. Murray*: —

"VENICE, January 25, 1819.

"You will do me the favour to *print privately, for private distribution, fifty copies of Don Juan*. The list of the men to whom I wish it presented I will send hereafter."

The poem, as will be remembered, begins with the meanest and foulest attack on his wife that ever ribald wrote, and put it in close neighborhood with scenes which every pure man or woman must feel to be the beastly utterances of a man who had lost all sense of decency.

Such a potion was too strong to be administered even in a time when great license was allowed, and men were not over-nice. But Byron chooses fifty armor-bearers of that class of men who would find indecent ribaldry about a wife a good joke, and talk about the "artistic merits" of things which we hope would make an honest boy blush.

At this time he acknowledges that his vices had brought him to a state of great exhaustion, attended by such debility of the stomach that nothing remained on it; and adds, "I was obliged to reform my way of life, which was conducting me from the yellow leaf to the ground with all deliberate speed." But as his health is a little better he employs it in making the way to death and hell elegantly easy for other young men, by breaking down the remaining scruples of a society not over-scrupulous.

Society revolted, however, and fought stoutly against the nauseous dose. Even his sister wrote to him that she heard such things said of it that *she* never would read it; and the outcry against it on the part of all women of his acquaintance was such that for a time he was quite overborne; and the Countess Guiccioli finally extorted a promise from him to cease writing it. Nevertheless, there came a time when England accepted *Don Juan*, -when Wilson, in the Noctes Ambrosianæ, praised it as a classic, and took every opportunity to reprobate Lady Byron's conduct.

When first it appeared the Blackwood came out with that indignant denunciation of which we have spoken, and to which Byron replied in the extracts we have already quoted. He did something more than reply. He marked out Wilson as one of the strongest literary men of the day, and set his "initiated" with their documents to work upon him. One of these documents to which he requested Wilson's attention was the private autobiography, written expressly to give his own story of all the facts of the marriage and separation.

In the indignant letter he writes Murray on the Blackwood article, Vol. IV. *Letter 350,* — under date December 10, 1819, — he says: —

"I sent home for Moore, and for Moore only (who has my journal also), my memoir written up to 1816, and I gave him leave to show it to whom he pleased, *but not to publish* on any account. *You* may read it, and you may let Wilson read it if he likes, — not for his public opinion, but his private, for I like the man, and care very little about the magazine.

And I could wish Lady Byron herself to read it, that she may have it in her power to mark anything mistaken or misstated. As it will never appear till after my extinction, it would be but fair she should see it; that is to say, herself willing. Your Blackwood accuses me of treating women harshly; but I have been their martyr; my whole life has been sacrificed to them and by them."

It was a part of Byron's policy to place Lady Byron in positions before the world where she *could* not speak, and where her silence would be set down to her as haughty, stony indifference and obstinacy. Such was the pretended negotiation through Madame de Staël, and such now this apparently fair and generous offer to let Lady Byron see and mark this manuscript.

The little Ada is now in her fifth year, -a child of singular sensibility and remarkable mental powers, — one of those exceptional children who are so perilous a charge for a mother.

Her husband proposes this artful snare to her, — that she shall mark what is false in a statement which is all built on a damning lie, that she cannot refute over that daughter's head, — and which would perhaps be her ruin to discuss.

Hence came an addition of two more documents, to be used "privately among friends," and which Blackwood uses after Lady Byron is safely out of the world to cast ignominy on her grave, — the wife's letter, that of a mother standing at bay for her daughter, knowing that she is dealing with a desperate, powerful, unscrupulous enemy.

"KIRKBY MALLORY, March 10, 1820.

"I received your letter of January 1, offering to my perusal a Memoir of part of your life. I decline to inspect it. I consider the publication or circulation of such a composition at any time as prejudicial to Ada's future happiness. For my own sake, I have no reason to shrink from publication; but, notwithstanding the injuries which I have suffered, I should lament some of the *consequences.*

"A. BYRON.

"To LORD BYRON."

Lord Byron, writing for the public, as is his custom, makes reply: —

"RAVENNA, April 3, 1820.

"I received yesterday your answer, dated March 10. My offer was an honest one, and surely could only be construed as such, even by the most malignant casuistry. I could answer you, but it is too late, and it is not worth while. To the mysterious menace of the last sentence, whatever its import may be, — and I cannot pretend to unriddle it, — I could hardly be very sensible even if I understood it, as, before it can take place, I shall be where 'nothing can touch him further.'.... I advise you, however, to anticipate the period of your intention, for, be assured, no power of figures can avail beyond the present; and if it could, I would answer with the Florentine: —

"'Ed io, che posto son con loro in croce..... e certo La fiera moglie, più ch' altro, mi nuoce.'

"BYRON.

"To LADY BYRON."

Two things are very evident in this correspondence. Lady Byron intimates that, if he

"And I, who with them on the cross am placed,... truly
My savage wife, more than aught else, doth harm me."

Inferno, Canto XVI., Longfellow translation. publishes his story, some *consequences* must follow which she shall regret.

Lord Byron receives this as a threat, and says he doesn't understand it. But directly after he says, "Before IT can take place, I shall be," &c.

The intimation is quite clear. He *does* understand what the consequences alluded to are. They are evidently that Lady Byron will speak out and tell her story. He says she cannot do this till *after he is dead,* and then he shall not care. In allusion to her accuracy as to dates and figures, he says: "Be assured no power of figures can avail beyond this present" (life); and then ironically *advises* her to *anticipate the period,* — i. e. to speak out while he is alive.

In Vol. VI. *Letter 518,* which Lord Byron wrote to Lady Byron, but did not send, he says: "I burned your last note for two reasons, — firstly, because it was written in a style not very agreeable; and, secondly, because I wished to take your word without documents, which are the resources of worldly and suspicious people."

It would appear from this that there *was* a last letter of Lady Byron to her husband, which he did not think proper to keep on hand, or show to the "initiated" with his usual unreserve; that this letter contained some kind of *pledge* for which he preferred to take her word, *without documents.*

Each reader can imagine for himself what that *pledge* might have been; but from the tenor of the three letters we should infer that it was a promise of silence for his lifetime, on *certain conditions,* and that the publication of the autobiography would violate those conditions, and make it her duty to speak out.

This celebrated autobiography forms so conspicuous a figure in the whole history, that the reader must have a full idea of it, as given by Byron himself, in Vol. IV. *Letter 344,* to Murray: —

"I gave to Moore, who is gone to Rome, my life in MS., — in seventy-eight folio sheets, brought down to 1816..... Also a journal kept in 1814. Neither are for publication during my life, but when I am cold you may do what you please. In the mean time, if you like to read them you may, and show them to anybody you like. I care not....."

He tells him also: —

"You will find in it a detailed account of my marriage and its consequences, as true as a party concerned can make such an account."

Of the extent to which this autobiography was circulated we have the following testimony of Shelton Mackenzie, in notes to the "Noctes" of June, 1824.

In the Noctes Odoherty says: —

"The fact is, the work had been copied for the private reading of a great lady in Florence."

The note says: —

"The great lady in Florence, for whose private reading Byron's autobiography was copied, was the Countess of Westmoreland..... Lady Blessington had the autobiography in her possession for weeks, and confessed to having copied every line of it. Moore remonstrated, and she committed her copy to the flames, but did not tell him that her sister, Mrs.

Home Purvis, now Viscountess of Canterbury, had also made a copy!.... From the quantity of' copy I have seen, — and others were more in the way of falling in with it than myself, -I surmise that at least half a dozen copies were made, and of these *five* are now in existence. Some particular parts, such as the marriage and separation, were copied separately; but I think there cannot be less than five full copies yet to be found."

This was written after the original autobiography was burned.

We may see the zeal and enthusiasm of the Byron party, — copying seventy-eight folio sheets, as of old Christians copied the Gospels. How widely, fully, and thoroughly, thus, by this secret process, was society saturated with Byron's own versions of the story that related to himself and wife! Against her there was only the complaint of an absolute silence. She put forth no statements, no documents; had no party, sealed the lips of her counsel, and even of her servants; yet she could not but have known, from time to time, how thoroughly and strongly this web of mingled truth and lies was being meshed around her steps.

From the time that Byron first saw the importance of securing Wilson on his side, and wrote to have his partisans attend to him, we may date an entire revolution in the Blackwood.

It became Byron's warmest supporter, — is to this day the bitterest accuser of his wife. Why was this wonderful silence? It appears by Dr. Lushington's statements, that, when Lady Byron did speak, she had a story to tell that powerfully affected both him and Romilly, — a story supported by evidence on which they were willing to have gone to public trial. Supposing, now, she had imitated Lord Byron's example, and, avoiding public trial, had put her story into private circulation; as he sent "Don Juan" to fifty confidential friends, suppose she had sent a written statement of her story to fifty judges as intelligent as the two that had heard it; or suppose she had confronted his autobiography with her own, — what would have been the result?

The first result would have been Mrs. Leigh's utter ruin. The world may finally forgive the man of genius anything; but for a woman there is no mercy and no redemption.

This ruin Lady Byron prevented by her utter silence and great self-command. Mrs. Leigh never lost position. Lady Byron never so varied in her manner toward her as to excite the suspicions even of her confidential old servant.

To protect Mrs. Leigh effectually, it must have been necessary to continue to exclude even her own mother from the secret, as we are assured she did at first; for, had she told Lady Milbanke, it is not possible that so high-spirited a woman could have restrained herself from such outward expressions as would at least have awakened suspicion. There was no resource but this absolute silence.

Lady Blessington, in her last conversation with Lord Byron, thus describes the life Lady Byron was leading. She speaks of her as "wearing away her youth in almost monastic seclusion, questioned by some, appreciated by few, seeking consolation alone in the discharge of her duties, and avoiding all external demonstrations of a grief that her pale cheek and solitary existence alone were vouchers for."

The main object of all this silence may be imagined, if we remember that if Lord Byron had not died, — had he truly and deeply repented, and become a thoroughly good man, and returned to England to pursue a course worthy of his powers, there was on record neither word nor deed from his wife to stand in his way.

His place was kept in society, ready for him to return to whenever he came clothed and in his right mind. He might have had the heart and confidence of his daughter unshadowed by a suspicion. He might have won the reverence of the great and good in his own land and all lands. That hope, which was the strong support, the prayer of the silent wife, it did not please God to fulfil.

Lord Byron died a worn-out man at thirtysix. But the bitter seeds he had sown came up, after his death, in a harvest of thorns over his grave; and there were not wanting hands to use them as instruments of torture on the heart of his widow.

Chapter 5

Resume of the Conspiracy

We have traced the conspiracy of Lord Byron against his wife up to its latest device. That the reader's mind may be clear on the points of the process, we shall now briefly recapitulate the documents in the order of time.

I. March 17, 1816. — While negotiations for separation were pending, — *"Fare thee well, and if forever."* While writing these pages, we have received from England the testimony of one who has seen the original draught of that "Fare thee well." This original copy had evidently been subjected to the most careful and acute revision. Scarcely two lines that were not interlined, scarcely an adjective that was not exchanged for a better; showing that the noble lord was not so far overcome by grief as to have forgotten his reputation. (Found its way to the public prints through the imprudence of *a friend*.)

II. March 29, 1816. — An attack on Lady Byron's old governess for having been born poor, for being homely, and for having unduly influenced his wife against him; promising that her grave should be a fiery bed, &c.; also praising his wife's perfect and remarkable truthfulness and discernment, that made it impossible for flattery to fool, or baseness blind her; but ascribing all his woes to her being fooled and blinded by this same governess. (Found its way to the prints by the imprudence of *a friend*.)

III. September, 1816. — Lines on hearing that Lady Byron is ill. Calls her a Clytemnestra, who has secretly set assassins on her lord; says she is a mean, treacherous, deceitful liar, and has entirely departed from her early truth, and become the most unscrupulous and unprincipled of women. Never printed till after Lord Byron's death, but circulated *privately* among the *"initiated."*

Aug. 9, 1817: Gives to M. G. Lewis a paper for circulation among friends in England, stating that what he most wants is public investigation, which has always been denied him; and daring Lady Byron and her counsel to come out publicly. Found in M. G. Lewis's portfolio after his death; never heard of before, except among the "initiated."

Having given M. G. Lewis's document time to work, —

January, 1818: Gives the fourth canto of "Childe Harold" to the public.

Jan. 25, 1819: Sends to Murray to print for private circulation among the "initiated" the first canto of "Don Juan."

August, 1819: Is nobly and severely rebuked for this insult to his wife by the "Blackwood,"

October, 1819: Gives Moore the manuscript Autobiography, with leave to show it to whom he pleases, and print it after his death.

Oct. 29, 1819: vol. iv. letter 344. — Writes to Murray, that he may read all this Autobiography, and show it to anybody he likes.

Dec. 10, 1819: Writes to Murray on this article in "Blackwood" against "Don Juan" and himself, which he supposes written by Wilson; sends a complimentary message to Wilson, and asks him to read his Autobiography sent by Moore. (Letter 350.)

March 15, 1820: Writes, and dedicates to I. Disraeli, Esq., a vindication of himself in reply to the "Blackwood" on "Don Juan," containing an indignant defence of his own conduct in relation to his wife, and maintaining that he never yet has had an opportunity of knowing whereof he has been accused;

accusing Sir S. Romilly of taking his retainer, and then going over to the adverse party, &c. Printed for *private circulation;* to be found in the standard English edition of Murray, vol. ix. p.57.

To this condensed account of Byron's strategy we must add the crowning stroke of policy which transmitted this warfare to his friends, to be continued after his death.

During the last visit Moore made him in Italy, and just before Byron presented to him his Autobiography, the following scene occurred, as narrated by Moore (vol. iv. p. 221):

"The chief subject of conversation, when alone, was his marriage, and the load of obloquy which it had brought upon him. He was most anxious to know *the worst* that had been alleged of his conduct; and, as this was our first opportunity of speaking together on the subject, I did not hesitate to put his candor most searchingly to the proof, not only by enumerating the various charges I had heard brought against him by others, but by specifying such portions of these charges as I had been inclined to think not incredible myself.

"To all this he listened with patience, and answered with the most unhesitating frankness; laughing to scorn the tales of unmanly outrage related of him, but at the same time acknowledging that there had been in his conduct but too much to blame and regret, and stating one or two occasions during his domestic life when he had been irritated into letting the 'breath of bitter words' escape him,... which he now evidently remembered with a degree of remorse and pain which might well have entitled them to be forgotten by others.

"It was, at the same time, manifest, that, whatever admissions he might be inclined to make respecting his own delinquencies, the inordinate measure of the punishment dealt out to him had sunk deeply into his mind, and, with the usual effect of such injustice, drove him also to be unjust himself; so much so, indeed, as to impute to the quarter to which he now traced all his ill fate a feeling of fixed hostility to himself, which would not rest, he thought, even at his grave, but continue to persecute his memory as it was now imbittering his life. So strong was this impression upon him, that, during one of our few intervals of seriousness, he conjured me by our friendship, if, as he both felt and hoped, I should survive him, not to let unmerited censure settle upon his name." In this same account, page 218, Moore testifies that "Lord Byron disliked his countrymen, but only because he knew that his morals were held in contempt by them. The English, themselves rigid observers of family duties, could not pardon him the neglect of his, nor his trampling on principles: therefore neither did he like being presented to them, nor did they, especially when they had wives with them, like to cultivate his acquaintance.

Still there was a strong desire in all of them to see him; and the women in particular, who did not dare to look at him but by stealth, said in an under-voice, 'What a pity it is!' If, however, any of his compatriots of exalted rank and high reputation came forward to treat him with courtesy, he showed himself obviously flattered by it. It seemed, that, to the wound which remained open in his ulcerated heart, such soothing attentions were as drops of healing balm, which comforted him."

When in society, we are further informed by a lady quoted by Mr. Moore, he was in the habit of speaking of his wife with much respect and affection, as an illustrious lady, distinguished for her qualities of heart and understanding; saying that all the fault of their cruel separation lay with himself.

Mr. Moore seems at times to be somewhat puzzled by these contradictory statements of his idol, and speculates not a little on what could be Lord Byron's object in using such language in public; mentally comparing it, we suppose, with the free handling which he gave to the same subject in his private correspondence. The innocence with which Moore gives himself up to be manipulated by Lord Byron, the *naïveté* with which he shows all the process, let us a little into the secret of the marvellous powers of charming and blinding which this great actor possessed. Lord Byron had the beauty, the wit, the genius, the dramatic talent, which have constituted the strength of some wonderfully fascinating women. There have been women able to lead their leashes of blinded adorers; to make them swear that black was white, or white black, at their word; to smile away their senses, or weep away their reason. No matter what these sirens may say, no matter what they may do, though caught in a thousand transparent lies, and doing a thousand deeds which would have ruined others, still men madly rave after them in life, and tear their hair over their graves. Such an enchanter in man's shape was Lord Byron.

He led captive Moore and Murray by being beautiful, a genius, and a lord; calling them "Dear Tom," and "Dear Murray," while they were only commoners. He first insulted Sir Walter Scott, and then witched his heart out of him by ingenuous confessions and poetical compliments; he took Wilson's heart by flattering messages and a beautifully-written letter; he corresponded familiarly with Hogg; and, before his death, had made fast friends, in one way or another, of the whole Noctes Ambrosianæ Club.

We thus have given the historical *résumé* of Lord Byron's attacks on his wife's reputation: we shall add, that they were based on philosophic principles, showing a deep knowledge of mankind. An analysis will show that they can be philosophically classified: —

1st, Those which addressed the sympathetic nature of man, representing her as cold, methodical, severe, strict, unforgiving.

2d, Those addressed to the faculty of association, connecting her with ludicrous and licentious images; taking from her the usual protection of womanly delicacy and sacredness.

3d, Those addressed to the moral faculties, accusing her as artful, treacherous, untruthful, malignant.

All these various devices he held in his hand, shuffling and dealing them as a careful gamester his pack of cards according to the exigencies of the game. He played adroitly, skilfully, with blinding flatteries and seductive wiles, that made his victims willing dupes. Nothing can more clearly show the power and perfectness of his enchantments than the masterly way in which he turned back the moral force of the whole English nation, which had risen at first in its strength against him. The victory was complete.

Chapter 6

Results After Lord Byron's Death

AT the time of Lord Byron's death, the English public had been so skilfully manipulated by the Byron propaganda, that the sympathy of the whole world was with him. A tide of emotion was now aroused in England by his early death, — dying in the cause of Greece and liberty. There arose a general wail for him, as for a lost pleiad, not only in England, but over the whole world; a great rush of enthusiasm for his memory, to which the greatest literary men of England freely gave voice. By general consent, Lady Byron seems to have been looked upon as the only cold-hearted, unsympathetic person in this general mourning.

From that time, the literary world of England apparently regarded Lady Byron as a woman to whom none of the decorums, nor courtesies of ordinary womanhood, nor even the consideration belonging to common humanity, were due.

"She that is a widow indeed, and desolate," has been regarded in all Christian countries as an object made sacred by the touch of God's afflicting hand, sacred in her very helplessness; and the old Hebrew Scriptures give to the Supreme Father no dearer title than "the widow's God." But, on Lord Byron's death, men not devoid of tenderness, men otherwise generous and of fine feeling, acquiesced in insults to his widow with an obtuseness that seems, on review, quite incredible.

Lady Byron was not only a widow, but an orphan. She had no sister for confidante; no father and mother to whom to go in her sorrows, — sorrows so much deeper and darker to her than they could be to any other human being. She had neither son nor brother to uphold and protect her. On all hands it was acknowledged, that, so far, there was no fault to be found in her but her utter silence. Her life was confessed to be pure, useful, charitable; and yet, in this time of her sorrow, the writers of England issued article upon article not only devoid of delicacy, but apparently injurious and insulting towards her, with a blind unconsciousness which seems astonishing.

One of the greatest literary powers of that time was the "Blackwood:" the reigning monarch on that literary throne was Wilson, the lion-hearted, the brave, generous, tender poet, and, with some sad exceptions, the noble man. But Wilson had believed the story of Byron, and, by his very generosity and tenderness and pity, was betrayed into injustice.

In "The Noctes" of November, 1824, there is a conversation of the Noctes club, in which North says, "Byron and I knew each other pretty well; and I suppose there's no harm in adding, that we appreciated each other pretty tolerably. Did you ever see his letter to me?"

The footnote to this says, "*This letter, which was* PRINTED *in Byron's lifetime, was not published till* 1830, when it appeared in Moore's Life of Byron. It is one of the most vigorous prose compositions in the language. Byron had the highest opinion of Wilson's genius and noble spirit."

In the first place, with our present ideas of propriety and good taste, we should reckon it an indecorum to make the private affairs of a pure and good woman, whose circumstances from any point of view were trying, and who evidently shunned publicity, the subject of public discussion in magazines which were read all over the world.

Lady Byron, as they all knew, had on her hands a most delicate and onerous task, in bringing up an only daughter, necessarily inheriting peculiarities of genius and great sensitiveness; and the many mortifications and embarrassments which such intermeddling with her private matters must have given, certainly should have been considered by men with any pretensions to refinement or good feeling.

But the literati of England allowed her no consideration, no rest, no privacy. In "The Noctes" of November, 1825, there is the record of a free conversation upon Lord and Lady Byron's affairs, interlarded with exhortations to push the bottle, and remarks on whiskey-toddy. Medwin's "Conversations with Lord Byron" is discussed, which, we are told in a note, appeared a few months after the *noble* poet's death.

There is a rather bold and free discussion of Lord Byron's character, — his fondness for gin and water, on which stimulus he wrote "Don Juan;" and James Hogg says pleasantly to Mullion, "O Mullion! it's a pity you and Byron could na ha' been acquaint. There would ha' been brave sparring to see who could say the wildest and the dreadfullest things; for he had neither fear of man or woman, and would ha' his joke or jeer, cost what it might."

And then follows a specimen of one of his jokes with an actress, that, in indecency, certainly justifies the assertion. From the other stories which follow, and the parenthesis that occurs frequently, ("Mind your glass, James, a little more!") it seems evident that the party are progressing in their peculiar kind of *civilization.*

It is in this same circle and paper that Lady Byron's private affairs come up for discussion. The discussion is thus elegantly introduced: —

Hogg. — "Reach me the black bottle. I say, Christopher, what, after all, is your opinion o' Lord and Leddy Byron's quarrel? Do you yoursel' take part with him, or with her? I wad like to hear your real opinion."

North. — "Oh, dear! Well, Hogg, since you will have it, I think Douglas Kinnaird and Hobhouse are bound to tell us whether there be any truth, and how much, in this story about the *declaration,* signed by Sir Ralph" [Milbanke].

The note here tells us that this refers to a statement that appeared in "Blackwood" immediately after Byron's death, to the effect, that, previous to the formal separation from his wife, Byron required and obtained from Sir Ralph Milbanke, Lady Byron's father, a statement to the effect that Lady Byron had no charge of moral delinquency to bring against him. (Note: Recently, Lord Lindsay has published another version of this story, which makes it appear that he has conversed with a lady who conversed with Hobhouse during his lifetime, in which this story is differently reported. In the last version, it is made to appear that Hobhouse got this declaration from Lady Byron herself.)

North continues: —

"And I think Lady Byron's letter, the 'Dearest Duck' one I mean, should really be forthcoming, if her ladyship's friends wish to stand fair before the public. At present, we have nothing but loose talk of society to go upon; and certainly, *if the things that are said be true, there must be thorough explanation from some quarter, or the tide will continue, as it has assuredly begun, to flow in a direction very opposite to what we were for years accustomed*. Sir, they must *explain this business of the letter*. You have, of course, heard about the invitation it contained, the warm, affectionate invitation, to Kirkby Mallory" —

Hogg interposes, —

"I dinna like to be interruptin' ye, Mr. North; but I must inquire, Is the *jug* to stand still while ye're going on at that rate?"

North. — "There, Porker! These things are part and parcel of the chatter of every bookseller's shop; *à fortiori*, of every drawing-room in May Fair. *Can* the matter stop here? Can a great man's memory be permitted to incur damnation while these saving clauses are afloat anywhere uncontradicted?"

And from this the conversation branches off into strong, emphatic praise of Byron's conduct in Greece during the last part of his life. The silent widow is thus delicately and considerately reminded in the "Blackwood" that she is the talk, not only over the whiskey-jug of the Noctes, but in every drawing-room in London; and that she *must* speak out and explain matters, or the whole world will set against her.

But she does not speak yet. The public persecution, therefore, proceeds. Medwin's book being insufficient, another biographer is to be selected. Now, the person in the Noctes club who was held to have the most complete information of the Byron affairs, and was, on that account, first thought of by Murray to execute this very delicate task of writing a Memoir which should include the most sacred domestic affairs of a noble lady and her orphan daughter, was *Maginn.*

Maginn, the author of the pleasant joke, that "man never reaches the apex of civilization till he is too drunk to pronounce the word," was the first person in whose hands the Autobiography, Memoirs, and Journals of Lord Byron were placed with this view.

The following note from Shelton Mackenzie, in the June number of "*The Noctes*," 1824, says,—

"At that time, had he been so minded, Maginn (Odoherty) could have got up a popular Life of Byron as well as most men in England. Immediately on the account of Byron's death being received in London, John Murray proposed that Maginn should bring out Memoirs,

Journals, and Letters of Lord Byron, and, with this intent, placed in his hand every line that he (Murray) possessed in Byron's handwriting.... The strong desire of *Byron's family and executors* that the Autobiography should be burned, to which desire Murray foolishly yielded, made such an hiatus in the materials, that Murray and Maginn agreed it would not answer to bring out the work then. Eventually Moore executed it."

The character of the times in which this work was to be undertaken will appear from the following note of Mackenzie's to "*The Noctes*" of August, 1824, which we copy, with the *author's own Italics:*—

"In the 'Blackwood' of July, 1824, was a poetical epistle by the renowned Timothy Tickler, to the editor of the *'John Bull'* magazine, on an article in his first number. This article... *professed* to be a portion of the veritable Autobiography of Byron which was burned, and was called '*My Wedding Night.*' It appeared to relate in detail *every thing* that occurred in the twenty-four hours immediately succeeding that in which Byron was married.

It had plenty of coarseness, and some to spare. It went into particulars such as hitherto had been given only by

Faublas; and it had, notwithstanding, many phrases and some facts which evidently did not belong to a mere fabricator. Some years after, I compared this '*Wedding Night*' with what I had all assurance of having been transcribed from the actual manuscripts of Byron, and was persuaded that the magazine-writer must have had the *actual* statement before him, or have had a perusal of it. The writer in '*Blackwood*' declared his conviction that it really was Byron's own writing."

The reader must remember that Lord Byron died April, 1824: so that, according to this, his Autobiography was made the means of this gross insult to his widow three months after his death.

If some powerful cause had not paralyzed all feelings of gentlemanly honor, and of womanly delicacy, and of common humanity, towards Lady Byron, throughout the whole British nation, no editor would have dared to open a periodical with such an article; or, if he had, he would have been overwhelmed with a storm of popular indignation, which, like the fire upon Sodom, would have left him a pillar of salt for a warning to all future generations.

"*Blackwood*" reproves "*The John Bull*" in a poetical epistle, recognizing the article as coming from Byron, and says to the *author,—*

"But that you, sir, a wit and a scholar like you,
Should not blush to produce what he blushed not to do,—
Take your compliment, youngster: this doubles, almost,
The sorrow that rose when his honor was lost."

We may not wonder that the Autobiography was burned, as Murray says in a recent account, by a committee of Byron's *friends,* including Hobhouse, his sister, and Murray himself.

Now, the "*Blackwood*" of July, 1824, thus declares its conviction that this outrage on every sentiment of human decency came from Lord Byron, and that his honor was lost. Maginn does not undertake the Memoir. No Memoir at all is undertaken; till finally Moore is selected, as, like Demetrius of old, a well-skilled gilder and "maker of silver shrines," though *not* for Diana. To Moore is committed the task of doing his best for this battered image, in which even the worshippers recognize foul sulphurous cracks, but which they none the less stand ready to worship as a genuine article that "fell down from Jupiter."

Moore was a man of no particular nicety as to moralities, but in that matter seems not very much below what this record shows his average associates to be. He is so far superior to Maginn, that his vice is rose-colored and refined. He does not burst out with such heroic stanzas as Maginn's frank invitation to Jeremy Bentham:—

"Jeremy, throw your pen aside,
And come get drunk with me;
And we'll go where Bacchus sits astride,
Perched high on barrels three."

Moore's, vice is cautious, soft, seductive, slippery, and covered at times with a thin, tremulous veil of religious sentimentalism. In regard to Byron, he was an unscrupulous, committed partisan: he was as much bewitched by him as ever man has been by woman; and therefore to him, at last, the task of editing Byron's Memoirs was given.

This Byron, whom they all knew to be obscene beyond what even their most drunken tolerance could at first endure; this man, whose foul license *spoke out* what most men conceal from mere respect to the decent instincts of humanity; whose "honor was lost," —was submitted to this careful manipulator, to be turned out a perfected idol for a world longing for one, as the Israelites longed for the calf in Horeb.

The image was to be invested with deceitful glories and shifting haloes,—admitted faults spoken of as peculiarities of sacred origin,-and the world given to understand that no common rule or measure could apply to such an undoubtedly divine production; and so the hearts of men were to be wrung with pity for his sorrows as the yearning pain of a god, and with anger at his injuries as sacrilege on the sacredness of genius, till they were ready to cast themselves at his feet, and adore.

Then he was to be set up on a pedestal, like Nebuchadnezzar's image on the plains of Dura; and what time the world heard the sound of cornet, sackbut, and dulcimer, in his enchanting verse, they were to fall down and worship.

For Lady Byron, Moore had simply the respect that a commoner has for a lady of rank, and a good deal of the feeling that seems to underlie all English literature,—that it is no matter what becomes of the woman when the man's story is to be told.

But, with all his faults, Moore was not a cruel man; and we cannot conceive such outrageous cruelty and ungentlemanly indelicacy towards an unoffending woman, as he shows in these Memoirs, without referring them to Lord Byron's own influence in making him an unscrupulous, committed partisan on his side.

So little pity, so little sympathy, did he suppose Lady Byron to be worthy of, that he laid before her, in the sight of all the world, selections from her husband's letters and journals, in which the privacies of her courtship and married life were jested upon with a vulgar levity; letters filled, from the time of the act of separation, with a constant succession of sarcasms, stabs, stings, epigrams, and vindictive allusions to herself, bringing her into direct and insulting comparison with his various mistresses, and implying their superiority over her.

There, too, were gross attacks on her father and mother, as having been the instigators of the separation; and poor Lady Milbanke, in particular, is sometimes mentioned with epithets so offensive, that the editor prudently covers the terms with stars, as intending language too gross to be printed.

The last mistress of Lord Byron is uniformly brought forward in terms of such respect and consideration, that one would suppose that the usual moral laws that regulate English family life had been specially repealed in his favour. Moore quotes with approval letters from Shelley, stating that Lord Byron's connection with La Guiccioli has been of inestimable benefit to him; and that he is now becoming what he should be, "a virtuous man."

Moore goes on to speak of the connection as one, though somewhat reprehensible, yet as having all those advantages of marriage and settled domestic ties that Byron's affectionate spirit had long sighed for, but never before found; and in his last *résumé* of the poet's character, at the end of the volume, he brings the mistress into direct comparison with the wife in a single sentence:

"The woman to whom he gave the love of his maturer years idolizes his name; and, *with a single unhappy exception,* scarce an instance is to be found of one brought... into relations of amity with him who did not retain a kind regard for him in life, and a fondness for his memory."

Literature has never yet seen the instance of a person, of Lady Byron's rank in life, placed before the world in a position more humiliating to womanly dignity, or wounding to womanly delicacy.

The direct implication is, that she has no feelings to be hurt, no heart to be broken, and is not worthy even of the consideration which in ordinary life is to be accorded to a widow who has received those awful tidings which generally must awaken many emotions, and call for some consideration, even in the most callous hearts.

The woman who we are told walked the room, vainly striving to control the sobs that shook her frame, while she sought to draw from the servant that last message of her husband which she was never to hear, was not thought worthy even of the rights of common humanity.

The first volume of the Memoir came out in 1830. Then for the first time came one flash of lightning from the silent cloud; and she who had never spoken before spoke out. The libels on the memory of her dead parents drew from her what her own wrongs never did.

During all this time, while her husband had been keeping her effigy dangling before the public as a mark for solemn curses, and filthy lampoons, and *secretly*-circulated disclosures, that spared no sacredness and violated every decorum, she had not uttered a word.

She had been subjected to nameless insults, discussed in the assemblies of drunkards, and challenged to speak for herself. Like the chaste lady in "*Comus,*" whom the vile wizard had bound in the enchanted seat to be "grinned at and chattered at" by all the filthy rabble of his dehumanized rout, she had remained pure, lofty, and undefiled; and the stains of mud and mire thrown upon her had fallen from her spotless garments.

Now that she is dead, a recent writer in "The London Quarterly" dares give voice to an insinuation which even Byron gave only a *suggestion* of when he called his wife Clytemnestra; and hints that she tried the power of youth and beauty to win to her the young solicitor Lushington, and a handsome young officer of high rank.

At this time, *such* insinuations had not been thought of; and the only and chief allegation against Lady Byron had been a cruel severity of virtue.

At all events, when Lady Byron spoke, the world listened with respect, and believed what she said. Here let us, too, read her statement, and give it the careful attention she solicits (Moore *Life of Byron*, vol. vi. p. 275): —

"I have disregarded various publications in which facts within my own knowledge have been grossly misrepresented; but I am called upon to notice some of the erroneous statements proceeding from one who claims to be considered as Lord Byron's confidential and authorized friend. Domestic details ought not to be intruded on the public attention: if, however, they *are* so intruded, the persons affected by them have a right to refute injurious charges.

Mr. Moore has promulgated his own impressions of private events in which I was most nearly concerned, as if he possessed a competent knowledge of the subject. Having survived Lord Byron, I feel increased reluctance to advert to any circumstances connected with the period of my marriage; nor is it now my intention to disclose them further than may be indispensably requisite for the end I have in view.

Self-vindication is not the motive which actuates me to make this appeal, and the spirit of accusation is unmingled with it; but when the conduct of my parents is brought forward in a disgraceful light by the passages selected from Lord Byron's letters, and by the remarks of his biographer, I feel bound to justify their characters from imputations which I *know* to be false.

The passages from Lord Byron's letters, to which I refer,

are, — the aspersion on my mother's character: 'My child is very well and flourishing, I hear; but I must see also. I feel no disposition to resign it to the *contagion of its grandmother's society.*' The assertion of her dishonorable conduct in employing a spy: 'A Mrs. C. (now a kind of housekeeper and *spy of Lady N.'s*), who, in her better days, was a washerwoman, is supposed to be — by the learned — very much the occult cause of our domestic discrepancies.'

The seeming exculpation of myself in the extract, with the words immediately following it, 'Her nearest relations are a— —;' where the blank clearly implies something too offensive for publication. These passages tend to throw suspicion on my parents, and give reason to ascribe the separation either to their direct agency, or to that of 'officious spies' employed by them.

From the following part of the narrative, it must also be inferred that an undue influence was exercised by them for the accomplishment of this purpose: 'It was in a few weeks after the latter communication between us (Lord Byron and Mr. Moore) that Lady Byron adopted the determination of parting from him.

She had left London at the latter end of January, on a visit to her father's house in Leicestershire; and Lord Byron was in a short time to follow her. They had parted in the utmost kindness, — she wrote him a letter, full of playfulness and affection, on the road; and, immediately on her arrival at Kirkby Mallory, her father wrote to acquaint Lord Byron that she would return to him no more.'

"In my observations upon this statement, I shall, as far as possible, avoid touching on any matters relating personally to Lord Byron and myself. The facts are, — I left London for Kirkby Mallory, the residence of my father and mother, on the 15th of January, 1816.

Lord Byron had signified to me in writing his absolute desire that I should leave London on the earliest day that I could conveniently fix. It was not safe for me to undertake the fatigue of a journey sooner than the 15th.

Previously to my departure, it had been strongly

impressed on my mind that Lord Byron was under the influence of insanity. This opinion was derived in a great measure from the communications made to me by his nearest relatives and personal attendant, who had more opportunities than myself of observing him during the latter part of my stay in town.

It was even represented to me that he was in danger of destroying himself. *With the concurrence of his family,* I had consulted Dr. Baillie, as a friend, respecting this supposed malady. On acquainting him with the state of the case, and with Lord Byron's desire that I should leave London, Dr. Baillie thought that my absence might be advisable as an experiment, *assuming* the fact of mental derangement; for Dr. Baillie, not having had access to Lord Byron, could not pronounce a positive opinion on that point.

He enjoined, that, in correspondence with Lord Byron, I should avoid all but light and soothing topics. Under these impressions, I left London, determined to follow the advice given by Dr. Baillie. Whatever might have been the nature of Lord Byron's conduct towards me from the time of my marriage, yet, supposing him to be in a state of mental alienation, it was not for *me,* nor for any person of common humanity, to manifest at that moment a sense of injury, On the day of my departure, and again on my arrival at Kirkby, I wrote to Lord Byron in a kind and cheerful tone, according to those medical directions.

"The last letter was circulated, and employed as a pretext for the charge of my having been subsequently *influenced* to 'desert' my husband. It has been argued that I parted from Lord Byron in perfect harmony; that feelings incompatible with any deep, sense of injury had dictated the letter which I addressed to him; and that my sentiments must have been changed by persuasion and interference when I was under the roof of my parents. These assertions and inferences are wholly destitute of foundation.

When I arrived at Kirkby Mallory, my parents were unacquainted with the existence of any causes likely to destroy my prospects of happiness; and, when I communicated to them the opinion which had been formed concerning Lord Byron's state of mind, they were most anxious to promote his restoration by every means in their power.

They assured those relations who were with him in London, that 'they would devote their whole care and attention to the alleviation of his malady;' and hoped to make the best arrangements for his comfort, if he could be induced to visit them.

"With these intentions, my mother wrote on the 17th to Lord Byron, inviting him to Kirkby Mallory. She had always treated him with an affectionate consideration and indulgence, which extended to every little peculiarity of his feelings. Never did an irritating word escape her lips in her whole intercourse with him.

The accounts given me after I left Lord Byron, by the persons in constant intercourse with him, added to those doubts which had before transiently occurred to my mind as to the reality of the alleged disease; and the reports of his medical attendant were far from establishing the existence of any thing like lunacy.

Under this uncertainty, I deemed it right to communicate to my parents, that, if I were to consider Lord Byron's past conduct as that of a person of sound mind, nothing could induce me to return to him. It therefore appeared expedient, both to them and myself, to consult the ablest advisers. For that object, and also to obtain still further information respecting the appearances which seemed to indicate mental derangement, my mother determined to go to London.

She was empowered by me to take legal opinions on a written statement of mine, though I had then reasons for reserving a part of the case from the knowledge even of my father and mother.

Being convinced by the result of these inquiries, and by the tenor of Lord Byron's proceedings, that the notion of insanity was an illusion, I no longer hesitated to authorize such measures as were necessary in order to secure me from being ever again placed in his power.

Conformably with this resolution, my father wrote to him

on the 2d of February to propose an amicable separation. Lord Byron at first rejected this proposal; but when it was distinctly notified to him, that, if he persisted in his refusal, recourse must be had to legal measures, he agreed to sign a deed of separation.

Upon applying to Dr. Lushington, who was intimately acquainted with all the circumstances, to state in writing what he recollected upon this subject, I received from him the following letter, by which it will be manifest that my mother cannot have been actuated by any hostile or ungenerous motives towards Lord Byron: —

"'Mydear Lady Byron, — I can rely upon the accuracy of my memory for the following statement. I was originally consulted by Lady Noel, on your behalf, whilst you were in the country. The circumstances detailed by her were such as justified a separation; but they were not of that aggravated description as to render such a measure indispensable. On Lady Noel's representation, I deemed a reconciliation with Lord Byron practicable, and felt most sincerely a wish to aid in effecting it.

There was not on Lady Noel's part any exaggeration of the facts; nor, so far as I could perceive, any determination to prevent a return to Lord Byron: certainly none was expressed when I spoke of a reconciliation. When you came to town, in about a fortnight, or perhaps more, after my first interview with Lady Noel, I was for the first time informed by you of facts utterly unknown, as I have no doubt, to Sir Ralph and Lady Noel.

On receiving this additional information, my opinion was entirely changed: I considered a reconciliation impossible. I declared my opinion, and added, that, if such an idea should be entertained, I could not, either professionally or otherwise, take any part towards effecting it.

Believe me, very faithfully yours,

Steph. Lushington.

GREAT GEORGE STREET, Jan. 31, 1830.'"

"I have only to observe, that, if the statements on which my legal advisers (the late Sir Samuel Romilly and Dr.

Lushington) formed their opinions were false, the responsibility and the odium should rest with *me only*. I trust that the facts which I have here briefly recapitulated will absolve my father and mother from all accusations with regard to the part they took in the separation between Lord Byron and myself.

"They neither originated, instigated, nor advised that separation; and they cannot be condemned for having afforded to their daughter the assistance and protection which she claimed. There is no other near relative to vindicate their memory from insult. I am therefore compelled to break the silence which I had hoped always to observe, and to solicit from the readers of Lord Byron's Life an impartial consideration of the testimony extorted from me.

"A. I. Noel Byron.

"*HANGER HILL*, Feb. 19, 1830."

The effect of this statement on the literary world may be best judged by the discussion of it by Christopher North (Wilson) in the succeeding May number of "*The Noctes*," where the bravest and most generous of literary men that then were — himself the husband of a gentle wife — thus gives sentence: the conversation is between North and the Shepherd: —

North. — "God forbid I should wound the feelings of Lady Byron, of whose character, known to me but by the high estimation in which it is held by all who have enjoyed her friendship, I have always spoken with respect!... But may I, without harshness or indelicacy, say, here among ourselves, James, that, by marrying Byron, she took upon herself, with eyes wide open and conscience clearly convinced, duties very different from those of which, even in common cases, the presaging foresight shadows... the light of the first nuptial moon?"

Shepherd. — "She did that, sir; by my troth, she did that."

North. — "Miss Milbanke knew that he was reckoned a rake and a *rouè*; and although his genius wiped off, by impassioned eloquence in love-letters that were felt to be irresistible, or hid the worst stain of, that reproach, still Miss Milbanke must have believed it a perilous thing to be the wife of Lord Byron.... But still, by joining her life to his in marriage, she pledged her troth and her faith and her love, under probabilities of severe, disturbing, perhaps fearful trials, in the future.

"But I think Lady Byron ought not to have printed that Narrative. Death abrogates not the rights of a husband to his wife's silence when speech is fatal... to his character as a man. Has she not flung suspicion, over his bones interred, that they are the bones of a — monster?... If Byron's sins or crimes — for we are driven to use terrible terms — were unendurable and unforgivable as if against the Holy Ghost, ought the wheel, the rack, or the stake to have extorted that confession from his widow's breast?...

But there was no such pain here, James: the declaration was voluntary, and it was calm. Self-collected, and gathering up all her faculties and feelings into unshrinking strength, she denounced before all the world -and throughout all space and all time — her husband, as excommunicated by his vices from woman's bosom.

"'Twas to vindicate the character of her parents that Lady Byron. wrote, — a holy purpose and devout, nor do I doubt sincere. But filial affection and reverence, sacred as they are, may be blamelessly, nay, righteously, subordinate to conjugal duties, which die not with the dead, are extinguished not even by the sins of the dead, were they as foul as the grave's corruption."

Here is what John Stuart Mill calls the literature of slavery for woman, in length and breadth; and, that all women may understand the doctrine, the Shepherd now takes up his parable, and expounds the true position of the wife. We render his Scotch into English: —

"Not a few such widows do I know, whom brutal, profligate, and savage husbands have brought to the brink of the grave, -as good, as bright, as innocent as, and far more forgiving than, Lady Byron. There they sit in their obscure, rarely-visited dwellings; for sympathy instructed by suffering knows well that the deepest and most hopeless misery is least given to complaint."

Then follows a pathetic picture of one such widow, trembling and fainting for hunger, obliged, on her way to the well for a can of water, her only drink, to sit down on a *"knowe"* and say a prayer.

"Yet she's decently, yea, tidily dressed, poor creature! in sair worn widow's clothes, a single suit for Saturday and Sunday; her hair, untimely gray, is neatly braided under her crape cap; and sometimes, when all is still and solitary in the fields, and all labour has disappeared into the house, you may see her stealing by herself, or leading one wee orphan by the hand, with another at her breast, to the kirkyard, where the love of her youth and the husband of her prime is buried."

"Yet," says the Shepherd, "he was a brute, a ruffian, a monster. When drunk, how he raged and cursed and swore! Often did she dread, that, in his fits of inhuman passion, he would have murdered the baby at her breast; for she had seen him dash their only little boy, a child of eight years old, on the floor, till the blood gushed from his ears; and then the madman threw himself down on the body, and howled for the gallows.

Limmers haunted his door, and he theirs; and it was hers to lie, not sleep, in a cold, forsaken bed, once the bed of peace, affection, and perfect happiness. Often he struck her; and once, when she was pregnant with that very orphan now smiling on her breast, reaching out his wee fingers to touch the flowers on his father's grave....

"But she tries to smile among the neighbors, and speaks of her boy's likeness to its father; nor, when the conversation turns on bygone times, does she fear to let his name escape her white lips, 'My Robert; the bairn's not ill-favored, but he will never look like his father,' — and such sayings, uttered in a calm, sweet voice.

Nay, I remember once how her pale countenance reddened with a sudden flush of pride, when a gossiping crone alluded to their wedding; and the widow's eye brightened through her tears to hear how the bridegroom, sitting that sabbath in his front seat beside his bonny bride, had not his equal for strength, stature, and all that is beauty in man, in all the congregation. That, I say, sir, whether right or wrong, *was — forgiveness.*"

Here is a specimen of how even generous men had been so perverted by the enchantment of Lord Byron's genius, as to turn all the pathos and power of the strongest literature of that day against the persecuted, pure woman, and for the strong, wicked man.

These "Blackwood" writers knew, by Byron's own filthy, ghastly writings, which had gone sorely against their own moral stomachs, that he was foul to the bone.

They could see, in Moore's Memoirs right before them, how he had caught an innocent girl's heart by sending a love-letter, and offer of marriage, at the end of a long friendly correspondence, — a letter that had been written to *show* to his libertine set, and sent on the tossup of a copper, because he cared nothing for it one way or the other.

They admit, that, having won this poor girl, he had been savage, brutal, drunken, cruel. They had read the filthy taunts in "Don Juan," and the nameless abominations in the Autobiography.

They had admitted among themselves that his honor was lost; but still this abused, desecrated woman must *reverence* her brutal master's memory, and not speak, even to defend the grave of her own kind father and mother.

That there was *no* lover of her youth, that the marriage-vow had been a hideous, shameless cheat, is on the face of Moore's account; yet the "Blackwood" does not see it nor feel it, and brings up against Lady Byron this touching story of a poor widow, who really had had a true lover once, — a lover maddened, imbruted, lost, through that very drunkenness in which the Noctes Club were always glorying.

It is because of such transgressors as Byron, such supporters as Moore and the Noctes Club, that there *are* so many helpless, cowering, broken-hearted, abject women, given over to the animal love which they share alike with the poor dog, — the dog, who, beaten, kicked, starved, and cuffed, still lies by his drunken master with great anxious eyes of love and sorrow, and with sweet, brute forgiveness nestles upon his bosom, as he lies in his filth in the snowy ditch, to keep the warmth of life in him.

Great is the mystery of this fidelity in the poor, loving brute, — most mournful and most sacred! But oh, that a noble man should have no higher ideal of the love of a high-souled, heroic woman! Oh, that men should teach women that they have no higher duties, and are capable of no higher tenderness, than this loving, unquestioning animal fidelity! The dog is ever-loving, ever-forgiving, because God has given him no high range of moral faculties, no sense of justice, no consequent horror at impurity and vileness.

Much of the beautiful patience and forgiveness of women is made possible to them by that utter *deadness to the sense of justice* which the laws, literature, and misunderstood religion of England have sought to induce in woman as a special grace and virtue.

The lesson to woman in this pathetic piece of special pleading is, that man may sink himself below the brute, may wallow in filth like the swine, may turn his home into a hell, beat and torture his children, forsake the marriage-bed for foul rivals; yet all this does *not* dissolve the marriage-vow on her part, nor free his bounden serf from her obligation to honor his memory, — nay, to sacrifice to it the honor due to a kind father and mother, slandered in their silent graves.

Such was the sympathy, and such the advice, that the best literature of England could give to a young widow, a peeress of England, whose husband, as they verily believed and admitted, might have done *worse* than all this; whose crimes might have been "foul, monstrous, unforgivable as the sin against the Holy Ghost."

If these things be done in the green tree, what shall be done in the dry? If the peeress *as a wife* has no rights, what is the state of the cotter's wife?

But, in the same paper, North again blames Lady Byron for not having come out with the whole story before the world at the time she separated from her husband. He says of the time when she first consulted counsel through her mother, keeping back one item, —

"How weak, and worse than weak, at such a juncture, on which hung her whole fate, to ask legal advice on an imperfect document! Give the delicacy of a virtuous woman its due; but at such a crisis, when the question was whether her conscience was to be free from the oath of oaths, delicacy should have died, and nature was privileged to show unashamed — if such there were — the records of uttermost pollution."

Shepherd. — "And what think ye, sir, that a' this pollution could hae been, that sae electrified Dr. Lushington?"

North. — "Bad — bad — bad, James. Nameless, it is horrible: named, it might leave Byron's memory yet within the range of pity and forgiveness; and, where they are, their sister affections will not be far; though, like weeping seraphs, standing aloof, and veiling their wings."

Shepherd. — "She should indeed hae been silent — till the grave had closed on her sorrows as on his sins."

North. — "*Even now she should speak,* — or some one else for her, —... and a few words will suffice. *Worse* the condition of the dead man's name cannot be — far, far better it might — I believe it would be — were *all* the truth somehow or other declared; and declared it must be, not for Byron's sake only, but for the sake of humanity itself; and then a mitigated sentence, or eternal silence." We have another discussion of Lady Byron's duties in a further number of "Blackwood."

The Memoir being out, it was proposed that there should be a complete annotation of Byron's works gotten up, and adorned, for the further glorification of his memory, with portraits of the various women whom he had delighted to honor.

Murray applied to Lady Byron for her portrait, and was met with a cold, decided negative. After reading all the particulars of Byron's harem of mistresses, and Moore's comparisons between herself and La Guiccioli, one might *imagine* reasons why a lady, with proper self respect, should object to appearing in this manner. One would suppose there might have been gentlemen who could well appreciate the *motive* of that refusal; but it was only considered a new evidence that she was indifferent to her conjugal duties, and wanting in that *respect* which Christopher North had told her she owed a husband's memory, though his crimes were foul as the rottenness of the grave.

Never, since Queen Vashti refused to come at the command of a drunken husband to show herself to his drunken lords, was there a clearer case of disrespect to the marital dignity on the part of a wife. It was a plain act of insubordination, rebellion against law and order; and how shocking in Lady Byron, who ought to feel herself but too much flattered to be exhibited to the public as the head wife of a man of genius!

Means were at once adopted to subdue her contumacy, of which one may read in a note to the "Blackwood" (Noctes), September, 1832. An artist was sent down to Ealing to take her picture by stealth as she sat in church.

Two sittings were thus obtained without her knowledge. In the third one, the artist placed himself boldly before her, and sketched, so that she could not but observe him. We shall give the rest in Mackenzie's own words, as a remarkable specimen of the obtuseness, not to say indelicacy of feeling, which seemed to pervade the literary circles of England at the time: —

"After prayers, Wright and his friend (the artist) were visited by an ambassador from her ladyship to inquire the meaning of what she had seen. The reply was, that Mr. Murray must have her portrait, and was compelled to take what she refused to give.

The result was, Wright was requested to visit her, which he did; taking with him, not *the* sketch, which was very good, but another, in which there was a strong touch of caricature. Rather than allow *that* to appear as her likeness (a very natural and womanly feeling by the way), she consented to sit for the portrait to W. J. Newton, which was engraved, and is here alluded to."

The artless barbarism of this note is too good to be lost; but it is quite borne out by the conversation in the Noctes Club, which it illustrates.

It would appear from this conversation that these Byron

beauties appeared successively in pamphlet form; and the picture of Lady Byron is thus discussed: —

Mullion. — "I don't know if you have seen the last brochure. It has a charming head of Lady Byron, who, it seems, sat on purpose: and that's very agreeable to hear of; for it shows her ladyship has got over any little soreness that Moore's Life occasioned, and is now willing to contribute any thing in her power to the real monument of Byron's genius."

North. — "I am delighted to hear of this: 'tis really very noble in the unfortunate lady. I never saw her. Is the face a striking one?"

Mullion. — "Eminently so, — a most calm, pensive, melancholy style of native beauty, — and a most touching contrast to the maids of Athens, Annesley, and all the rest of them. I'm sure you'll have the proof Finden has sent you framed for the Boudoir at the Lodge."

North. — "By all means. I mean to do that for all the Byron Beauties."

But it may be asked, Was there not a man in all England with delicacy enough to feel for Lady Byron, and chivalry enough to speak a bold word for her? Yes: there was one. Thomas Campbell the poet, when he read Lady Byron's statement, believed it, as did Christopher North; but it affected him differently.

It appears he did not believe it a wife's duty to burn herself on her husband's funeral-pile, as did Christopher North; and held the singular idea, that a wife had some rights as a human being as well as a husband.

Lady Byron's own statement appeared in pamphlet form in 1830: at least, such is the date at the foot of the document. Thomas Campbell, in "*The New Monthly Magazine*," shortly after, printed a spirited, gentlemanly defence of Lady Byron, and administered a pointed rebuke to Moore for the rudeness and indelicacy he had shown in selecting from Byron's letters the coarsest against herself, her parents, and her old governess Mrs. Clermont, and by the indecent comparisons he had instituted between Lady Byron and Lord Byron's last mistress.

It is refreshing to hear, at last, from somebody who is not

altogether on his knees at the feet of the popular idol, and who has some chivalry for woman, and some idea of common humanity. He says, —

"I found my right to speak on this painful subject, on its now *irrevocable publicity*, brought up afresh as it has been by Mr. Moore, to be the theme of discourse to millions, and, if I err not much, the cause of misconception to innumerable minds. I claim to speak of Lady Byron in the right of a man, and of a friend to the rights of woman, and to liberty, and to natural religion.

I claim a right, more especially, as one of the many friends of Lady Byron, who, one and all, feel aggrieved by this production. It has virtually dragged her forward from the shade of retirement, where she had hid her sorrows, and compelled her to defend the heads of her friends and her parents from being crushed under the tombstone of Byron. Nay, in a general view, it has forced her to defend *herself*; though, with her true sense and her pure taste, she stands above all special pleading.

To plenary explanation she *ought* not — she never shall be driven. Mr. Moore is too much a gentleman not to shudder at the thought of that; but if other Byronists, of a far different stamp, were to force the savage ordeal, it is her enemies, and not she, that would have to dread the burning ploughshares.

"We, her friends, have no wish to prolong the discussion: but a few words we *must* add, even to her admirable statement; for hers is a cause not only dear to her friends, but having become, from Mr. Moore and her misfortunes, a publicly agitated cause, it concerns morality, and the most sacred rights of the sex, that she should (and that, too, without more special explanations) be acquitted out and out, and honorably acquitted, in this business, of all share in the blame, which is one and indivisible.

Mr. Moore, on further reflection, may see this; and his return to candor will surprise us less than his momentary deviation path. "For the tact of Mr. Moore's conduct in this affair, I have not to answer; but, if indelicacy be charged upon me, I scorn the charge.

Neither will I submit to be called Lord Byron's accuser; because a word against him I wish not to say beyond what is painfully wrung from me by the necessity of owning or illustrating Lady Byron's unblamableness, and of repelling certain misconceptions respecting her, which are now walking the fashionable world, and which have been fostered (though Heaven knows where they were born) most delicately and warily by the Christian godfathership of Mr. Moore.

"I write not at Lady Byron's bidding. I have never humiliated either her or myself by asking if I should write, or what I should write; that is to say, I never applied to her for information against Lord Byron, though I was justified, as one intending to criticise Mr. Moore, in inquiring into the truth of some of his statements. Neither will I suffer myself to be called her champion, if by that word be meant the advocate of her mere legal innocence; for that, I take it, nobody questions.

"Still less is it from the sorry impulse of pity that I speak of this noble woman; for I look with wonder and even envy at the proud purity of her sense and conscience, that have carried her exquisite sensibilities in triumph through such poignant tribulations. But I am proud to be called her friend, the humble illustrator of her cause, and the advocate of those principles which make it to me more interesting than Lord Byron's.

Lady Byron (if the subject must be discussed) belongs to sentiment and morality (at least as much as Lord Byron); nor is she to be suffered, when compelled to speak, to raise her voice as in a desert, with no friendly voice to respond to her.

Lady Byron could not have outlived her sufferings if she had not wound up her fortitude to the high point of trusting mainly for consolation, not to the opinion of the world, but to her own inward peace; and, having said what ought to convince the world, I verily believe that she has less care about the fashionable opinion respecting her than any of her friends can have. But we, her friends, mix with the world; and we hear offensive absurdities about her, which we have a right to put down.

"I proceed to deal more generally with Mr. Moore's book. You speak, Mr. Moore, against Lord Byron's censurers in a tone of indignation which is perfectly lawful towards calumnious traducers, but which will not terrify me, or any other man of courage who is no calumniator, from uttering his mind freely with regard to this part of your hero's conduct.

I question your philosophy in assuming that all that is noble in Byron's poetry was inconsistent with the possibility of his being devoted to a pure and good woman; and I repudiate your morality for canting too complacently about 'the lava of his imagination,' and the unsettled fever of his passions, being any excuses for his planting the *tic douloureux* of domestic suffering in a meek woman's bosom.

"These are hard words, Mr. Moore; but you have brought them on yourself by your voluntary ignorance of facts known to me: for you might and ought to have known both sides of the question; and, if the subject was too delicate for you to consult Lady Byron's confidential friends, you ought to have had nothing to do with the subject. But you cannot have submitted your book even to Lord Byron's sister, otherwise she would have set you right about the imaginary spy, Mrs. Clermont."

Campbell now goes on to print, at his own peril, he says, and without time to ask leave, the following note from Lady Byron in reply to an application he made to her, when he was about to review Moore's book, for an "estimate as to the correctness of Moore's statements."

The following is Lady Byron's reply: —

"Dear mr. Campbell, — in taking up my pen to point out for your private information those passages in Mr. Moore's representation of my part of the story which were open to contradiction, I find them of still greater extent than I had supposed; and to deny an assertion *here and there* would virtually admit the truth of the rest.

If, on the contrary, I were to enter into a full exposure of the falsehood of the views taken by Mr. Moore, I must detail various matters, which, consistently with my principles and feelings, I cannot under the existing circumstances disclose. I may, perhaps, convince you better of the difficulty of the case by an example: It is not true that pecuniary embarrassments were the cause of the disturbed state of Lord Byron's mind, or formed the chief reason for the arrangements made by him at that time.

But is it reasonable for me to expect that you or any one else should believe this, unless I show you what were the causes in question? and this I cannot do. "I am, &c.,

"A. I. NOEL BYRON."

Campbell then goes on to reprove Moore for his injustice to Mrs. Clermont, whom Lord Byron had denounced as a spy, but whose respectability and innocence were vouched for by Lord Byron's own family; and then he pointedly rebukes one false statement of great indelicacy and cruelty concerning Lady Byron's courtship, as follows: —

"It is a further mistake on Mr. Moore's part, and I can prove it to be so, if proof be necessary, to represent Lady Byron, in the course of their courtship, as one inviting her future husband to correspondence by letters after she had at first refused him.

She never proposed a correspondence. On the contrary, he sent her a message after that first refusal, stating that he meant to go abroad, and to travel for some years in the East; that he should depart with a heart aching, but not angry; and that he only begged a verbal assurance that she had still some interest in his happiness.

Could Miss Milbanke, as a well-bred woman, refuse a courteous answer to such a message? She sent him a verbal answer, which was merely kind and becoming, but which signified no encouragement that he should renew his offer of marriage.

"After that message, he wrote to her a most interesting letter about himself, — about his views, personal, moral, and religious, — to which it would have been uncharitable not to have replied. The result was an insensibly increasing correspondence, which ended in her being devotedly attached to him. About that time, I occasionally saw Lord Byron; and though I knew less of him than Mr. Moore, yet I suspect I knew as much of him as Miss Milbanke then knew. At that time, he was so pleasing, that, if I had had a daughter with ample fortune and beauty, I should have trusted her in marriage with Lord Byron. "Mr. Moore at that period evidently understood Lord Byron better than either his future bride or myself; but this speaks more for Moore's shrewdness than for Byron's ingenuousness of character.

"It is more for Lord Byron's sake than for his widow's that I resort not to a more special examination of Mr. Moore's misconceptions. The subject would lead me insensibly into hateful disclosures against poor Lord Byron, who is more unfortunate in his rash defenders than in his reluctant accusers.

Happily, his own candor turns our hostility from himself against his defenders. It was only in wayward and bitter remarks that he misrepresented Lady Byron. He would have defended himself irresistibly if Mr. Moore had left only his acknowledging passages.

But Mr. Moore has produced a Life of him which reflects blame on Lady Byron so dexterously, that 'more is meant than meets the ear.' The almost universal impression produced by his book is, that Lady Byron must be a precise and a wan, unwarming spirit, a blue-stocking of chilblained learning, a piece of insensitive goodness.

"Who that knows Lady Byron will not pronounce her to be every thing the reverse? Will it be believed that this person, so unsuitably matched to her moody lord, has written verses that would do no discredit to Byron himself; that her sensitiveness is surpassed and bounded only by her good sense; and that she is

'Blest with a temper, whose unclouded ray
Can make to-morrow cheerful as to-day'?

"She brought to Lord Byron beauty, manners, fortune, meekness, romantic affection, and every thing that ought to have made her to the most transcendent man of genius — *had he been what he should have been* — his pride and his idol. I speak not of Lady Byron in the commonplace manner of attesting character: I appeal to the gifted Mrs.

Siddons and Joanna Baillie, to Lady Charlemont, and to other ornaments of their sex, whether I am exaggerating in the least when I say, that, in their whole lives, they have seen few beings so intellectual and well-tempered as Lady Byron. "I wish to be as ingenuous as possible in speaking of her. Her manner, I have no hesitation to say, is cool at the first interview, but is modestly, and not insolently, cool: she contracted it, I believe, from being exposed by her beauty and large fortune, in youth, to numbers of suitors, whom she could not have otherwise kept at a distance.

But this manner could have had no influence with Lord Byron; for it vanishes on nearer acquaintance, and has no origin in coldness. All her friends like her frankness the better for being preceded by this reserve. This manner, however, though not the slightest apology for Lord Byron, has been inimical to Lady Byron in her misfortunes.

It endears her to her friends; but it piques the indifferent. Most odiously unjust, therefore, is Mr. Moore's assertion, that she has had the advantage of Lord Byron in public opinion. She is, comparatively speaking, unknown to the world; for though she has many friends, that is, a friend in every one who knows her, yet her pride and purity and misfortunes naturally contract the circle of her acquaintance.

"There is something exquisitely unjust in Mr. Moore comparing her chance of popularity with Lord Byron's, the poet who can command men of talents, — putting even Mr. Moore into the livery of his service, — and who has suborned the favour of almost all women by the beauty of his person and the voluptuousness of his verses. Lady Byron has nothing to oppose to these fascinations but the truth and justice of her cause.

"You said, Mr. Moore, that Lady Byron was unsuitable to her lord: the word is cunningly insidious, and may mean as much or as little as may suit your convenience. But, if she was unsuitable, I remark that it tells all the worse against Lord Byron.

I have not read it in your book (for I hate to wade through it); but they tell me that you have not only warily depreciated Lady Byron, but that you have described a lady that would have suited him. If this be true, 'it is the unkindest cut of all,' — to hold up a florid description of a woman suitable to Lord

Byron, as if in mockery over the forlorn flower of virtue that was drooping in the solitude of sorrow.

"But I trust there is no such passage in your book. Surely you must be conscious of your woman, with her '*virtue loose about her, who would have suited Lord Byron,*' to be as imaginary a being as the woman without a head. A woman to suit Lord Byron! Poo, poo! I could paint to you the woman that could have *matched* him, if I had not bargained to say as little as possible against him.

"If Lady Byron was not suitable to Lord Byron, so much the worse for his lordship; for let me tell you, Mr. Moore, that neither your poetry, nor Lord Byron's, nor all our poetry put together, ever delineated a more interesting being than the woman whom you have so coldly treated.

This was not kicking the dead lion, but wounding the living lamb, who was already bleeding and shorn, even unto the quick. I know, that, collectively speaking, the world is in Lady Byron's favour; but it is coldly favorable, and you have not warmed its breath. Time, however, cures every thing; and even your book, Mr. Moore, may be the means of Lady Byron's character being better appreciated. "Thomas campbell."

Here is what seems to be a gentlemanly, high spirited, chivalric man, throwing down his glove in the lists for a pure woman. What was the consequence? Campbell was crowded back, thrust down, overwhelmed, his eyes filled with dust, his mouth with ashes.

There was a general confusion and outcry, which re-acted both on him and on Lady Byron. Her friends were angry with him for having caused this re-action upon her; and he found himself at once attacked by Lady Byron's enemies, and deserted by her friends.

All the literary authorities of his day took up against him with energy. Christopher North, professor of moral philosophy in the Edinburgh University, in a fatherly talk in "*The Noctes,*" condemns Campbell, and justifies Moore, and heartily recommends his Biography, as containing nothing materially objectionable on the score either of manners or morals. Thus we have it in "*The Noctes*" of May, 1830: —

"Mr. Moore's biographical book I admired; and I said so to my little world, in two somewhat lengthy articles, which many approved, and some, I am sorry to know, condemned."

On the point in question between Moore and Campbell, North goes on to justify Moore altogether, only admitting that "it would have been better had he not printed any coarse expression of Byron's about the old people; " and, finally, he closes by saying, –

"I do not think, that, under the circumstances, Mr. Campbell himself, had he written Byron's Life, could have spoken, with the sentiments he then held, in a better, more manly, and more gentlemanly spirit, in so far as regards Lady Byron, than Mr. Moore did: and I am sorry he has been deterred from 'swimming' through Mr. Moore's work by the fear of 'wading;' for the waters are clear and deep; nor is there any mud, either at the bottom or round the margin."

Of the conduct of Lady Byron's so-called friends on this occasion it is more difficult to speak. There has always been in England, as John Stuart Mill says, a class of women who glory in the utter self-abnegation of the wife to the husband, as the special crown of womanhood. Their patron saint is the Griselda of Chaucer, who, when her husband humiliates her, and treats her as a brute, still accepts all with meek, unquestioning, uncompla-ining devotion.

He tears her from her children; he treats her with personal abuse; he repudiates her, – sends her out to nakedness and poverty; he installs another mistress in his house, and sends for the first to be her handmaid and his own: and all this the meek saint accepts in the words of Milton, –

"My guide and head,
What thou hast said is just and right."

Accordingly, Miss Martineau tells us, that when Campbell's defence came out, coupled with a note from Lady Byron, –

"The first obvious remark was, that there was no real disclosure; and the whole affair had the appearance of a desire, on the part of Lady Byron, to exculpate herself, while yet no adequate information was given. Many, who had regarded her with favour till then, gave her up so far as to believe that feminine weakness had prevailed at last."

The saint had fallen from her pedestal! She had shown a human frailty! Quite evidently she is not a Griselda, but possessed with a shocking desire to exculpate herself and her friends. Is it, then, only to slandered men that the privilege belongs of desiring to exculpate themselves and their families and their friends from unjust censure?

Lord Byron had made it a life-long object to vilify and defame his wife. He had used for that one particular purpose every talent that he possessed. He had left it as a last charge to Moore to pursue the warfare after death, which Moore had done to some purpose;

Aand Christopher North had informed Lady Byron that her private affairs were discussed, not only with the whiskey-toddy of the Noctes Club, but in every drawing-room in May Fair; and declared that the *"Dear Duck"* letter, and various other matters, must be explained, and urged somebody to speak; and then, when Campbell does speak with all the energy of a real gentleman, a general outcry and an indiscriminate *mêlée* is the result.

The world, with its usual injustice, insisted on attributing Campbell's defence to Lady Byron. The reasons for this seemed to be, first, that Campbell states that he did *not* ask Lady Byron's leave, and that she did *not* authorize him to defend her; and, second, that, having asked some explanations from her, he prints a note in which she declines to give any.

We know not how a lady could more gently yet firmly decline to make a gentleman her confidant than in this published note of Lady Byron; and yet, to this day, Campbell is spoken of by the world as having been Lady Byron's confidant at this time. This simply shows how very trustworthy are the general assertions about Lady Byron's confidants.

The final result of the matter, so far as Campbell was concerned, is given in Miss Martineau's sketch, in the following paragraph: —

"The whole transaction was one of poor Campbell's

freaks. He excused himself by saying it was a mistake of his; that he did not know what he was about when he published the paper." It is the saddest of all sad things to see a man, who has spoken from moral convictions, in advance of his day, and who has taken a stand for which he ought to honor himself, thus forced down and humiliated, made to doubt his own better nature and his own honorable feelings, by the voice of a wicked world.

Campbell had no steadiness to stand by the truth he saw. His whole story is told incidentally in a note to "*The Noctes,*" in which it is stated, that in an article in " *Blackwood,*" January, 1825, on Scotch poets, the palm was given to Hogg over Campbell; "one ground being, that *he* could drink 'eight and twenty tumblers of punch, while Campbell is hazy upon seven.'" There is evidence in "*The Noctes,*" that in due time Campbell was reconciled to Moore, and was always suitably ashamed of having tried to be any more generous or just than the men of his generation.

And so it was settled as a law to Jacob, and an ordinance in Israel, that the Byron worship should proceed, and that all the earth should keep silence before him. "*Don Juan,*" that, years before, had been printed by stealth, without Murray's name on the title page, that had been denounced as a book which no woman should read, and had been given up as a desperate enterprise, now came forth in triumph, with banners flying and drums beating.

Every great periodical in England that had fired moral volleys of artillery against it in its early days, now humbly marched in the glorious procession of admirers to salute this edifying work of genius.

"*Blackwood,*" which in the beginning had been the most indignantly virtuous of the whole, now grovelled and ate dust as the serpent in the very abjectness of submission. Odoherty (Maginn) declares that he would rather have written a page of "*Don Juan*" than a ton of "*Childe Harold.*"

Timothy Tickler informs Christopher North that he means to tender Murray, as Emperor of the North, an interleaved copy of "*Don Juan,*" with illustrations, as the *only* work of

Byron's he cares much about; and Christopher North, professor of *moral* philosophy in Edinburgh, smiles approval!

We are not, after this, surprised to see the assertion, by a recent much-aggrieved writer in "*The London Era*," that "Lord Byron has been, more than any other man of the age, the *teacher of the youth* of England and that he has "seen his works on the bookshelves of *bishops'* palaces, no less than the tables of university under-graduates."

A note to "*The Noctes*" of July, 1822, informs us of another instance of Lord Byron's triumph over English morals: —

"The mention of this" (Byron's going to Greece) "reminds me, by the by, of what the Guiccioli said in her visit to London, where she was so lionized as having been the lady-love of Byron. She was rather fond of speaking on the subject, designating herself by some Venetian pet phrase, which she interpreted as meaning 'Love-Wife.'"

What was Lady Byron to do in such a world? She retired to the deepest privacy, and devoted herself to works of charity, and the education of her only child, — that brilliant daughter, to whose eager, opening mind the whole course of current litèrature must bring so many trying questions in regard to the position of her father and mother, — questions that the mother might not answer.

That the cruel inconsiderateness of the literary world added thorns to the intricacies of the path trodden by every mother who seeks to guide, restrain, and educate a strong, acute, and precociously intelligent child, must easily be seen.

What remains to be said of Lady Byron's life shall be said in the words of Miss Martineau, published in "The Atlantic Monthly:" —

"Her life, thenceforth, was one of unremitting bounty to society, administered with as much skill and prudence as benevolence. She lived in retirement, changing her abode frequently; partly for the benefit of her child's education and the promotion of her benevolent schemes, and partly from a restlessness which was one of the few signs of injury received from the spoiling of associations with *home*.

"She felt a satisfaction which her friends rejoiced in when

her daughter married Lord King, at present the Earl of Lovelace, in 1835; and when grief upon grief followed, in the appearance of mortal disease in her only child, her quiet patience stood her in good stead as before. She even found strength to appropriate the blessings of the occasion, and took comfort, as did her dying daughter, in the intimate friendship, which grew closer as the time of parting drew nigh.

"Lady Lovelace died in 1852; and, for her few remaining years, Lady Byron was devoted to her grandchildren. But nearer calls never lessened her interest in remoter objects. Her mind was of the large and clear quality which could comprehend remote interests in their true proportions, and achieve each aim as perfectly as if it were the only one.

Her agents used to say that it was impossible to mistake her directions; and thus her business was usually well done. There was no room, in her case, for the ordinary doubts, censures, and sneers about the misapplication of bounty.

"Her taste did not lie in the 'Charity-Ball" direction; her funds were not lavished in encouraging hypocrisy and improvidence among the idle and worthless; and the quality of her charity was, in fact, as admirable as its quantity. Her chief aim was the extension and improvement of popular education; but there was no kind of misery that she heard of that she did not palliate to the utmost, and no kind of solace that her quick imagination and sympathy could devise that she did not administer.

"In her methods, she united consideration and frankness with singular success. For one instance among a thousand: A lady with whom she had had friendly relations some time before, and who became impoverished in a quiet way by hopeless sickness, preferred poverty with an easy conscience to a competency attended by some uncertainty about the perfect rectitude of the resource.

Lady Byron wrote to an intermediate person exactly what she thought of the case. Whether the judgment of the sufferer was right or mistaken was nobody's business but her own: this was the first point. Next, a voluntary poverty could never be pitied by anybody: that was the second. But it was painful to others to think of the mortification to benevolent feelings which attends poverty; and there could be no objection to arresting that pain.

Therefore she, Lady Byron, had lodged in a neighboring bank the sum of one hundred pounds, to be used for benevolent purposes; and, in order to preclude all outside speculation, she had made the money payable to the order of the intermediate person, so that the sufferer's name need not appear at all.

"Five and thirty years of unremitting secret bounty like this must make up a great amount of human happiness; but this was only one of a wide variety of methods of doing good. It was the unconcealable magnitude of her beneficence, and its wise quality, which made her a second time the theme of English conversation in all honest households within the four seas. Years ago, it was said far and wide that Lady Byron was doing more good than anybody else in England; and it was difficult to imagine how anybody could do more.

"Lord Byron spent every shilling that the law allowed him out of her property while he lived, and left away from her every shilling that he could deprive her of by his will; yet she had, eventually, a large income at her command. In the management of it, she showed the same wise consideration that marked all her practical decisions. She resolved to spend her whole income, seeing how much the world needed help at the moment.

Her care was for the existing generation, rather than for a future one, which would have its own friends. She usually declined trammelling herself with annual subscriptions to charities; preferring to keep her freedom from year to year, and to achieve definite objects by liberal bounty, rather than to extend partial help over a large surface which she could not herself superintend.

"It was her first industrial school that awakened the admiration of the public, which had never ceased to take an interest in her, while sorely misjudging her character. We hear much now — and everybody hears it with pleasure — of the spread of education in 'common things;' but long before Miss

Coutts inherited her wealth, long before a name was found for such a method of training, Lady Byron had instituted the thing, and put it in thė way of making its own name.

"She was living at Ealing, in Middlesex, in 1834; and there she opened one of the first industrial schools in England, if not the very first. She sent out a master to Switzerland, to be instructed in De Fellenburgh's method. She took, on lease, five acres of land, and spent several hundred pounds in rendering the buildings upon it fit for the purposes of the school. A liberal education was afforded to the children of artisans and laborers during the half of the day when they were not employed in the field or garden.

The allotments were rented by the boys, who raised and sold produce, which afforded them a considerable yearly profit if they were good workmen. Those who worked in the field earned wages; their labour being paid by the hour, according to the capability of the young laborer. They kept their accounts of expenditure and receipts, and acquired good habits of business while learning the occupation of their lives. Some mechanical trades were taught, as well as the arts of agriculture.

"Part of the wisdom of the management lay in making the pupils pay. Of one hundred pupils, half were boarders. They paid little more than half the expenses of their maintenance, and the day-scholars paid three pence per week. Of course, a large part of the expense was borne by Lady Byron, besides the payments she made for children who could not otherwise have entered the school.

The establishment flourished steadily till 1852, when the owner of the land required it back for building purposes. During the eighteen years that the Ealing schools were in action, they did a world of good in the way of incitement and example.

The poor-law commissioners pointed out their merits. Land-owners and other wealthy persons visited them, and went home and set up similar establishments. During those years, too, Lady Byron had herself been at work in various directions to the same purpose.

"A more extensive industrial scheme was instituted on her Leicestershire property, and not far off she opened a girls' school and an infant school; and when a season of distress came, as such seasons are apt to befall the poor Leicestershire stocking-weavers, Lady Byron fed the children for months together, till they could resume their payments. These school were opened in 1840. The next year, she built a schoolhouse on her Warwickshire property; and, five years later, she set up an iron schoolhouse on another Leicestershire estate.

"By this time, her educational efforts were costing her several hundred pounds a year in the mere maintenance of existing establishments; but this is the smallest consideration in the case. She has sent out tribes of boys and girls into life fit to do their part there with skill and credit and comfort. Perhaps it is a still more important consideration, that scores of teachers and trainers have been led into their vocation, and duly prepared for it, by what they saw and learned in her schools.

As for the best and the worst of the Ealing boys, the best have, in a few cases, been received into the Battersea Training School, whence they could enter on their career as teachers to the greatest advantage; and the worst found their school a true reformatory, before reformatory schools were heard of. At Bristol, she bought a house for a reformatory for girls; and there her friend, Miss Carpenter, faithfully and energetically carries out her own and Lady Byron's aims, which were one and the same.

"There would be no end if I were to catalogue the schemes of which these are a specimen. It is of more consequence to observe that her mind was never narrowed by her own acts, as the minds of benevolent people are so apt to be. To the last, her interest in great political movements, at home and abroad, was as vivid as ever.

She watched every step won in philosophy, every discovery in science, every token of social change and progress in every shape. Her mind was as liberal as her heart and hand. No diversity of opinion troubled her: she was respectful to every sort of individuality, and indulgent to all constitutional peculiarities. It must have puzzled those who kept up the notion of her being 'strait-laced' to see how indulgent she was even to Epicurean tendencies, — the remotest of all from her own.

"But I must stop; for I do not wish my honest memorial to degenerate into panegyric. Among her latest known acts were her gifts to the Sicilian cause, and her manifestations on behalf of the antislavery cause in the United States. Her kindness to William and Ellen Craft must be well known there; and it is also related in the newspapers, that she bequeathed a legacy to a young American to assist him under any disadvantages he might suffer as an abolitionist.

"All these deeds were done under a heavy burden of ill health. Before she had passed middle life, her lungs were believed to be irreparably injured by partial ossification. She was subject to attacks so serious, that each one, for many years, was expected to be the last. She arranged her affairs in correspondence with her liabilities: so that the same order would have been found, whether she died suddenly or after long warning.

"She was to receive one more accession of outward greatness before she departed. She became Baroness Wentworth in November, 1856. This is one of the facts of her history; but it is the least interesting to us, as probably to her. We care more to know that her last days were bright in honor, and cheered by the attachment of old friends worthy to pay the duty she deserved.

Above all, it is consoling to know that she who so long outlived her only child was blessed with the unremitting and tender care of her grand-daughter. She died on the 16th of May, 1860. "The portrait of Lady Byron as she was at the time of her marriage is probably remembered by some of my readers. It is very engaging.

Her countenance afterwards became much worn; but its expression of thoughtfulness and composure was very interesting. Her handwriting accorded well with the character of her mind. It was clear, elegant, and womanly. Her manners differed with circumstances.

Her shrinking sensitiveness might embarrass one visitor;

while another would be charmed with her easy, significant, and vivacious conversation.

It depended much on whom she talked with. The abiding certainty was, that she had strength for the hardest of human trials, and the composure which belongs to strength. For the rest, it is enough to point to her deeds, and to the mourning of her friends round the chasm which her departure has made in their life, and in the society in which it is spent.

All that could be done in the way of personal love and honor was done while she lived: it only remains now to see that her name and fame are permitted to shine forth at last in their proper light."

We have simply to ask the reader whether a life like this was not the best, the noblest answer that a woman could make to a doubting world.

Chapter 7

The Attack on Lady Byron's Grave

WE have now brought the review of the antagonism against Lady Byron down to the period of her death. During all this time, let the candid reader ask himself which of these two parties seems to be plotting against the other.

Which has been active, aggressive, unscrupulous which has been silent, quiet, unoffending? Which of the two has labored to make a party, and to make that party active, watchful, enthusiastic?

Have we not proved that Lady Byron remained perfectly silent during Lord Byron's life, patiently looking out from her retirement to see the waves of popular sympathy, that once bore her up, day by day retreating, while his accusations against her were resounding in his poems over the whole earth?

And after Lord Byron's death, when all the world with one consent began to give their memorials of him, and made it appear, by their various "recollections of conversations," how incessantly he had obtruded his own version of the separation upon every listener, did she manifest any similar eagerness?

Lady Byron had seen the "Blackwood" coming forward, on the first appearance of "Don Juan," to rebuke the cowardly lampoon in words eloquent with all the unperverted vigor of an honest Englishman. Under the power of the great conspirator, she had seen *that* "Blackwood" become the very eager recipient and chief reporter of the stories against her, and the blind admirer of her adversary.

All this time, she lost sympathy daily by being silent. The

world will embrace those who court it; it will patronize those who seek its favour; it will make parties for those who seek to make parties: but for the often accused who do not speak, who make no confidants and no parties, the world soon loses sympathy.

When at last she spoke, Christopher North says "she astonished the world." Calm, clear, courageous, exact as to time, date, and circumstance, was that first testimony, backed by the equally clear testimony of Dr. Lushington.

It showed that her secret had been kept even from her parents. In words precise, firm, and fearless, she says, "If these statements on which Dr. Lushington and Sir Samuel Romilly formed their opinion were false, the responsibility and the odium should rest with me only." Christopher North did not pretend to disbelieve this statement. He breathed not a doubt of Lady Byron's word.

He spoke of the crime indicated, as one which might have been foul as the grave's corruption, unforgivable as the sin against the Holy Ghost. He rebuked the wife for bearing this testimony, even to save the memory of her dead father and mother, and, in the same breath, declared that she ought now to go farther, and speak fully the one awful word, and then — "a mitigated sentence, or eternal silence!"

But Lady Byron took no counsel with the world, nor with the literary men of her age. One knight, with some small remnant of England's old chivalry, set lance in rest for her: she saw him beaten back unhorsed, rolled in the dust, and ingloriously vanquished, and perceived that henceforth nothing but injury could come to any one who attempted to speak for her.

She turned from the judgments of man and the fond and natural hopes of human nature, to lose herself in sacred ministries to the downcast and suffering. What nobler record for woman could there be than that which Miss Martineau has given? Particularly to be noted in Lady Byron was her peculiar interest in reclaiming fallen women. Among her letters to Mrs. Prof. Follen of Cambridge was one addressed to a society of ladies who had undertaken this difficult work. It was full of heavenly wisdom and of a large and tolerant charity. Fénelon truly says, it is only perfection that can tolerate imperfection; and the very purity of Lady Byron's nature made her most forbearing and most tender towards the weak and the guilty.

This letter, with all the rest of Lady Byron's, was returned to the hands of her executors after her death. Its publication would greatly assist the world in understanding the peculiarities of its writer's character.

Lady Byron passed to a higher life in 1860. After her death, I looked for the publication of her Memoir and Letters as the event that should give her the same opportunity of being known and judged by her life and writings that had been so freely accorded to Lord Byron.

She was, in her husband's estimation, a woman of genius. She was the friend of many of the first men and women of her times, and corresponded with them on topics of literature, morals, religion, and, above all, on the benevolent and philanthropic movements of the day, whose principles she had studied with acute observation, and in connection with which she had acquired a large experience.

The knowledge of her, necessarily diffused by such a series of letters, would have created in America a comprehension of her character, of itself sufficient to wither a thousand slanders.

Such a Memoir was contemplated. Lady Byron's letters to Mrs. Follen were asked for from Boston; and I was applied to by a person in England, who I have recently learned is one of the existing trustees of Lady Byron's papers, to furnish copies of her letters to me for the purpose of a Memoir. Before I had time to have copies made, another letter came, stating that the trustees had concluded that it was not best to publish any Memoir of Lady Byron at all.

This left the character of Lady Byron in our American world precisely where the slanders of her husband, the literature of the Noctes Club, and the unanimous verdict of May Fair as recorded by "Blackwood", had placed it. True, Lady Byron had nobly and quietly lived down these slanders in England by deeds that made her name revered as a saint among all those who valued saintliness. But in France and Italy, and in these United States, I have had abundant opportunity to know that Lady Byron stood judged and condemned on the testimony of her brilliant husband, and that the feeling against her had a vivacity and intensity not to be overcome by mere allusions to a virtuous life in distant England.

This is strikingly shown by one fact. In the American edition of Moore "Life of Byron", by Claxton, Remsen, and Haffelfinger, Philadelphia, 1869, which I have been consulting, Lady Byron's statement, which is found in the Appendix of Murray's standard edition, *is entirely omitted.* Every other paper is carefully preserved.

This one incident showed how the tide of sympathy was setting in this New World. Of course, there is no stronger power than a virtuous life; but, for a virtuous life to bear testimony to the world, its details must be *told,* so that the world may know them.

Suppose the memoirs of Clarkson and Wilberforce had been suppressed after their death, how soon might the coming tide have wiped out the record of their bravery and philanthropy! Suppose the lives of Francis Xavier and Henry Martyn had never been written, and we had lost the remembrance of what holy men could do and dare in the divine enthusiasm of Christian faith! Suppose we had no Fénelon, no Book of Martyrs!

Would there not be an outcry through all the literary and artistic world if a perfect statue were allowed to remain buried forever because some painful individual history was connected with its burial and its recovery? But is not a noble life a greater treasure to mankind than any work of art?

We have heard much mourning over the burned Autobiography of Lord Byron, and seen it treated of in a magazine as "the lost chapter in history." The lost chapter in history is *Lady* Byron's Autobiography in her life and letters; and the suppression of them is the root of this whole mischief. We do not in this intend to censure the parties who came to this decision.

The descendants of Lady Byron revere her memory, as they have every reason to do. That it was *their* desire to have a Memoir of her published, I have been informed by an individual of the highest character in England, who obtained the information directly from Lady Byron's grandchildren.

But the trustees in whose care the papers were placed drew back on examination of them, and declared, that, as Lady Byron's papers could not be fully published, they should regret any thing that should call public attention once more to the discussion of her history.

Reviewing this long history of the way in which the literary world had treated Lady Byron, we cannot wonder that her friends should have doubted whether there was left on earth any justice, or sense that any thing is due to woman as a human being with human rights.

Evidently this lesson had taken from them all faith in the moral sense of the world. Rather than re-awaken the discussion, so unsparing, so painful, and so indelicate, which had been carried on so many years around that loved form, now sanctified by death, they sacrificed the dear pleasure of the memorials, and the interests of mankind, who have an indefeasible right to all the help that can be got from the truth of history as to the living power of virtue, and the reality of that great victory that overcometh the world.

There are thousands of poor victims, suffering in sadness, discouragement, and poverty; heart-broken wives of brutal, drunken husbands; women enduring nameless wrongs and horrors which the delicacy of their sex forbids them to utter, — to whom the lovely letters lying hidden away under those seals might bring courage and hope from springs not of this world.

But though the friends of Lady Byron, perhaps from despair of their kind, from weariness of the utter injustice done her, wished to cherish her name in silence, and to confine the story of her virtues to that circle who knew her too well to ask a proof, or utter a doubt, the partisans of Lord Byron were embarrassed with no such scruple.

Lord Byron had artfully contrived during his life to place

his wife in such an antagonistic position with regard to himself, that his intimate friends were forced to believe that one of the two had deliberately and wantonly injured the other. The published statement of Lady Byron contradicted boldly and point-blank all the statement of her husband concerning the separation: so that, unless *she* was convicted as a false witness, *he* certainly was.

The best evidence of this is Christopher North's own shocked, astonished statement, and the words of the Noctes Club. The noble life that Lady Byron lived after this hushed every voice, and silenced even the most desperate calumny, *while she was in the world*. In the face of Lady Byron as the world saw her, of what use was the talk of Clytemnestra, and the assertion that she had been a mean, deceitful conspirator against her husband's honor in life, and stabbed his memory after death?

But when she was in her grave, when her voice and presence and good deeds no more spoke for her, and a new generation was growing up that knew her not, *then* was the time selected to revive the assault on her memory, and to say over her grave what none would ever have dared to say of her while living.

During these last two years, I have been gradually awakening to the evidence of a new crusade against the memory of Lady Byron, which respected no sanctity, — not even that last and most awful one of death. Nine years after her death, when it was fully understood that no story on her side or that of her friends was to be forthcoming, then her calumniators raked out from the ashes of her husband's sepulchre all his bitter charges, to state them over in even stronger and more indecent forms.

There seems to be reason to think that the materials supplied by Lord Byron for such a campaign yet exist in society. To "*The Noctes*" of November, 1824, there is the following note *apropos* to a discussion of the Byron question:—

"Byron's Memoirs, given by him to Moore, were burned, as everybody knows. But, before this, Moore had lent them to several persons. Mrs. Home Purvis, afterwards Viscountess of

Canterbury, is *known* to have sat up all one night, in which, aided by her daughter, she had a copy made. I have the strongest reason for believing that one other person made a copy; for the description of the first twenty-four hours after the marriage ceremonial has been in my hands. *Not until after the death of Lady Byron, and Hobhouse,* who was the poet's literary executor, can the poet's Autobiography see the light; *but I am certain it will be published.*"

Thus speaks Mackenzie in a note to a volume of "*The Noctes,*" published in America in 1854. Lady Byron died in 1860. Nine years after Lady Byron's death, when it was ascertained that her story was not to see the light, when there were no means of judging her character by her own writings, commenced a well-planned set of operations to turn the public attention once more to Lord Byron, and to represent him as an injured man, whose testimony had been unjustly suppressed.

It was quite possible, supposing copies of the Autobiography to exist, that this might occasion a call from the generation of to-day, in answer to which the suppressed work might appear. This was a rather delicate operation to commence; but the instrument was not wanting. It was necessary that the subject should be first opened by some irresponsible party, whom more powerful parties might, as by accident, recognize and patronize, and on whose weakness they might build something stronger.

Just such an instrument was to be found in Paris. The mistress of Lord Byron could easily be stirred up and flattered to come before the world with a book which should re-open the whole controversy; and she proved a facile tool. At first, the work appeared prudently in French, and was called "Lord Byron jugé par les Témoins de sa Vie," and was rather a failure. Then it was translated into English, and published by Bentley.

The book was inartistic, and helplessly, childishly stupid as to any literary merits, — a mere mass of gossip and twaddle; but after all, when one remembers the taste of the thousands of circulating-library readers, it must not be considered the less likely to be widely read on that account. It is only once in a century that a writer of real genius has the art to tell his story so as to take both the cultivated few and the average many. De Foe and John Bunyan are almost the only examples. But there is a certain class of reading that sells and spreads, and exerts a vast influence, which the upper circles of literature despise too much ever to fairly estimate its power.

However, the Guiccioli book did not want for patrons in the high places of literature. The "*Blackwood*" — the old classic magazine of England; the defender of conservatism and aristocracy; the paper of Lockhart, Wilson, Hogg, Walter Scott, and a host of departed grandeurs — was deputed to usher into the world this book, and to recommend it and its author to the Christian public of the nineteenth century.

The following is the manner in which "*Blackwood*" calls attention to it:—

"One of the most beautiful of the songs of Béranger is that addressed to his Lisette, in which he pictures her, in old age, narrating to a younger generation the loves of their youth; deckt with flowers at each returning spring, and reciting the verses that had been inspired by her vanished charms:—

'When youthful eyes your wrinkles shall explore
To see what beauties once inspired my lays,
Then will they say to thee, "Who was that friend
So loved, so wept, so sung in ceaseless praise?"
Paint to their eyes, if possible, my love,
Its ardors, its deliriums, e'en its fears;
And, good old friend, beside thy peaceful fire
Repeat the love-songs of my early years.
"Ah!" will they say, "was he so lovely, then?"
And thou without a blush shalt say, "I loved."
"Of wrong or evil was he guilty ever?"
And thou with noble pride shalt answer, "Never!"'

"This charming picture," "*Blackwood*" goes on to say, "has been realized in the case of a poet greater than Béranger, and by a mistress more famous than Lisette. The Countess Guiccioli has at length given to the world her 'Recollections of Lord Byron.' The book first appeared in France under the title of ' Lord Byron jugé par les Témoins de sa Vie,' without the name of the countess. A more unfortunate designation could hardly have been selected. The 'witnesses of his life' told us nothing but what had been told before over and over again; and the uniform and exaggerated tone of eulogy which pervaded the whole book was fatal to any claim on the part of the writer to be considered an impartial judge of the wonderfully mixed character of Byron.

"*When, however, the book is regarded as the avowed production of the Countess Guiccioli, it derives value and interest from its very faults.* * There is something inexpressibly touching in the picture of the old lady calling up the phantoms of half a century ago; not faded and stricken by the hand of time, but brilliant and gorgeous as they were when Byron, in his manly prime of genius and beauty, first flashed upon her enraptured sight, and she gave her whole soul up to an absorbing passion, the embers of which still glow in her heart, (italics were added by Stowe)

"To her there has been no change, no decay. The god whom she worshipped with all the ardor of her Italian nature at seventeen is still the 'Pythian of the age' to her at seventy. To try such a book by the ordinary canons of criticism would be as absurd as to arraign the authoress before a jury of British matrons, or to prefer a bill of indictment against the Sultan for bigamy to a Middlesex grand jury."

This, then, is the introduction which one of the oldest and most classical periodicals of Great Britain gives to a very stupid book, simply because it was written by Lord Byron's mistress. *That fact,* we are assured, lends grace even to its faults.

Having brought the authoress upon the stage, the review now goes on to define her position, and assure the Christian world that

"The Countess Guiccioli was the daughter of an impoverished noble. At the age of sixteen, she was taken from a convent, and sold as third wife to the Count Guiccioli, who was old, rich, and profligate. A fouler prostitution never profaned the name of marriage. A short time afterwards, she accidentally met Lord Byron.

Outraged and rebellious nature vindicated itself in the

deep and devoted passion with which he inspired her. With the full assent of husband, father, and brother, and in compliance with the usages of Italian society, he was shortly afterwards installed in the office, and invested with all the privileges, of her 'Cavalier Servente.'"

It has been asserted that the Marquis de Boissy, the late husband of this Guiccioli lady, was in the habit of introducing her in fashionable circles as "the Marquise de Boissy, my wife, formerly mistress to Lord Byron"! We do not give the story as a verity; yet, in the review of this whole history, we may be pardoned for thinking it quite possible.

The mistress, being thus vouched for and presented as worthy of sympathy and attention by one of the oldest and most classic organs of English literature, may now proceed in her work of glorifying the popular idol, and casting abuse on the grave of the dead wife.

Her attacks on Lady Byron are, to be sure, less skilful and adroit than those of Lord Byron. They want his literary polish and tact; but what of that? "*Blackwood*" assures us that even the faults of manner derive a peculiar grace from the fact that the narrator is Lord Byron's mistress; and so we suppose the literary world must find grace in things like this:—

"She has been called, after his words, the moral Clytemnestra of her husband. Such a surname is severe: but the repugnance we feel to condemning a woman cannot prevent our listening to the voice of justice, which tells us that the comparison is still in favour of the guilty one of antiquity; for *she*, driven to crime by fierce passion overpowering reason, at least only deprived her husband of physical life, and, in committing the deed, exposed herself to all its consequences; while Lady Byron left her husband at the very moment that she saw him struggling amid a thousand shoals in the stormy sea of embarrassments created by his marriage, and precisely when he more than ever required a friendly, tender, and indulgent hand to save him.

"Besides, she shut herself up in silence a thousand times more cruel than Clytemnestra's poniard: *that* only killed the body; whereas Lady Byron's silence was destined to kill the soul, -and such a soul! — leaving the door open to calumny, and making it to be supposed that her silence was magnanimity destined to cover over frightful wrongs, perhaps even depravity. In vain did he, feeling his conscience at ease, implore some inquiry and examination. She refused; and the only favour she granted was to send him, one fine day, two persons to see whether he were not mad.

"And why, then, had she believed him mad? Because she, a methodical, inflexible woman, with that unbendingness which a profound moralist calls the worship rendered to pride by a feelingless soul, — because she could not understand the possibility of tastes and habits different to those of ordinary routine, or of her own starched life.

Not to be hungry when she was; not to sleep at night, but to write while she was sleeping, and to sleep when she was up; in short, to gratify the requirements of material and intellectual life at hours different to hers, — all that was not merely annoying for her, but it must be *madness;* or, if not, it betokened depravity that she could neither submit to nor tolerate without perilling her own morality.

"Such was the grand secret of the cruel silence which exposed Lord Byron to the most malignant interpretations, to all the calumny and revenge of his enemies.

"She was, perhaps, the only woman in the world so strangely organized,—the only one, perhaps, capable of not feeling happy and proud at belonging to a man superior to the rest of humanity; and fatally was it decreed that this woman *alone* of her species should be Lord Byron's wife!"

In a note is added, —

"If an imaginary fear, and even an unreasonable jealousy, may be her excuse (just as one excuses a monomania), can one equally forgive her silence? Such a silence is morally what are physically the poisons which kill at once, and defy all remedies; thus insuring the culprit's safety. This silence it is which will ever be her crime; for by it she poisoned the life of her husband."

The book has several chapters devoted to Lord Byron's peculiar virtues; and, under the one devoted to magnanimity and heroism, his *forgiving* disposition receives special attention. The climax of all is stated to be that he forgave Lady Byron. All the world knew that, since he had declared this fact in a very noisy and impassioned manner in the fourth canto of "Childe Harold," together with a statement of the wrongs which he forgave; but the Guiccioli thinks his virtue, at this period, has not been enough appreciated. In her view, it rose to the sublime. She says of Lady Byron, –

"An absolute moral monstrosity, an anomaly in the history of types of female hideousness, had succeeded in showing itself in the light of magnanimity. But false as was this high quality in Lady Byron, so did it shine out in him true and admirable.

The position in which Lady Byron had placed him, and where she continued to keep him by her harshness, silence, and strange refusals, was one of those which cause such suffering, that the highest degree of self-control seldom suffices to quiet the promptings of human weakness, and to cause persons of even slight sensibility to preserve moderation. Yet, with his sensibility and the knowledge of his worth, how did he act what did he say? I will not speak of his 'Farewell;' of the care he took to shield her from blame by throwing it on others, by taking much too large a share to himself."

With like vivacity and earnestness does the narrator now proceed to make an incarnate angel of her subject by the simple process of denying every thing that he himself ever confessed, -every thing that has ever been confessed in regard to him by his best friends. He has been in the world as an angel unawares from his cradle.

His guardian did not properly appreciate him, and is consequently mentioned as that *wicked* Lord Carlisle. Thomas Moore is never to be sufficiently condemned for the facts told in his Biography. Byron's own frank and lawless admissions of evil are set down to a peculiar inability he had for speaking the truth about himself, -sometimes about his near relations; all which does not in the least discourage the authoress from giving a separate chapter on "Lord Byron's Love of Truth."

In the matter of his relations with women, she

complacently repeats (what sounds rather oddly as coming from her) Lord Byron's own assurance, that he *never* seduced a woman; and also the equally convincing statement, that he had told *her* (the Guiccioli) that his married fidelity to his wife was perfect. She discusses Moore's account of the mistress in boy's clothes who used to share Byron's apartments in college, and ride with him to races, and whom he presented to *ladies* as his brother. She has her own view of this matter. The disguised boy was a lady of rank and fashion, who sought Lord Byron's chambers, as we are informed noble ladies everywhere, both in Italy and England, were constantly in the habit of doing; throwing themselves at his feet, and imploring permission to become his handmaids.

In the authoress's own words, "Feminine overtures still continued to be made to Lord Byron; but the fumes of incense never hid from his sight his IDEAL." We are told, that, in case of these poor ladies, generally "disenchantment took place on his side without a corresponding result on the other: THENCE many heart-breakings."

Nevertheless, we are informed that there followed the indiscretions of these ladies "none of those proceedings that the world readily forgives, but which his feelings as a man of honor would have condemned." As to drunkenness, and all that, we are informed he was an anchorite. Pages are given to an account of the biscuits and soda-water that on this and that occasion were found to be the sole means of sustenance to this ethereal creature.

As to the story of using his wife's money, the lady gives, directly in the face of his own Letters and Journal, the same account given before by Medwin, and which caused such merriment when talked over in the Noctes Club, — that he had with her only a marriage-portion of £10,000; and that, on the separation, he not only paid it back, but doubled it.

So on the authoress goes, sowing right and left the most transparent absurdities and misstatements with what Carlyle well calls "a composed stupidity, and a cheerful infinitude of ignorance." Who *should* know, if not she, to be sure? Had not Byron told her all about it and was not his family motto *Crede*

Byron? The "Blackwood," having a dim suspicion that this confused style of attack and defence in reference to the two parties under consideration may not have great weight, itself proceeds to make the book an occasion for re-opening the controversy of Lord Byron with his wife.

The rest of the review is devoted to a powerful attack on Lady Byron's character, — the most fearful attack on the memory of a dead woman we have ever seen made by a living man. The author proceeds, like a lawyer, to gather up, arrange, and restate, in a most workmanlike manner, the confused accusations of the book.

Anticipating the objection, that such a reopening of the inquiry was a violation of the privacy due to womanhood and to the feelings of a surviving family, he says, that though marriage usually is a private matter which the world has no right to intermeddle with or discuss, yet —

Lord Byron's was an exceptional case. It is not too much to say, that, had his marriage been a happy one, the course of events of the present century might have been materially changed; that the genius which poured itself forth in 'Don Juan' and 'Cain' might have flowed in far different channels; that the ardent love of freedom which sent him to perish at six and thirty at Missolonghi might have inspired a long career at home; and that we might at this moment have been appealing to the counsels of his experience and wisdom at an age not exceeding that which was attained by Wellington, Lyndhurst, and Brougham.

"Whether the world would have been a gainer or a loser by the exchange is a question which every man must answer for himself, according to his own tastes and opinions; but the possibility of such a change in the course of events warrants us in treating what would otherwise be a strictly private matter as one of public interest.

"More than half a century has elapsed, the actors have departed from the stage, the curtain has fallen; and whether it will ever again be raised so as to reveal the real facts of the drama, may, as we have already observed, be well doubted. But the time has arrived when we may fairly gather up the fragments of evidence, clear them as far as possible from the incrustations of passion, prejudice, and malice, and place them in such order, as, if possible, to enable us to arrive at some probable conjecture as to what the skeleton of the drama originally was."

Here the writer proceeds to put together all the facts of Lady Byron's case, just as an adverse lawyer would put them as against her, and for her husband. The plea is made vigorously and ably, and with an air of indignant severity, as of an honest advocate who is thoroughly convinced that he is pleading the cause of a wronged man who has been ruined in name, shipwrecked in life, and driven to an early grave, by the arts of a bad woman, — a woman all the more horrible that her malice was disguised under the cloak of religion.

Having made an able statement of facts, adroitly leaving out ONE, of which he could not have been ignorant had he studied the case carefully enough to know all the others, he proceeds to sum up against the criminal thus. –

"We would deal tenderly with the memory of Lady Byron. Few women have been juster objects of compassion. It would seem as if Nature and Fortune had vied with each other which should be most lavish of her gifts, and yet that some malignant power had rendered all their bounty of no effect. Rank, beauty, wealth, and mental powers of no common order, were hers; yet they were of no avail to secure her happiness.

The spoilt child of seclusion, restraint, and parental idolatry, a fate (alike evil for both) cast her into the arms of the spoilt child of genius, passion, and the world. What real or fancied wrongs she suffered, we may never know; but those which she inflicted are sufficiently apparent.

"It is said that there are some poisons so subtle that they will destroy life, and yet leave no trace of their action. The murderer who uses them may escape the vengeance of the law; but he is not the less guilty. So the slanderer who makes no charge; who deals in hints and insinuations; who knows melancholy facts he would not willingly divulge, — things too painful to state; who forbears, expresses pity, sometimes even affection, for his victim, shrugs his shoulders, looks with

'The significant eye,
Which learns to lie with silence,' —

is far more guilty than he who tells the bold falsehood which may be met and answered, and who braves the punishment which must follow upon detection.

"Lady Byron has been called
'The moral Clytemnestra of her lord.'

The 'moral Brinvilliers' would have been a truer designation.

"The conclusion at which we arrive is, that there is no proof whatever that Lord Byron was guilty of any act that need have caused a separation, or prevented a re-union, and that the imputations upon him rest on the vaguest conjecture; that whatever real or fancied wrongs Lady Byron may have endured are shrouded in an impenetrable mist of her own creation, — a poisonous miasma in which she enveloped the character of her husband, — raised by her breath, and which her breath only could have dispersed.

'She dies, and makes no sign. O God! forgive her.'"

As we have been obliged to review accusations on Lady Byron founded on old Greek tragedy, so now we are forced to abridge a passage from a modern conversations-lexicon, that we may understand what sort of comparisons are deemed in good taste in a conservative English review, when speaking of ladies of rank in their graves.

Under the article "Brinvilliers", we find as follows: —

"Marguerite D'aubrai, Marchioness of Brinvilliers. — The Singular Atrocity Of This Woman Gives her a sort of infamous claim to notice. She was born in Paris in 1651; being daughter of D'Aubrai, lieutenant-civil of Paris, who married her to the Marquis of Brinvilliers. Although possessed of attractions to captivate lovers, she was for some time much attached to her husband, but at length became madly in love with a Gascon officer.

Her father imprisoned the officer in the Bastille; and, while there, he learned the art of compounding subtle and most mortal poisons; and, when he was released, he taught it to the lady, who exercised it with such success, that, in one year, her father, sister, and two brothers, became her victims. She professed the utmost tenderness for her victims, and nursed them assiduously.

On her father she is said to have made eight attempts before she succeeded. She was *very religious*, and devoted to works of charity; and visited the hospitals a great deal, where it is said she tried her poisons on the sick."

People have made loud outcries lately, both in America and England, about violating the repose of the dead. We should like to know what they call this. Is this, then, what they mean by *respecting* the dead?

Let any man imagine a leading review coming out with language equally brutal about his own mother, or any dear and revered friend. Men of America, men of England, what do you think of this?

When Lady Byron was publicly branded with the names of the foulest ancient and foulest modern assassins, and Lord Byron's mistress was publicly taken by the hand, and encouraged to go on and prosper in her slanders, by one of the oldest and most influential British reviews, what was said and what was done in England?

That is a question we should be glad to have answered. Nothing was done that ever reached us across the water. And why was nothing done? Is this language of a kind to be passed over in silence? Was it no offence to the house of Wentworth to attack the pure character of its late venerable head, and to brand her in her sacred grave with the name of one of the vilest of criminals?

Might there not properly have been an indignant protest of family solicitors against this insult to the person and character of the Baroness Wentworth?

If virtue went for nothing, benevolence for nothing, a long life of service to humanity for nothing, one would at least have thought, that, in aristocratic countries, rank might have had its rights to decent consideration, and its guardians to rebuke the violation of those rights. We Americans understand little of the advantages of rank; but we did understand that it secured certain decorums to people, both while living and when in their graves. From Lady Byron's whole history, in life and in death, it would appear that we were mistaken.

What a life was hers! Was ever a woman more evidently desirous of the delicate and secluded privileges of womanhood, of the sacredness of individual privacy? Was ever a woman so rudely dragged forth, and exposed to the hardened, vulgar, and unfeeling gaze of mere curiosity? — her maiden secrets of love thrown open to be handled by *roués;* the sanctities of her marriage-chamber desecrated by leering satyrs; her parents and best friends traduced and slandered, till one indignant public protest was extorted from her, as by the rack, — a protest which seems yet to quiver in every word with the indignation of outraged womanly delicacy!

Then followed coarse blame and coarser comment, — blame for speaking at all, and blame for not speaking more. One manly voice, raised for her in honorable protest, was silenced and overborne by the universal roar of ridicule and reprobation; and henceforth what refuge? Only this remained: "Let them that suffer according to the will of God commit the keeping of their souls to him as to a faithful Creator."

Lady Byron turned to this refuge in silence, and filled up her life with a noble record of charities and humanities. So pure was she, so childlike, so artless, so loving, that those who knew her best, feel, to this day, that a memorial of her is like the relic of a saint. And could not all this preserve her grave from insult? O England, England!

I speak in sorrow of heart to those who must have known, loved, and revered Lady Byron, and ask them, Of what were you thinking when you allowed a paper of so established literary rank as the "Blackwood" to present and earnestly recommend to our New World such a compendium of lies as the Guiccioli book?

Is the great English-speaking community, whose waves toss from Maine to California, and whose literature is yet to come back in a thousand voices to you, a thing to be so despised? If, as the solicitors of the Wentworth family observe, you might be entitled to treat with silent contempt the slanders of a mistress against a wife, was it safe to treat with equal contempt the indorsement and recommendation of those slanders by one of your oldest and most powerful literary authorities? No European magazine has ever had the weight and circulation in America that the

"Blackwood" has held. In the days of my youth, when New England was a comparat-ively secluded section of the earth, the wit and genius of the "Noctes Ambrosianæ" were in the mouths of men and maidens, even in our most quiet mountain-towns. There, years ago, we saw all Lady Byron's private affairs discussed, and felt the weight of Christopher North's decisions against her.

Shelton Mackenzie, in his American edition, speaks of the American circulation of *"Blackwood"* being greater than that in England. It was and is now reprinted monthly; and, besides that, *Littell's Magazine* reproduces all its striking articles, and they come with the weight of long-established position. From the very fact that it has long been considered the Tory organ, and the supporter of aristocratic orders, all its admissions against the character of individuals in the privileged classes have a double force.

When " *Blackwood,"* therefore, boldly denounces a lady of high rank as a modern Brinvilliers, and no sensation is produced, and no remonstrance follows, what can people in the New World suppose, but that Lady Byron's character was a point entirely given up; that her depravity was so well established and so fully conceded, that nothing was to be said, and that even the defenders of aristocracy were forced to admit it?

I have been blamed for speaking on this subject without consulting Lady Byron's friends, trustees, and family. More than ten years had elapsed since I had had any intercourse with England, and I knew none of them. How was I to know that any of them were living? It was perfectly fair for me to conclude that they were not; for, if they had been, they certainly must have taken some public steps to stop such a scandal.

I was astonished to learn, for the first time, by the solicitors' letters, that there were trustees, who held in their hands all Lady Byron's carefully-prepared proofs and documents, by which this falsehood might immediately have been refuted. If they had spoken, they might have saved all this confusion. Even if bound by restrictions for a certain period of time, they still might have called on, a Christian public to frown down such a cruel and indecent attack on the character of a noble lady who had been a benefactress to so many in England.

They might have stated that the means of wholly refuting the slanders of the "*Blackwood*" were in their hands, and only delayed in coming forth from regard to the feelings of some in this generation. Then might they not have announced her Life and Letters, that the public might have the same opportunity as themselves for knowing and judging Lady Byron by her own writings?

Had this been done, I had been most happy to have remained silent. I have been astonished that any one should have supposed this speaking on my part to be any thing less than it is, — the severest act of self-sacrifice that one friend can perform for another, and the most solemn and difficult tribute to justice that a human being can be called upon to render.

I have been informed that the course I have taken would be contrary to the wishes of my friend. I think otherwise. I know her strong sense of justice, and her reverence for truth. Nothing ever moved her to speak to the public but an attack upon the honor of the dead. In her statement, she says of her parents, "There is no other near relative to vindicate their memory from insult: I am therefore compelled to break the silence I had hoped always to have observed."

If there was any near relative to vindicate Lady Byron's memory, I had no evidence of the fact; and I considered the utter silence to be strong evidence to the contrary. In all the storm of obloquy and rebuke that has raged in consequence of my speaking, I have had two unspeakable sources of joy: first, that they could not touch *her*; and, second, that they could not blind the all-seeing God. It is worth being in darkness to see the stars.

It has been said that I have drawn on Lady Byron's name greater obloquy than ever before. I deny the charge. Nothing fouler has been asserted of her than the charges of the "*Blackwood,*" because nothing fouler *could* be asserted. No satyr's hoof has ever crushed this pearl deeper in the mire than the hoof of the "*Blackwood;*" but none of them have so defiled it or trodden it so deep that God cannot find it in the day "when he maketh up his jewels."

I have another word, as an American, to say about the contempt shown to our great people in thus suffering the materials of history to be falsified to subserve the temporary purposes of family feeling in England.

Lord Byron belongs not properly either to the Byrons or the Wentworths. He is not one of their family jewels, to be locked up in their cases. He belongs to the world for which he wrote, to which he appealed, and before which he dragged his reluctant, delicate wife to a publicity equal with his own: the world has, therefore, a right to judge him.

We Americans have been made accessories, after the fact, to every insult and injury that Lord Byron and the literary men of his day have heaped upon Lady Byron. We have been betrayed into injustice, and a complicity with villany.

After Lady Byron had nobly lived down slanders in England, and died full of years and honors, the "*Blackwood*" takes occasion to re-open the controversy by recommending a book full of slanders to a rising generation who knew nothing of the past.

What was the consequence in America? My attention was first called to the result, not by reading the "*Blackwood*" article, but by finding in a popular monthly magazine two long articles, — the one an enthusiastic recommendation of the Guiccioli book, and the other a lamentation over the burning of the Autobiography as a lost chapter in history.

Both articles represented Lady Byron as a cold, malignant, mean, persecuting woman, who had been her husband's ruin. They were so full of falsehoods and misstatements as to astonish me. Not long after, a literary friend wrote to me, "*Will* you, *can* you, reconcile it to your conscience to sit still and allow that mistress so to slander that wife, — you, perhaps, the only one knowing the real facts, and able to set them forth?"

Upon this, I immediately began collecting and reading the various articles and the book, and perceived that the public of this generation were in a way of having false history created, uncontradicted, under their own eyes.

I claim for my country men and women our right to *true* history. For years, the popular literature has held up publicly before our eyes the facts as to this man and this woman, and called on us to praise or condemn. Let us have *truth* when we are called on to judge. It is our *right.*

There is no conceivable obligation on a human being greater than that of *absolute justice.* It is the deepest personal injury to an honorable mind to be made, through misrepresentation, an accomplice in injustice. When a noble name is accused, any person who possesses truth which might clear it, and withholds that truth, is guilty of a sin against human nature and the inalienable claims of justice. I claim that I have not only a right, but an obligation, to bring in my solemn testimony upon this subject.

For years and years, the silence-policy has been tried; and what has it brought forth? As neither word nor deed could be proved against Lady Byron, her silence has been spoken of as a monstrous, unnatural crime, "a poisonous miasma," in which she enveloped the name of her husband.

Very well: since silence is the crime, I thought I would tell the world that Lady Byron had spoken. Christopher North, years ago, when he condemned her for speaking, said that she should speak further, —

"She should speak, or some one for her. One word would suffice."

That one word I have spoken.

Chapter 8

Byron and Lady Caroline Ponsoby Lamb

Lady Caroline Ponsonby Lamb was the daughter of the earl of Bessborough and Henrietta Ponsonby, and the niece of the duchess of Devonshire. As a child she was a tomboy - and a spirit of recklessness and disdain for convention never left her. She had no formal education and was unable to read until late adolescence.

But she was intelligent and witty; as an adult, she wrote poetry and prose and drew portraits. She was the first woman of Byron's class to captivate the poet completely. He treated Caroline badly after the grand infatuation faded.

But while it lasted, he was demanding and possessive, goading her to admit she loved him more than her husband. He pursued her with abandon, once planning to flee England with her. Caroline's reaction to the break-up is understandable; Byron led her to believe he loved her. It was her sad fate to discover Byron's interpretation of love - a mad, passionate obsession which is abandoned as soon as curiosity and desire are sated.

When they met in 1812, Byron was 24 years old and already famous as the melancholy writer of 'Childe Harold.' Caroline was 27 years old, married and mother of an autistic son. Her husband was William Lamb, the younger son of Byron's friends, Lord and Lady Melbourne. It was Lady Melbourne to whom Byron addressed some of his most personal and scandalous letters; she was one of his great confidantes and supporters. The family lived at Melbourne

House in Whitehall and played host to many fashionable and lively gatherings. They were also cousins of Lady Anne Isabella (Annabella) Milbanke, later to become Byron's wife.

Caroline and William had married when she was 17 and the union began happily enough. But the death of one child and the health problems of another, as well as William's growing interest in a political career, caused a rift between the couple.

There is also some evidence that William Lamb was sexually promiscuous and made disturbing demands upon his wife, as Caroline implied in a letter to Lady Melbourne in 1810: 'He called me prudish - said I was strait-laced, - amused himself with instructing me in things I need never have heard or known - & the disgust that I at first felt for the world's wickedness I till then had never even heard of - in a very short time this gave way to a general laxity of principles which little by little unperceived of you all has been undermining the few virtues I ever possessed.' Despite these problems, however, they remained affectionate.

Caroline had read 'Childe Harold' before meeting Byron, having been lent the poem by a mutual friend. She was told that Byron 'has a club-foot, and bites his nails' but Caroline replied, 'If he was as ugly as Aesop I must know him.' She had the transparent nature of a child, with little ability to dissemble or play coy, and developed passionate attachments.

Upon reading the poem, she conjured a romantic image of the poet which Byron's reputation did nothing to dispel. She wrote him an anonymous fan letter - 'You deserve to be and you shall be happy....' A few days later, she left Lady Westmoreland's before meeting him. He had been surrounded by other women and she was nervous. Already she had written her impression of him - 'mad - bad - and dangerous to know.' This remains the Byronic epitaph.

Byron, of course, always preferred women he had to pursue. Once Caroline Lamb had avoided the introduction, Byron was determined to meet her. They were introduced at Lord and Lady Holland's, but Byron was initially disappointed. Caroline did not resemble his traditional conquests, or his concept of feminine beauty. She was tall and very thin, with short, curly blonde hair and hazel eyes. After the meeting, he told his friend Medwin, 'The lady had scarcely any personal attractions to recommend her.'

Her figure 'was too thin to be good' and her eccentric habit of dressing as a page shocked him. She had none of the 'retired modesty' which later attracted him to Annabella Milbanke. But Caroline was attracted to him instantly; she wrote, 'That beautiful pale face is my fate.'

In truth, Caroline possessed an instinctive disregard of opinion which Byron always coveted. However much he postured as the ne'er-do-well lord, he remained an aristocrat who desired the good opinion of other aristocrats.

This changed only when his marriage failed and he grew careless of opinion and terribly cynical. Caroline was a vivacious and flirtatious woman and Byron suspected she wanted him for the notoriety and to feed her vanity. He was always insecure, a quality he hid beneath the 'Childe Harold' pose. Caroline sensed this insecurity but it only increased his charm.

He soon overcame his initial response to her attractiveness, or lack thereof. They became lovers and shocked London with their affair through much of April and May 1812. Byron had long believed women were truly incapable of understanding male thoughts and desires. With Caroline, he was forced to abandon this notion. They read together, discussed poetry - and argued fiercely.

His supposed flirtations with other women and her open affection for her husband and other admirers caused most of the fighting. Some arguments ended 'without any verbal explanation', Byron told a friend. He was particularly jealous of her waltzing with other men. And since Byron could not dance with his club-foot, Caroline now sat with him, no longer the life of her parties.

When she was not invited to a party he attended, she would wait out in the street for him. If he needed money, she told him, he could pawn her jewels. She wrote letters constantly, confided in her diary - and Byron wrote to her as well, an equal partner in the affair. But such passion never lasts. Byron was a victim of his own contradictory personality - he loved to pursue women but, once captured, he longed to leave them. Paradoxically, he could not rest easy without their complete adoration. He could not be simply Caroline's lover, a participant in a scandalous (but tolerated) affair; he must be her grand passion, her true love - she must belong to him alone. But once she capitulated, he grew bored and irritated with her.

Though Caroline was instantly infatuated, she at first refused Byron's most heated demands. She would not admit she loved him more than her husband William; Byron told her, 'My God, you shall pay for this, I'll wring that obstinate little heart.'

But soon she loved him enough to contemplate leaving her husband, at Byron's suggestion in May 1812. He was probably testing her commitment for it is unlikely he meant to flee England with her. But he needed to know she loved him more than anything, even her very comfortable life, and so he hinted at 'elopement.' His friends, particularly the sensible John Hobhouse, were already shocked by the affair; it had grown increasingly open and hysterical. Byron was eventually persuaded to leave London.

At Newstead, Caroline bombarded him with letters. Hobhouse cautioned Byron to not respond, warning him that he was risking his reputation. Once again, it was one thing to pose as a cad but quite another to be one (and in such a public manner.) At Melbourne House, Caroline was confused and hurt.

Byron did not answer her letters but he returned to London on 13 June. Then the long, slow death of their passionate affair began. He avoided her but was still attracted to her. Hobhouse, still fearful of a potential elopement, again persuaded him to leave, this time for Harrow. They were to leave Wednesday 29 July, for Caroline had threatened to visit alone on that day.

Such a visit would have been disastrous for them both. An affair conducted with a modicum of restraint and discretion contains a detailed account of the horrors which ended in the extinction of one of the noblest and richest families of that city during the Pontificate of Clement VIII, in the year 1599" ("Preface," 238).

The violent sequence of the Cenci tragedy comprises Count Cenci's calculated rape of his daughter Beatrice, the murder of the Count, and the Pope's execution of Beatrice and her allies. Although it happened two centuries before his arrival at Rome (1818), Shelley notes that this tragic family history was not only widely known among "all ranks of" contemporary Romans, but never failed to generate their "deep and breathless interest," or "a romantic pity for the wrongs, and a passionate exculpation of the horrible deed to which they urged [Beatrice]" ("Preface," 239).

Shelley's emphasis in his "Preface" on the Romans' sympathetic attitude towards Beatrice seems to have stemmed from his projection of the audience's sympathetic reception of his play at home, especially since he strongly wished for its production on the London stage. With an eye to his British readership in an increasingly reactionary milieu, Shelley stresses both his own "delicate" approach to the subject and its highly "dramatic" (tragic, aesthetic) nature, while downplaying the political implication of Beatrice's active involvement in parricide: "The highest moral purpose aimed at in the highest species of the drama, is the teaching the human heart, through its sympathies and antipathies, the knowledge of itself".

Shelley thus asks his readership to suspend "vulgar" and "dogmatic" moral judgment of Beatrice's act. Such a view also corresponds with his later description of drama (or dramatic lyric) in the Defense of Poetry (1821): "In a drama of the highest order there is little food for censure or hatred; it teaches rather self-knowledge and self-respect".

Since Shelley proposes teaching the knowledge of the human heart itself through a literary representation of a historical event, the question of how he does it in the play becomes his great concern: "I have endeavoured as nearly as possible to represent the characters as they probably were, and have sought to avoid the error of making them actuated by my own conceptions of right or wrong, false or true, thus under a thin veil converting names and actions of the sixteenth century into cold impersonations of my own mind" ("Preface," 240; emphasis added). This concern with representation leads him to a related query on poetic language:

I have avoided with great care in writing this play the introduction of what is commonly called mere poetry, and I imagine there will scarcely be found a detached simile or a single isolated description, unless Beatrice's description of the chasm appointed for her father's murder should be judged to be of that nature.

In a dramatic composition the imagery and the passion should interpenetrate one another, the former being reserved simply for the full development and illustration of the latter. Imagination is as the immortal God which should assume flesh for the redemption of mortal passion. (241; emphasis added)

On the one hand, Shelley expresses his alliance with Wordsworthian poetics especially where dramatic poetry is concerned ("it must be the real language of men in general, and not that of any particular class to whose society the writer happens to belong" [241-42]); on the other, the climactic point of the play, Beatrice's parricide (and its unnameable cause—the Father's rape of her), is construed through a literary trope, because it is perhaps beyond "the real language of men in general." And the precise links between imagination and passion, imagination and "real language," remain open to interpretation.

While constructing Beatrice's "chasm" as unrepresentable by "real" language, Shelley nonetheless turns to an exemplary and "just" representation of her character—the famous "Guido portrait of Beatrice Cenci." In the well-known painting of Beatrice that Shelley saw at Palazzo Colonna (22nd of April, 1819), he finds a paragon of the fearful symmetry of gentleness and energy, and simplicity and profundity. It was perhaps this paradoxical combination of beauty and terror that intrigued and inspired the English poet in exile to draft a five-act play in two months:

beyond the grave for you, and in refraining from this, must my motives be misunderstood? I care not who knows this, what use is made of it.... I was an am yours freely and most entirely, to obey, to honor, love, - and fly with you when, where, and how you yourself *might* and *may* determine.'

The winter of 1812 and 1813 also found Byron engaged in another affair, with Jane Elizabeth, countess of Oxford. An older woman with six children, politically active and the veteran of other love affairs, she was at first more discreet and less demanding than Caroline. She was also a friend of Caroline's, though she quickly destroyed the friendship by encouraging Byron's disdain for his former lover.

Caroline wrote to Byron from Ireland and the letters reached him at Lady Oxford's home of Eywood. There Byron and his new lover would read the letters and compose replies. On her way home to London in early November 1812, Caroline received one such reply sealed with Lady Oxford's initials. Its contents were reproduced in her novel 'Glenarvon' four years later:

'I am no longer your lover; and since you oblige me to confess it, by this truly unfeminine persecution, - learn, that I am attached to another; whose name it would of course be dishonourable to mention. I shall ever remember with gratitude the many instances I have received of the predilection you have shewn in my favour.

I shall ever continue your friend, if your Ladyship will permit me so to style myself; and, as a first proof of my regard, I offer you this advice, correct your vanity, which is ridiculous; exert your absurd caprices upon others; and leave me in peace.'

The effect upon Caroline was brutal. She was physically ill and had to seek rest in Cornwall, where she was also bled. Upon her arrival in London, she began to write Lady Oxford as well, threatening to tell Lord Oxford of the affair. The countess laughed at the threat but Byron was understandably troubled.

Byron soon returned to London and saw Caroline at various social events. Face-to-face, the poet could not be particularly nasty. They had a few brief civil conversations.

Caroline was still torn by jealousy and regrets. In the last year, with Byron safely away, she had struggled to repair her marriage but heartbreak and indecision left their mark. She was now emotionally agitated and her figure increasingly emaciated.

Byron remarked to Lady Melbourne that he was 'haunted by a skeleton.' He was both repulsed and fascinated by her devotion. During the Christmas season, while Byron stayed with the Oxfords, Caroline held a dramatic bonfire at the Melbourne country home in Hertfordshire.

Village girls dressed in white danced while Caroline threw copies of his letters and other tokens into the fire. A figure of Byron was even burned in effigy while her page recited lines she had written: 'Burn, fire, burn, while wondering boys exclaim,/ And gold and trinkets glitter in the flame.'

The return to London society in early 1813 witnessed more indiscretions. Caroline would visit at inappropriate hours, once inscribing on a book at his desk: 'Remember me!' The book, not coincidentally, was written by the homosexual William Beckford. The message was a reminder that she knew of his transgressions. In a fit of pique at the clumsy blackmail, Byron wrote a poem of the same name which captured his feelings:

Remember thee! remember thee!
Till Lethe quench life's burning stream
Remorse and shame shall cling to thee,
And haunt thee like a feverish dream!
Remember thee! Aye, doubt it not.
Thy husband too shall think of thee:
By neither shalt thou be forgot,
Thou false to him, thou fiend to me!

She then forged a note in Byron's handwriting to his publisher John Murray, requesting a painted miniature of the poet. Murray complied, none the wiser. Byron was again furious. It was up to Lady Melbourne to have a copy made for Caroline and return the original to Byron. When Caroline requested a lock of his hair, Byron played a cruel trick. He sent her a lock of the countess of Oxford's hair instead, later remarking 'it was a lucky coincidence of colour & shape for manifestation of "Beatrice," is inscribed in Shelley's main text in multifarious ways, even if he, at the same time, seems to avoid presenting Beatrice's countenance in a direct authorial voice. For any writer, representing Beatrice's gaze would be a fundamentally paradoxical task, not only because to do so would imply freezing the active force of a body into a still image, but more profoundly, because her subjectivity lies beyond the writer's conscious grasp.

Such alterity, in fact, might have been what haunted Shelley and inspired his impossible Utopian passion to give a face to the broken fragments of an image, despite his ambivalence about a "chasm" or "casuistry" in Beatrice's character. A woman rebellious against a matrix of masculinist, authoritarian and systemic violence thus emerges through the "imagination . . . that assumes flesh for the redemption of mortal passion". Reconstructing "a thing-world of destructive forces in which human autonomy was drowned," Shelley ironically gives face (the painting) to a name (Beatrice), brings "the dead" to life, and remaps the conflicting forces of the past.

With its relevance and cross-references to his contemporary world (which outraged the self-designated bourgeois moralists), The Cenci is an attempt not only to destabilize the norms and values of his contemporary culture but to re-write history through and through, restaging the present according to a re-imagined past. Shelley's endeavor to represent Beatrice's "casuistical" gaze shows the blindness and insight of the author's desire to grasp the alterity in the other and the problematics of representation.

REVOLUTIONARY VIOLENCE AND SEXUAL DIFFERENCES

... the monster of my thought... grew familiar to desire...
—Giacomo from The Cenci, V.i.23-24

"The real difference between Byron and Shelley is this: those who understand them and love them rejoice that Byron died at thirty-six, because if he lived he would have become a reactionary bourgeois. They grieve that Shelley died at twenty-nine because he was essentially a revolutionist and he would always have been one of the advanced guard of socialism." This famous remark by Karl Marx, underlining the revolutionary impetus in Shelley, could be substantiated by lines from The Cenci, such as "what a world we make/ The oppressor and the oppressed" (V.iii.74-75).

But Beatrice's remark towards the end of the play connotes layers of implications, especially because the sentence is in the active voice. It also suggests Shelley's continuous struggle to conceptualize and configure social relations and revolutionary ideas in literary form. In a letter to his publisher, Charles Ollier, dated Aug. 16, 1819 (as he completed the tragedy), Shelley links the agony of an intellectual faced with the Peterloo Massacre directly to Beatrice Cenci's situation in his dramatic poem: "I was anxiously [waiting to] hear how the Country will express its sense of this bloody murderous oppression of its destroyers. 'Something must be done.... What yet I know not.'"

Indeed, "Something must be done.... What yet I know not" is the urgent question on which victims of any social injustice have to reflect. That Beatrice has to deal with intense shame and guilt after victimization and that she cannot forget or escape from it could be seen as the tragic social condition under which such domestic crimes were calculated, committed and perpetrated. Sharply contrasted with Cenci's assertion of phallic will ("It [the rape of Beatrice] must be done; it shall be done. I swear"), the regressive attitude shown in her haunting thought, "What have I done?" (III.i.69) shares in the self-reproaching, "self-lacerating mystification" that Eagleton analyzes in his study of the rape of Clarissa. Even different from Orsino's "what may be done," her "what is to be done?" impels her to assert that "neither life [n]or death can give me rest" (III.i.140). Later in her conversation with Lucretia, Beatrice says "O, fear not/ What may be done, but what is left undone:/ The act seals all" (IV.iii.5-7).

Beatrice's profound question as to the gap between action and inaction can be seen as the theme of Shelley's writing of the period, including Laon and Cythna (The Revolt of Islam), Prometheus Unbound, A Philosophical View of Reform and The Masque of Anarchy. The inscription of a revolutionary balk and return to sanity. Though he may have used other women as distractions, Byron still ignored Caroline. Ironically, her love for him typified the 'Byronic' spirit in all its heedless emotion. But Byron was far less enamored of reckless abandon than many believed. Though he often acted impulsively, he was deeply aware of his faults.

He was never dismissive of his sins and too often obsessed over them. Caroline shared this obsessive spirit. But she and Byron had shared their last private conversation sometime in June. After his death, she told a mutual friend that Byron had kissed her at his home: '....the last time we parted for ever, as he pressed his lips on mine (it was in the Albany) he said 'poor Caro, if every one hates me, you, I see, will never change - No, not with ill usage!' & I said, 'yes, I *am* changed, & shall come near you no more.' - For then he showed me letters, & told me things I cannot repeat, & all my attachment went.'

The last statement was perhaps optimistic and an attempt to save face. Their final public confrontations in early July had been so scandalous and humiliating that nothing was left but regret and anger. By 1814, Byron was preparing to wed Caroline's cousin Annabella Milbanke. It was his first romantic attachment of a purely conventional nature. There was no need to be clandestine or discreet; there was nothing forbidden about courtship with a respectable and studious heiress.

Therein lay its attraction and danger. Caroline accepted the news calmly, though Byron had feared otherwise. They had not seen each other for months, even as Byron continued to write regularly to her mother-in-law. Caroline now viewed Byron with a wounded eye. As for Annabella, she was never threatened by her cousin, remarking she found her 'quite virtuous' compared to other former lovers. But when Byron and Annabella separated in 1816, Caroline sought her revenge against the poet. Caroline claimed that Byron had confessed to an incestuous relationship with his half-sister Augusta Leigh at their last private meeting.

This was supposedly what ended her 'attachment.' During the initial separation between Annabella and Byron in 1816, Caroline played both sides against one another, spreading rumors about Byron and Augusta while writing to Byron through mutual friends. He suspected her duplicity and was disgusted. In turn, she wrote: 'I know not from what quarter the report originates. You accused *me,* and falsely; but if you could hear all that is said at this moment, you would hear one, who....would perhaps die to save you.'

But she had already arranged a meeting with Annabella, now desperate for some power over her husband. Annabella, meticulous as always, took notes at the meeting. Caroline alleged that Byron told her of a 'criminal intercourse' between him and Augusta, even 'boasting at the ease of his conquest.' And there were other 'unnatural crimes' - young boys he had corrupted - 'He mentioned 3 schoolfellows whom he had thus perverted.' Annabella now had the information necessary to ensure a divorce on her terms. But having betrayed Byron with rumors and slander, Caroline was desperate to hide her deceit. She wrote to him again. He never responded and she came close to madness.

Later, Caroline traveled with her husband to Paris and Brussels where she humiliated him again, pursuing various army officers. Her most famous conquest was the duke of Wellington. Yet Byron remained the greatest passion of her life. She wrote a novel about him called 'Glenarvon', an open condemnation of his character which revealed her continuing obsession. In 1820, when the first cantos of 'Don Juan' were causing a sensation in London, Caroline appeared at a masked ball dressed as the character. The newspapers made note of her appearance. When Byron died in 1824, she wanted to know his last words - and she wanted her letters to him returned.

Instead, Hobhouse asked to have the letters Byron had written her, but she refused to part with them. She said, 'I am very sorry I ever said one unkind word against him.' Caroline's last years found her increasingly melancholy and restless. She wrote two more novels and separated from her husband in 1825. But she and William remained close and he was at her bedside when she died in 1828. He never married again and continued working in politics. He eventually became Prime Minister and one of Queen Victoria's favorite advisers.

intervention into the family affair under Cenci's control. Part of the reason that Beatrice's entreaty to the guests proves vain is that Cenci curtails it with a most effective appeal—to the affinity in position between them as fathers/patriarchs ("I hope my good friends here/ Will think of their own daughters—or perhaps / Of their own throats-before they lend an ear/ To this wild girl" [I.iii.129-32: emphasis added]): it is not so much their fear of Cenci's power that keeps them in check as it is their anxiety about breaking bond with the bellowing male head and risking questioning the precondition of the patriarchal social order itself.

Half dismayed and half disturbed by the implications and consequences of Beatrice's serious charges against her father for murdering her brothers, they conspiratorially silence their doubts and agree not to disrupt Cenci's authority as Father. This incident thus results only in their retreat to their safe homes, and in strengthening Cenci's desire to crush Beatrice's daring resistance.

On the other end of the spectrum of violence, revolutionary violence has culturally been constituted as male, with an association with parricide—sons against fathers. This gendering of political and social discourses is witnessed in a typical British representation of the French Revolution: "That the French Maniacs should pay such adoration to Roman murderers as to adore the statue of Brutus, who stabbed his father (as Caesar certainly was) is not to be wondered at, when we read of a Frenchman bringing his father and mother's heads to the Jacobin club." Such logistics of power often go unquestioned by the revolutionary forces as well (as exemplified in the typology of the "manly" revolutionary forces usurping aristocratic regime).

When driven to take action, Giacomo assumes the role of rebellious son, as does Demogorgon in Prometheus Unbound. Soon the vague idea becomes a more clear argument for revolutionary violence:

Does my destroyer know his danger? We Are now no more, as once, parent and child, But man to man; the oppressor to the oppressed; The slanderer to the slandered; foe to foe:

He has cast Nature off, which was his shield, And Nature casts him off, who is her shame; And I spurn both. Is it a father's throat Which I will shake,...

(III.i.282-89; emphasis added)

In this reconceptualization of the father-son relationship as man-to-man rivalry. male subjects are cast as the active forces engaged in the power struggle, while the feminine remnants are obscured into the familiar topos of nature which functions as a "symptom" of social men. With his compassion towards Beatrice, Giacomo assumes that she needs to be represented and protected. Yet from the moment he and Orsino plot parricide in Act II Scene ii, he shows a hesitation that arises from his own status as a male head of a family. Giacomo vacillates between anger or rebellion against the common oppressor and recognition of his patriarchal affinity with the father's position. Sensing his own fate through self-identification with a patriarch, he trembles at the implication of his Oedipal desire: "That word parricide,/ Although I am resolved, haunts me like fear" (III.i.340-41).

Verbalizing the dynamic of patricide, Giacomo thus states poignantly: "the monster of my thought . . . grew familiar to desire . . ." (V.i.23-24). This pithy statement strikingly depicts the uncanniness of the generative will to power—the revolutionary iconography of father-son rivalry. Yet, his identification with his father intensifies when he reflects upon his own position to his son:

My son will then perhaps be waiting thus, Tortured between just hate and vain remorse; Chiding the tardy messenger of news Like those which I expect. I almost wish He [the Count] be not dead, although my wrongs are great.

Later, in the face of prosecution, the escalated tension in Giacomo that has driven him to parricide finally collapses into the pole of identification: "Alas! Alas!/ It was a wicked thought, a piteous deed,/ To kill an old and hoary-headed father".

Given the sexual economy that naturalizes male aggression and female victimization, Beatrice's parricidal desire could strike one as even more monstrous than Giacomo's. The basis for the "inevitability" of such action,

In burst of outrage spread your judgements wide,
And to your wrath cry out, "Be thou our guide."
(The Poems, 2: 739-40)

For Wordsworth, the tygers of wrath are clearly not wiser than the horses of instruction; and when the people allow themselves to be guided by anger, they become bewildered, deceived, mistaken, desperate, and lost. Such an attitude towards public wrath owes a great deal to Wordsworth's experience of the French Revolution and the Terror, and also to his disapproval of the angry rhetoric of the popular press, that "theoretic feud" of "scandalous tongues" leading the citizens astray.

As Wordsworth wrote in response to what he saw as Carlyle's overly enthusiastic account of the French Revolution, "Hath it not long been said the wrath of Man / Works not the righteousness of God?" (*The Poems,* 2: 881). The agitation surrounding the Reform Bill was England's version of the revolutionary conflicts in France, and Wordsworth saw in both only an outraged blindness dangerous to the people and the nation. In Book 10 of *The Prelude,* Wordsworth recalls his experiences in Paris in 1792, just after the September Massacres and the declaration of the Republic, both of which put him at great unease:

But at best it seemed a place of fear,
Unfit for the repose of night,
Defenceless as a wood where tigers roam.
(1805 Prelude, Book 10, lines 80-82)

Wordsworth's image of unfenced tigers prowling the *civitas* is meant to register his sense that the state should police the anger of citizens rather than encourage it. But even Wordsworth would have recognized that, like it or no, the Revolution had resulted in a new place for anger within the public sphere. How much had changed in regard to anger can be seen by comparing two passages that recall Wordsworth's from *The Prelude.*

The first is from Edward Young's *A Vindication of Providence,* written in 1728, when the anger of the monarch was still the monarch of the political jungle:

> *It is elegantly said, the King's anger is as a roaring lion, which Description of it is confin'd to Kings, only as to its Efficacy; it is strong, though not as successful in other Men. By a King it is let loose into the large Field of Power; in others it bites the Bars that confine it. (Young 28)*

Young recognizes that anger is our fundamental political emotion, the ferocity of which is equal in all men. By picturing the common man's anger as a caged lion that "bites the Bars that confine it," Young implies that instruments of control (i.e., chains and prisons) are the only things that separate the king — both physically and ontologically — from his subjects.

Approximately one hundred years later, Sir Walter Scott looked back on the period leading up to the fateful meeting of the Estates-General (on May 5, 1789), and wondered at the provoking behaviour of Louis XVI's government:

> The conduct of the government... towards the nation whose representatives it was shortly to meet, resembled that of an insane person, who should by a hundred teazing and vexatious insults irritate into frenzy the lion, whose cage he was about to open, and to whose fury he must necessarily be exposed. (Scott, *Life of Buonaparte,* 1: 4)

The political role of the angry citizen had changed utterly between Young's era and Scott's; the enraged populace (one of the larger cats of history) had been let out of the bag, and had entered the "large Field of Power" as a legitimate force for political change.

Like the unfenced tigers that Wordsworth imagines in Paris, the uncaged lion offers to tear apart the old order in the name of the people's wrath. Even Edmund Burke, in the final sentence of his reactionary *Reflections on the Revolution in France,* admits the virtue of personal rage — as if he recognizes that the events in Paris, however deplorable, have instituted a new relation between the anger of citizens and the conduct of the state. Burke concludes his great work by describing himself as "one in whose breast no anger durable or vehement has ever been kindled, but by what he considered as tyranny" (*Reflections* 376).

So, despite his talk of the bestial madness of the French

nothing else/ But pleasure" (I.i.9-94, 96, 10-104). This libidinal self-attention symptomatically explains Cenci's drive for phallic identification. When his authority is challenged by Beatrice at the banquet scene, Cenci, in reaction, immediately debases her by resorting to typical misogynist tropes: "Thou painted viper!/ Beast that thou art! Fair and yet terrible!/ I know a charm shall make thee meek and tame" (I.iii.165-67). This battle between the tyrannical father and the rebellious daughter takes the form of a battle of the sexes, triggering his desire to control her and obliterate any excess in women (to quell her "stubborn will," to make her "stoop . . . low" [IV.i.10, 11]). Acted out by the male gaze ("one look, one smile" in Beatrice's words [II.i.64]), Cenci's masculine fantasy grows to be the self-fulfilling force of "one supplication, one desire [and] one hope".

In Lacanian terms, Beatrice figures now for Cenci as the Law or Name-of-the-Father, "the censorious, castrating agency which places a taboo on the very desire it provokes into being." Since the phallus is the effect of an imaginary fantasy of bodily completion, to Cenci, Beatrice embodies the fetishistic signifier of male power and desire. And since the phallus is the object of desire, insofar as Beatrice is Cenci's object of desire, she is the phallus, a "phallic woman." In Beatrice the Count Cenci sees the recalcitrantly integral phallus, and his desire to penetrate the imaginary selfhood in Beatrice is precipitated after the banquet scene:

Be thou [the wine] . . . . . . manhood's purpose stern, And age's firm, cold, subtle villainy; As if thou were indeed my children's blood Which I did thirst to drink! The charm works well; It must be done; It shall be done. I swear! (I.iii.173—78; emphasis added)

With a self-serving logic of elevated urgency ("It must be done; it shall be done"), accompanied by an orgiastic fervor ("I did thirst to drink"), Count Cenci reveals his intent to Beatrice:

. . . from this day and hour Never again, I think, with fearless eye, And brow superior, and unaltered cheek, And that lip made for tenderness or scorn, Shalt thou strike dumb the meanest of mankind; Me least of all. Now get thee to thy chamber! Thou too, loathed image of thy cursed mother, [To Bernardo. Thy milky, meek face makes me sick with hate! [Exeunt Beatrice and Bernardo.] (Aside.) So much passed between us as must make Me bold, her fearful!

(II.i.115—24; emphasis added)

While Beatrice's countenance is delineated through Count Cenci's gaze, what is traceable, if disavowed by the Count, is indeterminacy in Beatrice-"the lip made for tenderness or scorn." Cenci is driven to compensate for the humiliation caused by Beatrice's challenge in front of the banquet guests; even the presence of his unmasculine son ("Thy milky, meek face") compels him to strengthen his phallic identity by subjugating his strong-willed daughter ("me bold, her fearful"). By penetrating the imaginary whole of Beatrice's body, Cenci attempts psychically to subjugate her: he boasts his intention to "drag her, step by step,/ Through infamies unheard of among men" (IV.i.80—81), and ultimately to "poison and corrupt her soul" (IV.i.44).

Even in a state of shock, fear, delirium, and inertia after the rape, Beatrice sees the sexual economy as well: "'Twere better not to struggle any more./ Men, like my father, have been dark and bloody" (II.i.54—55). Highlighting her father's masculinity, Beatrice equates him with other men who share the same subject position. After all, she lives in a society where men perpetrate brutal and inexplicable sexual crimes, while female sexuality is considered to be a "circulating property which cements the system of male dominance."

Such sexual dynamics become precariously intensified when they occur within the confines of the family circle in which the power imbalance between family members plays a critical role. Considered as a private realm, a family is insulated from outside intervention, and the patriarch can have full access to female family members and exert absolute power over them. The most crucial aspect of the Count's rape of his daughter in The Cenci is that while such a heinous crime is easy for the Father to commit, it has no name and thus no appropriate channel to be exposed and prosecuted.

Better to reign in Hell than serve in Heaven.
(Paradise Lost 1.170; 261-63)(5)

Self-reliance is the order of the day, and Satan's trouble with his pronouns in this passage demonstrates the powerfully alienating drive of anger. "We may reign," Satan opines democratically to his equally outraged fellow, and yet he follows immediately with talk of "my choice / To reign," as if his anger were driving him constantly towards isolation and further forms of exile. When Satan announces later, "My self am Hell" (4:75), he confirms this drive, and makes it clear that, at one level, his angry rebellion against Heaven amounts only to a wish for personal sovereignty.

In promoting Jesus, God alienates Satan; in rebelling against God, Satan confirms that alienation. In sending Satan to Hell, God makes the alienation permanent; and in claiming he chose to reign in Hell, Satan turns it into an industry of his own. At each moment, anger compels both parties to envision their doings as actions rather than reactions — as products of an individual will, not as belated responses. Of course, God's omniscience makes belatedness on his part impossible — and so his anger is really nothing but judgment expressed as punishment. Satan's rage, on the other hand, is always reactive, like our own — an identity that William Blake deplored.

Alienating, defensive, reactive: such descriptions — and they were the dominant ones in the eighteenth and early nineteenth centuries — begin to explain why writing anger was such a problem for the Romantic poets, who, in an age of the ascendancy of lyricism, were to express their own emotions rather than creating dramatic or narrative characters to enact them.

In most circumstances, angry rhetoric wards off readerly sympathy, the primary goal of the archetypal Romantic poet, and institutes a scene of distance and distrust. No emotion invites judgment from its audience so readily, because our experience of others' anger, unlike that of other strong passions, is always informed by rational measures.

How much anger is justified under the circumstances? Is this particular pound of flesh too much or too little in the way of vengeance? Has this angry person gone too far? In *Revenge Tragedy: Aeschylus to Armageddon*, John Kerrigan has shown that the deep connections between revenge and theater have a basis in our eagerness to make such evaluations.

For the lyric speaker whose art depends upon a sincere and sympathetic voice, anger invites the encroachment of the dramatic and the juridical, and thus threatens to break down lines of imagined communion between poet and reader.

What, though, of satiric poetry? Between the Augustans and the Romantics, Thomas Lockwood finds a widening split between satire and poetry: it is not that satire was not being written, but that critical canons were changing, dismissing wit, reason, and politics as components alien to "pure" poetry.

In his influential study of Romantic theory, *The Mirror and the Lamp* (1953), M.H. Abrams traces the Romantic substitution of internal for external verisimilitude as the end of poetry. The work of art, which before 1800 aimed to mirror nature, now aimed to project the artist's emotional state, without deceit or distortion.

Primarily under Rousseau's influence, English poetry came to be governed by an aesthetic ideology of (authorial) sincerity and (readerly) sympathy that prohibited the essential theatricality and confrontational implications of angry satire. As the voice of poetry became more disembodied and more isolated in order to avoid imputations of theatricality, anger — a violent passion that relies on tone, gesture, and facial expression for its communication to others — necessarily grew problematic for lyric poets.

How does one become angry without a body, a voice, or an established dramatic context? One answer is to write very strongly worded imprecations and curses. Yet such a strategy invites charges of overreaction and overacting, or madness and insincerity, as the career of Lord Byron demonstrates.

Indeed, when one considers the dialogue between Romantic lyricism and ill-tempered theatricality, Byron's poetic procedures come first to mind. However, studies of Byron's engagement with satire tend to downplay the importance of anger, probably because *Don Juan* bestrides his who can feign no image in my mind Of that which has transformed me. I, whose thought Is like a ghost shrouded and folded up In its own formless horror.

For Beatrice, the Cenci Palace is the prison-house where Cenci's will is the will of Heaven (IV.i.138), and where her father can drag her "from hall to hall by the entangled hair," where such utmost violence swirls into the dark void of silence, where her scream for help is submerged under "a gloomy pile of feudal architecture" ("Preface" 242): "Never to change, never to pass away. / Why so it is. This is the Cenci palace" (III.i.63-64).

Competing with her acknowledgment of the persistence of the existent symbolic economy, however, is the urge to initiate a change through obliterating the "lasting circumstance of life": "If I try to speak/ I shall go mad. Aye, something must be done". Beatrice takes up an active role by engaging herself in the parricidal plot and indeed by "becoming" a rival to the father and patriarchal authority. Traditional readings of Beatrice's "reproduction" of patriarchal modes in her violent revolt, emphasizing her lack of endurance or lack of conscience in confessing her crime, miss the point in explaining the gender-specific quality in Beatrice's struggle.

The crux of the matter of mad Beatrice, however, is that she is situated in the mad dening network of the sex-gender system, not that she lacks patience. The paradox and complexity of Beatrice's action as a female victim against the rule of the father (including that of the Pope) can never be fully explained if we put her in the same position as her father.

At the outset, the Count and the daughter seem to share one quality: both he who violates his daughter's body so readily and she who revolts against her tyrannical father so radically pose direct challenges to the idealized notion of a "natural family." In contrast to the dominant fiction of family as an organic unit composed of domestic bliss, fatherly love and family bonding, the Cenci family shows how institutionality itself generates criminality. Family structure as a central apparatus of patriarchal social relations effectively silences the voice of discontent: Beatrice thus deplores:

. . . In this mortal world There is no vindication and no law Which can adjudge and execute the doom Of that through which I suffer. (III.i.134-37)

The naturalized notion of family bonding is continuously put into question as Beatrice raises epistemological questions: "What thing am I" (III.i.38); "Thou are not what thou seemest . . ." (III.i.58). Cenci condemns his murdered sons as "most unnatural sons" at the banquet scene and in his conversation with Lucretia (II.i.133); Lucretia and Beatrice speak of Cenci's "unnatural pride," "unnatural desire" and unspeakable violence, and reevaluate sacrosanct codings; finally, Giacomo declares that "She [Beatrice] . . . alone in this unnatural work [parricide],/ Stands like God's angel ministered upon/ By fiends" (V.i.42-45; emphasis added). Here dialectical movement allows the whole incident to be seen from an alternative perspective, in which Beatrice alone is an avenger of the "unnatural" world.

The Cenci certainly questions the roles of home, family, and father in the Count's crime through laying bare the disruption and fragmentation of socially assumed identities and subject positions, and through resituating family as a social construct that also organizes individual subjects [daughters, wives] according to the interests of patriarchal structure. Giacomo offers a textual test-ground for family organization: as the inverse of Cenci, meek and pusillanimous Giacomo lives with a disillusioned family romance. Irrevocably tarnished by Count Cenci's manipulation, Giacomo's family resentfully enacts hollow repetitions of coded activities:

It is my wife complaining in her sleep: I doubt not she is saying bitter things Of me; and all my children round her dreaming That I deny them sustenance.

Indeed when he realizes that because of his father's exploitation he cannot live up to the fiction of an affective family, he declares, "I looked, and saw that home was hell". In this light, an altercation between Orsino and Beatrice, where Orsino asks "what is he who has thus injured you?" and Beatrice answers, "The man they call my faher: a dread name,"

Yet, as McGann explains, Byron's genius lies in his refusal to abide within a strictly ironic vision; his commitment to contradiction includes contradiction itself. This means that Byron sometimes grounds his work in sincere and consistent emotions, whose vehement certainty exempts them from the play of irony and contradiction. Not surprisingly, the first of these emotions are anger and hatred. As McGann says of Don Juan:

Romantic irony is not the work's ground of truth either. We glimpse this even through the example of Southey, who is not known in Don Juan through the plays of Romantic irony. He is known rather through hatred — the same way Brougham and Castlereagh are known....Byron can be witty at his own expense, or at Southey's expense, but his wit is not engaged in the face of the Byron/Southey parallel....because Southey is not in the end a figure of fun for Byron, he is a figure of all that is hateful and despicable. (TLK 55)

Before turning to a closer examination of Byron's work, we should sort out the connections between Romantic sincerity and sympathy, and how anger cuts against them. Clearly, as dramatic action, anger can produce a powerful sympathetic response in an audience.

From Oedipus forward, the history of tragedy has found its centre in anger and revenge, as John Kerrigan has shown. Because anger arises from the perception of unjust injury, we take great interest in the circumstances and consequences surrounding it; if we think that someone's anger is appropriate to the injury, we grant him our sympathy. The complex ethical economy of anger makes the stage its proper home, where the nuances of situation and response can be presented.

Furthermore, since anger emerges most often from some dramatic relation, its artistic expression is typically most effective as dialogue; it takes two (or more) to make an argument. Finally, and perhaps most crucially, the expression of anger depends on tone, gesture, and facial expression for its communication to others — things available to actors but not to lyric poets.

Charles Lamb, in his "On the Tragedies of Shakespeare"

(1811), sees anger as the most appropriate emotion for the stage, where the goal is the overt display of passion:

> *The glory of scenic art is to personate passion, and the turns of passion; and the more coarse and palpable the passion is, the more hold upon the eyes and ears of the spectators the performer obviously possesses. For this reason, scolding scenes, scenes where two persons talk themselves into a fit of fury...have always been the most popular on our stage.*
>
> (qtd. in *Romantics on Shakespeare* 114)

Anger is "coarse and palpable," best represented in dialogue as a "scene," attractive to spectators who naturally prefer scenes full of sound and fury, regardless of what they signify. However, to express anger using pen and ink alone, the poet may feel obliged to resort to very strongly worded imprecations and curses.

Yet, faced with such outbursts, the reader typically assumes the poet is either over-acting (or thus insincere) or overreacting (and thus unsympathetic). In either case, the sincerity effect is disabled and the poem becomes a spectacle, returning in effect to theater. Such readerly detachment opens a gap into which rush hermeneutic suspicions and judgments.

The "sincerity" that characterizes Wordsworthian Romanticism depends wholly on sympathy — precisely that which the decontextualized anger of the lyric has trouble evoking, particularly when it appears spontaneous: that is, uncalled for.

Robert Langbaum has written, "*Einfühlung*," or sympathy, "is the specifically Romantic way of knowing," and the Romantic speaker is "a pole of sympathy — the means by which reader and writer project themselves into the poem" (*Poetry of Experience* 52). We call sincere the poetry that effectively provokes such sympathetic projection. Of course, as Langbaum and McGann both recognize, sincere poetry is, at one level, an oxymoron. Langbaum writes, "the anti-rhetorical style is itself a rhetoric.

For there remains, between the sincere feeling in the heart and the effect of sincerity on the page, the art of incest, and highlighted the "unnatural" character of the violence while rendering Beatrice's suffering invisible or ambiguous. The Monthly Review, for example, declares that "we honestly confess that the story of the Cenci, chosen as a subject for tragedy in the twentieth [sic] century, does indeed astonish and revolt us: for it involves incest committed by a father, and murder perpetrated by a daughter."

If The British Review and London Critical Journal labels the Count's crime as incestuous rape, it still argues that "incestuous rape, murder, the rack, and the scaffold are not the proper materials of the tragic Muse: crimes and punishments are not in themselves dramatic." On the character of Count Cenci the reviewer also says:

. . . no such being as Cenci existed: none such could exist. The historical fact was in itself disgustingly shocking; and, in Mr Shelley's hands, the fable becomes even more loathsome and less dramatic than the fact . . . the most hateful forms of vice and suffering, preceded by involuntary pollution and followed by voluntary parricide, are the materials of this mix-called tragedy. They who can find dramatic poetry in such representations of human life must excuse us for wondering of what materials their minds are composed.... The ties of father and daughter, of husband and wife, ought not to be profaned as they are in this poem. It is in vain to plead, that the delineations are meant to excite our hatred; they ought not to be presented to the mind at all....

On the British reviewers' part, such a radical destablization of the "natural" affective family-Beatrice's parricidal desire as much as Count Cenci's rape-was indeed threatening, especially since the ideology of affective family was a badly needed fuel for bourgeois nationalist moralism, especially at its burgeoning imperialist stage. Furthermore, the main player of the revolt is the daughter of the family, the moral backbone of the system.

Among the strident attacks Shelley evoked with the publication of the play, The Literary Gazette typifies the hostile criticism poured onto the work. According to its reviewer, "Of all the abominations which intellectual perversion, and poetical atheism, have produced in our times, this tragedy appears to us to be most abominable." It is "the dish of carrion, seasoned with sulphur as spice, which Mr. Shelley serves up to his friend Mr. Leigh Hunt." This characteristic response sent a sobering message to Shelley's rather optimistic expectation of The Cenci's reception. Although Shelley never lacked adversaries among the conservative reviewers of his time, the ferocious attacks on The Cenci seem peculiarly vicious. The London Magazine recapitulates the most disturbing aspect of the play as follows:

[Shelley's] style, though disgraced by occasional puerilities, and simpering affectations, is in general bold, vigorous, and manly; but the disgraceful fault to which we object in his writings, is the scorn he every where evinces for all that is moral or religious. If he must be sceptical—if he must be lax in his human code of excellence, let him be so; but in God's name let him not publish his principles, and cram them down the throats of others. (emphasis added)

Valorizing the notion of masculinity on the one hand, the reviewer emphasizes the writer's need to exercise self-censorship against the dissemination of such "unnatural" or "immoral" material on the other. Often such ideologues advocate complete suppression of the discourse of "incest" or parricide, while erasing the logic of power couched in such repressive hypotheses. The New Monthly Magazine argues, for instance, for the voluntary suppression of literary transgression by resorting to the dictum, "Where there is no law, there is no transgression." Evoking the golden rule of the control of information, and denouncing the already existing law of prohibition, the ideological pretension of decency reaches its apogee: "The exposure of a crime too often pollutes the very soul which shudders at its recital, and destroys that unconsciousness of ill which most safely preserves its sanctities."

Assuming the role of moral guardian, the reviewer not only denounces the crime but actually denies its possibility, resorting to essentialist logic in explaining the "nature" of "ordinary" people's minds and souls. However, the

Clermont. "It was this poem," writes McGann, "that brought down the general public attack" on Byron in 1816, and led to his departure from England (CPW, vol. 3, p. 495). Reading the poem is still unpleasant:

If like a snake she steal within your walls,
Till the black slime betray her as she crawls;
If like a viper to the heart she wind,
And leave the venom there she did not find; –
What marvel that this hag of hatred works
Eternal evil latent as she lurks
To make a Pandemonium where she dwells,
And reign the Hecate of domestic Hells.

By foregrounding his "Private Life" and "domestic Hells," Byron draws the reader into a realm of personal anger where the subject of poetry is Byron's enemy and the object is revenge. "A Sketch" is a disturbingly intimate poem, whose problem is not theatricality but its relentless sincerity. By bringing his anger and hatred to the lyric, Byron reveals the dark side of the 'true voice of feeling' and the 'spontaneous overflow' of emotion that characterize Romanticism.

Of this aspect of Byron's poetry McGann writes, "When feeling comes to the aid of feeling in the Byronic and Baudelairean world, the sympathetic event is not confined to a horizon of benevolence". In other words, some emotions are hellish, and Byron's poetry based in those emotions can be malevolent indeed, particularly for the Romantic reader accustomed to engaging sympathetically with the speaker of the poem.

Byron's angry curses rebuff sympathy and introduce a set of agonistic relations amongst himself, his poetry, his readers, and his victims. The resulting spectacle invites judgment, criticism, and uneasy voyeurism. In fact, Byron's unique style emerges under direct pressure from his anger, as he develops ways to engage readers despite his spite. One favorite method is to portray himself as one who has patiently suffered many betrayals, who endures despite having been unreasonably provoked. McGann calls this role "the figure of the suffering poet, whose (audience) reciprocal is the sympathetic reader".

Yet the angry Byron frequently lets this mask slip, as he plays the role of *poète maudit* with strong overtones of vindictiveness. To this his audience typically responds not with sympathy, but with a disturbed fascination; by means of its angry moods, the Byronic personality compels attention.

A mysterious, deliberately provocative blend of confession and accusation fairly defines the Byronic curse. Perhaps the most famous example of this occurs in Canto IV of *Childe Harold's Pilgrimage,* during the scene in the Roman Coliseum where Byron addresses "Time, the avenger!" He first asserts his patience, even as he hopes for revenge:

If calmly I have:..
Reserved my pride against the hate
Which shall not whelm me, let me not have worn
This iron in my soul in vain — shall they not mourn?
(lines 1176-79)

"Thou shalt take / The vengeance" (lines 1194-95), Byron declares to "great Nemesis" (line 1181); "I sleep, but thou shalt yet awake" (line 1197); the poet's emotional equivocation and displacement do not mask his outrage. As Peter Manning puts it, we can perceive "the vindictive impulses surviving beneath the proclamation of sincerity" (Manning 23); one might say 'thriving' and be closer to the poem's spirit.

Vindication (that is, revenge and its justification) remains central to Byron's poetry. By fusing anger and patience, or outburst and deferral, Byron creates a seductive mode of intense expression that opens up a space for readers' sympathy, even as it alienates them. We keep reading Byron in expectation of either catching him in outright evil or finding him to be a saint — in a moment of unalloyed judgment or sympathy. His curse of forgiveness exemplifies this mode:

a far hour shall wreak
The deep prophetic fulness of this verse,
And pile on human heads the mountain of my curse!
That curse shall be Forgiveness.—Have I not—
Hear me, my mother Earth! behold it, Heaven!—
Have I not had to wrestle with my lot?
Have I not suffered things to be forgiven?

cancelled from people's minds, a necessity which they were all to agree had existed but was not to be spoken of, a crime which to punish was to proclaim and make real,—any thing, in short, but that a daughter killed her father. It is a lie told, as it were, for the sake of nature, to save it the shame of a greater contradiction.

Attuned to the polemics involved in reviewing rhetoric, Hunt here exaggerates the notion of the patricide as unthinkable and unspeakable and thus masterfully plays upon the reviewers' deeply held assumptions. If they think the unthinkable crime should be suppressed, it is only natural that Beatrice suppress it herself. At the same time, in his desire to solve the mystery of Beatrice's "contradiction," Hunt rushes into reducing her into a time-honored feminine icon.

Shelley must also have anticipated the conservative camp's dogmatic moralizing. The troubling ethical question of Beatrice's "inconsistency," especially her unequivocal refusal to accept her involvement in parricide at the trial, constitutes the crux of what Shelley calls the "chasm" in Beatrice: in the "Preface" he argues that the "crimes and miseries in which [Beatrice] was an actor and a sufferer are as the mask and the mantle in which circumstances clothed her for her impersonation on the scene of the world."

One might argue that Beatrice's earlier experiences of the futility of protest (her plea at the banquet and her intercepted appeal to the Pope) compel her to redefine the "official" process of seeking justice. Beatrice's absolutely unflinching denial of her criminality inscribes a certain unarticulated insistence that the patriarchal structure itself be subjected to a rigorous interrogation. Still, Shelley expresses his ambivalence about the excess in Beatrice that he associates with parricide:

Undoubtedly, no person can be truly dishonoured by the act of another; and the fit return to make to the most enormous injuries is kindness and forebearance, and a resolution to convert the injurer from his dark passions by peace and love. Revenge, retaliation, atonement, are pernicious mistakes. If Beatrice had thought in this manner she would have been wiser and better; but she would never have been a tragic character.

. . . . . ("Preface" 240). This rare judgmental moment (of downplaying his sympathy and fascination with Beatrice's character) comes hand in hand with his emphasis on the aesthetic quality of her character (echoing the classical concept of the tragic flaw). Beatrice in fact ends up becoming a traditional tragic scapegoat, who assumes the sins of the community as a precursor of change. But here does Shelley at the same time reinscribe the saintly victimhood as the ultimate way to deal with the unrelenting tyranny, while silencing precisely what has driven Beatrice to make the "pernicious" mistake in the first place?

In light of that question, Shelley's invention of the Pope's death warrant for Cenci after his murder needs further investigation. Clearly differentiating his text from the transcribed version of the historical incident (in which there is no such voluntary attempt to prosecute Cenci on the Pope's part), Shelley inserts his ambivalence about the necessity of the parricidal act. Shelley's distancing strategy thus allows him to preempt his contemporary critics' attacks on the "excessive" political content of The Cenci.

At the same time, Shelley offers in the "Preface" to define Beatrice's involvement in the parricide and her firm refusal to admit it before the law in terms of "casuistry": "It is in the restless and anatomizing casuistry with which men seek the justification of Beatrice, yet feel that she has done what needs justification; it is in the superstitious horror with which they contemplate alike her wrongs and their revenge; that the dramatic character of what she did and suffered, consists".

Here, casuistry "is that part of ethics which resolves cases of conscience, applying the general rule of religion and morality to particular instances in which circumstances alter cases, or in which there appears to be a conflict of duties". Earl Wasserman highlights the concept of "sublime casuistry" which Shelley uses to explain Falkland's nature in Godwin's Caleb Williams: "Inherent purity of character can coexist with moral error; and, since sublime casuistry reveals that error cannot be reconciled with the purity, that purity is unaltered by the error."

poetry. On the other hand, the "Nemesis" passage from *Childe Harold's Pilgrimage* strongly implies what the "Time & Nemesis" letter to Augusta confirms: that Byron wants his wife and her allies to suffer for what he has convinced himself was treachery.

As might be expected, Byron's angriest writing can be found in cancelled lines, fragments, personal letters, and private notations. However, these outbursts merely illuminate the larger patterns of anger and revenge that structure his more public works of art. In his communications to others, poetic and otherwise, Byron makes a spectacle of the conflicts of his intimate life. Take, as another example, the letter that should be paired with "A Sketch from Private Life." Soon after composing that poem of abuse directed at Jane Clermont, Byron wrote of her to his wife:

She came as a guest—she remained as a spy—she departed as an informer—&reappeared as an evidence—if false—she belied—if true she betrayed me. The worst of treacheries—a "bread and salt traitress" she ate & drank & slept & awoke to sting me.

The curse of my Soul light upon her & hers forever!—may my Spirit be deep upon her in her life &—in her death—may her thirst be unquenchable—&her wretchedness irrevocable—may she see herself only & eternally—may the fulfillment of her wishes become the destruction of her hopes—may she dwell in the darkness of her own heart & shudder now & for existence. Her last food will be the bread of her enemies. I have said it.

(BLJ, vol. 5, p. 64)

Byron presented a poetic version of this curse at least twice, once as "A Sketch from Private Life," and again as an "Incantation" or "Chorus in an unfinished Witch Drama" that later found its way into *Manfred*. As Daniel McVeigh observes, the two poems resemble one another so that "it seems reasonable to suspect with Marchand that the Incantation's vitriol came originally from the same reservoir of hate as this heartfelt curse against Clermont"; McVeigh also cites the letter to Lady Byron (McVeigh 603-4).

Furthermore, McGann has exposed the wicked double-meaning of "unfinished Witch Drama" as a reference to Byron's tormenting marriage ("Truth in Masquerade" 16-17).

It seems that a recurring accompaniment of Byronic anger is the transgression of boundaries between the public and the private: while this personal letter performs its anger self-consciously as a curse, the public poems (one, a drama) encode personal conflicts and outbursts at their foundations.

Combining the satirist's enthusiasm for punishment, the dramatist's sense of anger as spectacle, and the lyricist's confessional mode and matter, Byron creates poetry to stage his revenge.

Particularly when he broods upon personal injuries and betrayals, the result is a strangely confessional and performative invective, filled with curses. In fact, the construction of the Byronic subject typically depends upon a curse, pronounced by or upon him, which enacts his alienation from the rest of humanity; one thinks of Childe Harold, of Manfred, of the Giaour, of Cain.

In choosing the curse as vehicle, Byron situates his angry poetry between the precincts of sincerity and performance, since cursing performs its meaning (i.e., revenge) according to the authentic fervor of the curser.

In other words, a curse is a dramatic attempt to compel the sympathy of the world, and it depends for its power on both sincerity and spectacle, or private emotion and public rage. Byron's poetic experiments with the angry curse thus provoke both sympathy and judgment, and help create the Byronic persona— so alien to Wordsworthian Romanticism — that prefigures the dramatic monologists of the Victorian era.

spectacle, object, and fetish, the Medusan gaze evokes an unappropriable realm of female power. Medusa's petrifying gaze monstrously disrupts any narrative, bringing to a standstill the timehonored expectation of the virtuous damsel, saintly-martyr, maternal or sisterly muse, despite all the patriarchal apparatuses of appropriation, containment, or "othering."

How could Shelley stage such Medusan gaze of Beatrice Cenci? The very first account of her gaze is given by Orsino, who encapsulates the powerful yet mysterious effect of that gaze:

Yet I fear

Her subtle mind, her awe-inspiring gaze, Whose beams anatomize me nerve by nerve And lay me bare, and make be blush to see My hiding thoughts.—Ah, no! A friendless girl Who clings to me, as to her only hope:—I were a fool, not less than if a panther Were panic-stricken by the Antelope's eye, If she escape me.

In spite of his apparent condescension towards the helpless "antelope" from the eye of the powerful "panther," Orsino is irrevocably struck by her anatomizing gaze. "Laid bare," and incapacitated, Orsino faces the spectacle of himself as seen by the Other, with a disavowed recognition that Beatrice will ultimately escape his grasp.

This "anatomizing" gaze is a prominent and awful feature to her father, who is plotting the rape of his daughter. While apparently subjecting her to his power, the Count still expresses his frustration over her "fearless" eyes:

. . . from this day and hour Never again, I think, with fearless eye, And brow superior, and unaltered cheek, And that lip made for tenderness or scorn, Shalt thou strike dumb the meanest of mankind; Me least of all.

(II.i.11-121; emphasis added)

While imposing his will just before the rape, the Count exhibits a curious hesitation with the insertion, "I think." Count Cenci's fetishistic attempt to define Beatrice tells more about his state of mind—i.e., his phallic drive and obsession—than about hers. At once admitting that he is stupefied, speechless, by her gaze, Cenci is now determined to crush her with an overpowering masculine will. Finally, in the trial scene of Act V, Shelley construes "the gaze of the Other," obliquely enough, through Marzio's final declaration of Beatrice's innocence (in Marzio's words, to comply with "a higher truth").

Beatrice advances towards Marzio, the Count's assassin, who consequently "covers his face, and shrinks back," shouting "Oh, dart/ The terrible resentment of those eyes/ On the dead earth! Turn them away from me!/ They wound: 'twas torture forced the truth" (V.ii.29-32). Beatrice asks him to "fix shine eyes on mine;/ Answer to what I ask, . . . What! wilt thou say/ That I did murder my own father?" (81-82; 8687), to which Marzio exclaims, "Oh! Spare me! . . . Let her not look on me!" (88; 90).

In the face of impending death, Marzio sees ungraspable, intractble, and almost sublime power in Beatrice's Medusan eyes that wound: Beatrice's transvaluational claim of innocence with a dramatic miming of the judges results in the mysterious submission of Marzio to her power and logic.

Marzio finally declares: "A keener pain has wrung a higher truth/ From my last breath. She is most innocent!" (164-65). Beatrice's gaze cuts across class-differentiation by also turning Camillo, in effect, to a "soul-less" thing: "I would pledge my soul/ That she is guiltless" (V.ii.61-62). Beatrice's gaze thus thrusts the allegorical, self-reflexive structure of the play to the fore. As if to defy even the author's desire for a just representation, it effects "an alien viewpoint with a voiding force, functioning as the reverse side of consciousness, and elides itself."

Put face to face with the "blind" law that refuses to recognize how patriarchal oppression fosters crimes, and after identifying the nature of her struggle as the battleground of power and meaning, Beatrice refuses to be represented and tried by the state's legal apparatus.

Beatrice's gaze allegorizes that otherness in her character, an "excess" or alterity of her subjectivity, that cannot be contained by the all-pervasive symbolic order. Stubbornly refusing to be a part of the system, Beatrice makes an friend Hobhouse and his half-sister, Augusta Leigh, was committed to the flames after Byron's death. The publication of his poems—especially the third and fourth cantos of *Childe Harold* and *Manfred*—greatly increased Byron's reputation as a poet, and his fame spread from England to the continent.

The resemblance of *Manfred* to *Faust* stimulated the interest of the most famous of Byron's literary contemporaries, Goethe, who, henceforth, showed a lively regard for the younger poet's genius and character.

A correspondence sprang up between them; Byron dedicated to Goethe, in language of sincere homage, his tragedy *Sardanapalus* (1821), and, after Byron's death, Goethe honoured his memory by introducing him as Euphorion, child of Helen and Faust, of Hellenism and the renascence, in the second part of *Faust*. In the spring of 1819 began Byron's connection with Theresa, countess Guiccioli, the young wife of the sexagenarian count Guiccioli, whose home was at Ravenna.

On either side the attachment was one of passionate devotion: the lady was prepared to make supreme sacrifices for the man she loved, and her influence upon him was ennobling. She lifted him out of the mire of Venetian libertinism and aroused his interest in the cause of Italian freedom; she inspired one of his sublimest poems, *The Prophecy of Dante,* while such was her power over him that, for her sake, he desisted, for a time, from the continuation of *Don Juan* after the completion of the fifth canto.

In December, 1819, Byron broke up his home at Venice and moved to Ravenna, in order to be nearer to the countess. Here, he was visited by Shelley, who, in a letter to Mrs. Shelley, dated 8 August, 1821, speaks as follows of the change which had come over his friend:

Lord Byron is greatly improved in every respect. In genius, in temper, in moral views, in health, in happiness. The connection with La Guiccioli has been an inestimable benefit to him.... He has had mischievous passions, but these he seems to have subdued, and he is becoming, what he should be, a virtuous man. The interest which he took in the politics of Italy, and the actions he performed in consequence of it, are subjects not fit to be *written,* but are such as will delight and surprise you. In the preceding year, the countess had obtained a papal decree of separation from her husband, and was now living in a villa belonging to her borther, count Gamba, about fifteen miles from Ravenna.

Byron's literary activity remained unabated in his new home. To the Ravenna period belong, in addition to his *Prophecy of Dante, Francesca of Rimini* and his translation of the first canto of Pulci's *Morgante Maggiore,* most of his dramatic writings. Drama had always interested him keenly, and, while living in London, after his return from the east, he had been elected a member of the Drury lane theatre committee, and had thus gained some first-hand knowledge of the stage.

His earliest play, *Manfred,* had been begun in Switzerland and completed at Venice in the spring of 1817; after his removal to Ravenna, he turned his attention to historical tragedy, and, in little more than a year, produced his two tragedies of Venetian history, *Marino Faliero* and *The Two Foscari,* together with his oriental *Sardanapalus.*

Following upon these came the two "mysteries," *Cain* and *Heaven and Earth,* both written *currente calamo* between the July and October of 1821. These plays were not intended for the stage, and the only one acted during the author's lifetime was *Marino Faliero,* which was performed at Drury lane, against Byron's express wish, in April, 1821.

To the Ravenna period also belongs Byron's *Letter to John Murray, Esq. on the Rev. W. L. Bowles's Strictures on the Life and Writings of Pope,* in which the poet came forward as the champion of Pope and the Augustan school of poetry against the attacks directed upon them by the romanticists. The controversy is chiefly interesting as an indication of Byron's regard for the classical principles of literary taste and, arising out of this, his uncritical exaltation of the poetry of Crabbe and Rogers over the great romantic poets of his own day. Of far greater consequence was his attack upon Southey, which followed a little later.

The feud between the two poets was an old one: Southey

had attacked Byron in an article contributed to *Blackwood's Magazine* (August, 1819) and the younger poet had replied with *Some Observations* on the attack, in which he brought a charge of apostasy and slander against the poet laureate.

In 1821 appeared Southey's fatuous *A Vision of Judgment,* prefixed to which was a gross onslaught upon *Don Juan* as "a monstrous combination of horror and mockery, lewdness and impiety," and a reference to its author as the founder of "the Satanic school" inspired by the spirit of Belial in their lascivious parts, and the spirit of Moloch in those loathsome images of atrocities and horrors which they delight to represent.

To all this, Byron's effective rejoinder was his own *The Vision of Judgment,* published in Leigh Hunt's magazine, *The Liberal,* in 1822. Byron's victory was complete and uncontestable, though the British government brought against the publisher a charge of "calumniating the late King and wounding the feelings of his present Majesty," and won their suit. Byron's connection with countess Guiccioli brought him, as already stated, into direct relationship with the Carboneria, one of the many secret societies of the time in Italy, which had its headquarters in Naples, and of which count Pietro Gamba was an enthusiastic leader.

Its ultimate aim was the liberation of Italy from foreign domination and the establishment of constitutional government. To Byron, this was "a grand object—the very poetry of politics," and to it he devoted, at this time, both his wealth and his influence.

But the movement, owing to lack of discipline and resolution on the part of its adherents, proved abortive, and the Papal States confiscated the property of the Gambas and exiled them from the Romagna. They fled to Pisa in the autumn of 1821, where Byron soon joined them, and shared with them the palazzo Lanfranchi.

The change of residence brought Byron into closer contact with Shelley, whose home, at this time, was in Pisa, and, through Shelley, he made the acquaintance of captain Medwin, the author of the *Journal of the Conversations of Lord Byron* (1824). Here, too, he first met captain Trelawny, who subsequently accompanied the poet to Greece and, many years after Byron's death, published his *Recollections of the last days of Shelley and Byron* (1858).

In April, 1822, a heavy blow fell upon the poet through the death of his natural daughter Allegra, whose mother was Jane Clairmont, a half-sister of Mary Shelley; and, in the following month, in consequence of a street-brawl with an Italian dragoon who had knocked Shelley from his horse, the little circle of friends at Pisa was broken up. Byron and the Gambas retired to a villa near Leghorn, while the Shelleys, with Trelawney, left for Lerici. The tragic death of Shelley in the gulf of Spezia took place two months later.

CHILDE HAROLD

The surprising success of the first two cantos of *Childe Harold* on their first appearance in 1812 was in no small measure due to the originality of the design, and to Byron's extension of the horizon of romance. Before this time, poets had made certain attempts to set forth in verse the experiences of their foreign travels.

Thus, Goldsmith's *Traveller* is the firstfruits of the tour which he had made, flute in hand, through Flanders, France and Italy, in 1756. But the eighteenth century spirit lay heavy on Goldsmith: broad generalisations take the place of the vivid, concrete pictures which, in a more propitious age, he might have introduced into his poem, and racy description is sacrificed to the Augustan love of moralising.

Byron, for his part, is by no means averse to sententious rhetoric; but he has, also, the supreme gift of vivid portrayal, whether it be that of a Spanish bull-fight, the voice of a muezzin on the minaret of a Turkish mosque, or the sound of revelry on the night before Waterloo. The creation of an ideal pilgrim as the central figure before whom this kaleidoscopic survey should be displayed, though good in idea, proved but a partial success.

There was much that appealed to the jaded tastes of English society under the regency in the conception of Childe Harold as "Pleasure's palled victim," seeking distraction from disappointed love and Comus revelry in travel abroad; but, placed amid scenes which quiver with an intensity of light and colour, Childe Harold remains from first to last an unreal, shadowy form.

He is thrust into the picture as fitfully as the Spenserian archaisms are thrust into the text, and, when, in the last canto, he disappears altogether, we are scarcely conscious of his absence. In his prose, Byron denies again and again the identity of Childe Harold with himself; but, in his verse, he comes nearer to the truth by his confession that his hero is a projection of his own intenser self into human form:

Tis to create, and in creating live
A being more intense, that we endow
With form our fancy, gaining as we give
The life we image, even as I do now.

When *Childe Harold* was begun at Janina in Albania, in 1809, the hero may well have seemed to his creator as an imaginary figure; but, between the composition of the first two cantos and the third, there intervened for Byron a course of experiences which converted what was ideal and imaginary into bitter reality. The satiety, the lonely heart-sickness and the loathing for his native land, with which the poet imbues his hero in the opening stanzas of the first canto, had won an entrance into Byron's own heart when he bade farewell to England in 1816.

It was, accordingly, no longer had necessary for him to create an ideal being, for the creator and the creation become one. The third and fourth cantos show, in comparison with the first two, a far greater intensity of feeling and a deeper reading of life. Something of the glitter of rhetoric remains; but it is no longer cold, for a lava-flood of passion has passed over it. The poet is still a master of vivid description; but the objects that he paints are now seen quivering in an atmosphere of personal emotion. The human interest of the poem has also deepened; in the second canto, while recalling the historic associations of Greece, he sketched no portrait of Athenian poet, sage, or statesman: but, in his description of Switzerland, he seems unable to escape from the personality of Rousseau, and, in northern Italy, his progress is from one poet's shrine to another. Side by side with this deeper human interest, there is, also, a profounder insight into external nature.

Not only does he describe with incisive power majestic scenes like that of the Alps towering above the lake of Geneva, or that of the foaming cataract of Terni: he also enters, though only as a sojourner, into that mystic communion with nature wherein mountains, sea and sky are felt to be a part of himself and he of them. Among the solitudes of the Alps, Byron becomes, for a while, and, perhaps through his daily intercourse with Shelley, a true disciple of the great high-priest of nature, Wordsworth, whom elsewhere he often treats with contemptuous ridicule. Yet, even when he approaches Wordsworth most nearly, we are conscious of the gulf which separates them from one another.

Byron seeks communion with nature in order to escape from man; high mountains become "a feeling" to him when the hum of human cities is a torture; but Wordsworth hears in nature the music of humanity, and the high purpose of his life is to sing the spousal verse of the mystic marriage between the discerning intellect of man and the goodly universe.

In his letter to Moore, prefixed to *The Corsair,* Byron confesses that the Spenserian stanza is the measure most after his own heart, though it is well to remember that when he wrote these words he had not essayed the *ottava rima.* Disfigured as the stanzas of *Childe Harold* often are by jarring discords, it must be confessed that this ambitious measure assumed, in Byron's hands, remarkable vigour, while its elaborately knit structure saved him from the slipshod movement which is all too common in his blank verse.

Yet, this vigour is purchased at a heavy price. Rarely in Byron do we meet with the stately, if slow-moving, magnificence with which Spenser has invested the verse of his own creation; the effect produced on our ears by the music of *The Faerie Queene* is that of a symphony of many strings, whereas, in *Childe Harold,* we listen to a trumpetcall, clear and resonant, but wanting the subtle cadence and rich vowel-harmonies of the Elizabethan master.

Chapter 11

Lord Byron: What makes go?

Strong determinations—public/private—of imperial errancy private mean the singular and traumatic, contingent and coincidental materiality of the signifier that makes Lord Byron unique. By public I intend the publishing process that transfigured Byron into a stereotypical signified for public consumption, as well as the global, geopolitical and sociohistorical situation that set the stage for both his life-writing and his theatrical performance of this life of writing. The deleuzo-guattarian notion of deterritorialization is difficult to define. The simplest way to do so is to call on one of Deleuze and Guattari's exemplary cases: "Bird-songs: the bird sings to mark its territory."

This aggressive and defensive territorialization becomes more complex until it is transformed into a "song of courtship," a reaching outwards, a pure singing for the sake of sound that enables the bird to exceed its territorial limits, to mate with birds of the opposite sex, and to interact with the ecosphere: "Many birds 'imitate' the songs of other species" (TP 324, 331). Deterritorialization can also be defined in world-historical terms—that is, in terms of emergent capitalism.

The Reformation produces a sectarian proliferation that un-grounds "God" as a foundational "despotic signifier," while emergent globalization uproots economic exchange both from the land, in particular from the Island England (the ideological, imaginary or egological 'unity' of the British Isles), and from the feudal mastery encoded by the terms "Lord" and "King."

The emergence of capitalism transforms the English

experience of the world-system into a wild circulation of signs: counterfeit coinage, paper speculation, ad-venture capital, the reflexivity of Elizabethan theatrical representations, militant Puritan factions, emigrants, colonists, etc. King James the First's arbitrary dispensation of titles reduces knighthood to an empty performative, while his sovereign abuses, excesses and transgressions irreversibly void the doctrine of absolute kingship.

James, given the rise of the modern family, predictably appeals to the signifier Father—the King as Father of the nation—to bolster his absolutist claims, yet the "name of the father" inevitably loses its unconditional aura as the signifiers King, God and Lord whirl about the "distracted globe" of "the book and volume of my brain":

"'The body is with the King, but the King is not with the body. The King is a thing—' / 'A thing, my lord?' / 'Of nothing.'" If this fantasmic situation is one of global deterritorialization, then James's anachronistic reliance on the paternal signifier to legitimate authoritarian control of a distended social body, is, like Shakespeare's nostalgic investment of a feudal coat of arms—Non Sanz Droit—a reterritorialization.

If I write that I will "situate Lord Byron's errancy," I do so to distance myself from a tendency to take deterritorialization as a fait accompli: to reduce writing to a consumable feast that compensates for the lack of a politically viable alternative to the rigidly segregated and over-coded social body of capitalism. The writings of Deleuze and Guattari—writings to which this essay is obviously indebted—evidence this reductive tendency when the dynamic duo represent deterritorialization as an ecriture of becoming opposed to the fixities of Being:

One writes, then, on the same level as the real of an unformed matter, at the same time as that matter traverses and extends all of nonformal language: a becoming-animal like Kafka's mouse, Hofmannsthal's rats, Moritz's calves. A revolutionary machine, all the more abstract for being real. A regime that no longer operates by the signifier or the subjective.

It is as if writing incarnates the ontological reality of a cosmic deterritorialization, a "revolutionary machine" or "the real" of "matter" itself.

To conceive of the cosmos as a kind of metaphysical Thing is, however, unhelpful if one is trying to relate a deterritorializing life-writing to political struggles. Instead of attempting to mediate the relations between writing and the social, Deleuze-Guattari seek to perform deterritorialization as if this textual performative of a "literary enunciation" was sufficient to alter "objective conditions"—relations of production, uneven spatial relations, social institutions of domination, etc.:

"When a statement is produced by a bachelor or an artistic singularity, it occurs necessarily as a function of a national, political, and social community, even if the objective conditions of this community are not yet given to the moment except in literary enunciation." There is, in other words, little attention paid to how the artist speaks for or represents (in the sense of political representation) class fractions by means of aesthetic presentations within a pre-existing force field of "objective conditions."

Since deterritorialization is "a function of a national, political, and social community," insofar as this social body is doubly overdetermined by unspeakably private and unrepresentably global dimensions, it is to these "objective conditions" that I now turn.

I begin, however, with Jerome Christensen's Lord Byron's Strength: Romantic Writing and Commercial Society (1993), a very strong book indeed, for Christensen is a dedicated historicist, a savvy post-structural theorist and a fierce reader. I cite: "It is in [Byron's] invention that his strength appears. And it is as an ethos of invention that his poetry matters".

Christensen is attempting "to acknowledge the `essential importance of a concept of action' and to `elaborate a satisfactory account of the competent and knowledgeable human agent' without `relapsing into a subjectivist view, and without failing to grasp the structural components of the social institutions which outlive us'" (Anthony Giddens, The

Constitution of Society: Outline of a Theory of Structuration [1984]; quoted in CH xxii). A post-subjective accounting of this type replicates the deleuzo-guattarian stricture against operating in terms of "the subjective," but does not banish the signifier in favour of a non-materialist (in the Marxist sense) transcendental empiricism of immanence.

Christensen is more concerned with the Lacanian "agency [instance]" or "materiality of the signifier" (parapraxes, puns, freudian slips, literal overdeterminations of figural meaning), since it is this rhetorical drift of language—exemplified by the Byronic digression and employed by Byron's endlessly inventive strength—that prevents the poet from being reduced to the stereotypes reiterated by public consumption.

Byron is this drift: "the mattering of the signifier whose eccentric and inexorable itinerary is its Romantic biography". To trace these drifts—biographic and excursive—is to track the travails—local and global—of his errant letters: To find out what makes Lord Byron go. Deleuze and Guattari's conception of "unformed matter," on the other hand, refuses the chaotic, not-yet-meaningful flux instanced by the materiality of the signifier.

Their insistence that writing, once they have reconceived it as reading ("Kafka's mouse, Hofmannsthal's rats, Moritz's calves..."), instantiates the ontological truth of the "Chaosmos," performs a political displacement from agency to consumption, a displacement that repeats, mutatis mutandis, the fetishization of Byron's writing into the Byronic hero by the reading public as a compensation for political agency and as a defense-formation against being ingloriously implicated in Imperialism.

Byron initiates, as my conclusion will stress, this compensatory defense-formation by desiring to arrest the "mattering" of his writing. The reflexivity of the signifier, however, frames this desire as an arrested development of the Byronic drift.

How does a public worlding of geopolitical worlds relate to Byron's eccentricity, an errancy riddled through and through by trauma? What mode of reading will enable us to forge or mediate this relation between emergent globalization and a secret, private and traumatic past? Christensen adapts Abraham and Torok to trace the "secret impulse" that pushed Byron into writing. He reads "the strength of the encrypted inscription" in terms of "a past that persists in the present by virtue of its encrypted alterity".

My more globally oriented trajectory will be overdetermined by the "encrypted alterity" of "Augusta" (Byron's half-sister-cum-object of an incestuous affair) vis-a-vis "Augusta" (an ancient, Roman name for London popular in the 18th-Century); Albania (a way-station on Byron's pilgrimage) in relation to Albion (an archaic, nationalist name for Imperial Britain); and cryptonyms of ingenium. The aim of my essay is, if you get my drift, simple: to globalize Byron's case history:

Un gros meuble a tiroirs encombre de bilans, De vers, de billets doux, de proces, de romances, Avec de lourd cheveux roules dans des quittances, Cache moins de secrets que mon triste cerveau. C'est une pyramide, un immense caveau, Qui contient plus de morts que la fosse commun.

What, then, is Byron's problem: "all the woes we see—And worse, the woes we see not—which throb through the immedicable soul, with heart-aches ever new" (Childe Harold IV.1132-34)? Yet to insist on a "handily metaphoric secret (such as incest or homosexuality)" is to traduce the Byronic text by fixating on a stereotype of Byron produced by the publishing process: the capitalist exigencies of production, distribution and consumption.

The traumatic secret must remain secret, "the absence of the cause" that makes the text go, thereby catalyzing the historical overdeterminants that inflect its itness: private and singular, productive and inventive. An overdetermined drift, as it were.

Overdetermination is my sortie into a psychoanalytic mode of biographic reading that supplements a strictly "poststructuralist biographical criticism" (CH xxii) by attempting to get beyond Oedipal stereotypes, a "pas au-dela" or "pas du pas" that has been stressed, in different ways, by

Derrida, Deleuze and Guattari, Abraham and Torok (as read by Derrida or de Man). Byron encrypts, as I will detail, the figure of the incestuous ingenue, a trope, and not the biographical persona named Augusta Leigh. Incest is, according to the Anti-Oedipal critique, a key articulation of the stereotypical Oedipal triangle of mommy-daddy-me: "Only incest is possible...

Answer daddy-and-mommy when I speak to you!'". Fantasms of incest displace and re-articulate the barred desire for the Mother that upholds the patriarchal coding of the history of sexuality as a reiteration of "the repressive hypothesis."

Repression, in turn, presupposes and re-articulates the desire for a true or "full speech," or, in romanticist terms, a lyrical selfhood. My "step beyond" Oedipus and the social body this centered discourse over-codes is, in other words, simultaneously an attempt to get beyond a belief in the possibility of extracting the self-determining truth-content of a life-writing.

Fredric Jameson has pointed out that the "hysterical" extremity of Deleuze and Guattari's critique of "the Oedipus complex" presupposes that a grain of truth inheres in the object of this critique. Oedipus names the truth of the social structuration of sexuality "we" have been acting out from the Romantic Century onwards. I am unconcerned with the lived truth—content of Byron's relation to his incestuous relations, and am interested, instead, in the encrypted readability—local and global, national and geopolitical—of the ingenue figure.

By readability I do not mean a concatenation of themes that can be accessed via a textual exegesis of the Byronic figurative experience of a private/public double bind. I prefer an a-thematic style of reading that will, of course, have no other option than to proceed by explicating the matedality of the text in terms of themes in order to traverse thematic fantasms "such as incest," "homosexuality," or "daddy-mommy."

The Byronic figurative experience in question is, however, the situation of the reader adrift in the signifying materiality of Byron's text. To follow the Byronic drift is to uncover a "drive-structure" [Triebstruktur] that explicates romanticism's enthusiasm for empire, while also explicating—the drive is, after all, fundamentally ambivalent—resistance to imperialism. To resist empire is also a death drive, since id amounts, I argue, to an embrace of the being-put-to-death that makes writing mean beyond the imperial intent of the scriptor (George Gordon Byron).

Death is not a soft name for M(Other) Oedipus. The Thanatotic dramatrauma has been theatrically over-inflated into irrelevance. To die, simply means, as Derrida noted long ago, to commit oneself, always already, to writing.

Lastly, empire is not a moralistic term of condemnation (except insofar as this moral book-keeping or "culture of culpability" is explicitly inscribed by Byron's articulation of a Protestant guilt-complex), but the concrete condition—sine qua non—of Byron's ambivalent desire for the name globally distributed by Fame, a canonization that is required if the resistant encryptions are to be given a chance to get beyond, exceed or outwit the stereotypes Fame rests on.

To resist empire is to resist the social field of communication—an "imaginary community" of print capitalism gone deliriously global—that infrastructures the theatrical staging of one's life-writing, a staging of self that is resisted by the writing's interminable drive-structure and not by the life (1788-1824).

A psychoanalytic mode of bio-graphic reading enacts, in other words, the death of the biographical subject—that ubiquitous hidden mover of literary formalism, criticism and historicism—and the after-Barthes of the reader as the writerly explicator of a not-quite global historical situation, a not-quiteness that remains, nevertheless, the lived experience of globalization.

Incipit Lord Byron as a "fantasy or protonarrative structure," "as the vehicle for our experience of the real," or, as far as the fantasmic figure (in contradistinction to the historical) Lord Byron is concerned, for our figurative experience of "emergent globalization." How, then, to situate his Lordship's death-by-writing in relation to the material mise-en-mot of the public/private aporia within which Byron finds, or, rather, fails to find, himself? Two key words adrift in Christensen are "virtue" and "invention." Invention translates the Greek term heurein (to find out or discover), a term used by Aristotle's Rhetoric to describe the deployment of topoi—the content and form of rhetorical invention—in the construction of arguments. Latin rhetoricians translated heurein as invenire.

Cicero's youthful work on rhetoric was entitled De inventione. A persuasive inventiveness depends, according to Latin rhetorical theory, on an indeterminate, innate quality (natural disposition, taste, genius, capacity, or inclination, in sum, strength) called ingenium. The figure of Cicero serves, in turn, to save rhetoric from the charge of sophistry that has always accompanied it, for he spoke out in the name of the Republic, and died trying to save it from the Imperial ambitions of the dictatorial Second Triumvirate.

The 18th-Century ideal of civic humanism set itself up against the automatic machinations of commercial society reified by political economy. The ideal raged against the splenetic machine by attempting to reincarnate the rhetorical virtue of right speaking in the name of a moralized political praxis that was already anachronistic in relation to the reign of Old Corruption and the ministerial cabalism typified by Walpole.

Yet the connection between rhetoric and a hygienic moralization of politics continued to be taught in the schools (as opposed to dissenting, provincial and peripheral schools defined by a more practical pedagogy of rhetoric).

Lord Byron, destined by his newly discovered title to serve in the upper house of Parliament, imbibed this potent mixture at Harrow, where he declared his dream to become "a Parliamentary orator." Byron's desire for a public rhetoric impelled him to claim his seat in the House of Lords before embarking on his pilgrimage to Iberia, Greece, Albania and the Ottoman Empire—a voyage in excess of the eurocentric Grand Tour detailed in the subject of my geopsychanalysis: Childe Harold's Pilgrimage, Cantos I and II.

Yet his claim to his seat in the House of Lords and to his right to be called the sixth Lord Byron was problematic. Earl Carlile, his patron, refused to guarantee the young Lord's paternity, and an embarrassing delving into the archives ensued.

This refusal is significant, for it caused a split between Byron and his most valued confidante-cum-epistolary addressee, his half-sister Augusta, who was on close terms with the Earl. As a result, Byron did not write to her during his continental excursion.

The letters Byron writes during this excursion and during his rewriting of this life-writing (i.e., Childe Harold) can therefore be regarded as the active encryption of his relation to the figure of the incestuous ingenue. Variations on the name Augusta fill in the repressed blanks in Byron's writing, not because she is the centric reference, but because his pained awareness of her absence makes her name into a cryptic articulation for Byron's unconscious inscription of the private/public aporia.

The importance of Augusta Byron Leigh to Byron's life is in inverse proportion to the amount of effort expended in destroying incriminating evidence. It is thought that they commenced an incestuous affair in 1813. Byron's sexuality was, however, already highly unusual, for he had fallen in love with a little Scotch girl named Mary Duff when he was not quite eight, "and yet my misery, my love for that girl were so violent that I sometimes doubt if I have ever really been attached since."

Since this journal entry saved from the flames was written in 1813, the encryption of incest with Augusta is evidently yet another repetition of an idealized asexual or pre-pubescent relation to Mary.

Things became even more traumatic for Byron, as he was all but certainly sexually abused in his ninth year by a servant named May Grey. He soon fell head over heels in love with two of his cousins, the first named Margaret Parker and the second Mary Chaworth. The latter was a descendent of Mr. Chaworth, a relative infamously killed in a shady duel with the "Wicked Lord," the fifth Lord Byron, thereby disgracing the name Byron was so eager to assume.

Byron's attachment to Mary Chaworth was virulent, for he was crushed by her subsequent marriage, a "violent" affect he repeated in a finer tone when he was "thrown into convulsions" on finding out "Mary Duffwas married".

It is therefore a little too self-evident that he was driven to cathect or invest (besetzen) his cousin ('s name) by a desire to efface the stain from his title: "But one sad losel soils a name for aye, / However mighty in the olden time, / Nor all that heralds rake from coffin'd clay / Nor florid prose, nor honied lies of rhyme / Can blazon evil deeds, or consecrate a crime" (Childe Harold I.23-27).

Byron's figuration of the love-relation (and the name that encrypts it) as a purgative for "bad" genealogical blood is consequently repeated in his desire for an innocent (or non-noxious) relation to his wife-to-be, as a letter to Augusta after his return from the East attests: "Well, I must marry to repair the ravages of myself & prodigal ancestry"

(August 30, 1811). The names of Byron's jejune amours, as well as the name of the traumatic figure who sexually abused him, all begin with M, thereby encrypting the M(other) Byron came to hate, as is expressed by letters he wrote to Augusta before their split: "Mrs. Byron I have shaken off for two years, and I shall not resume her yoke in future... I never can forgive that woman, or breathe in comfort under the same roof" (November 30, 1808; BLJ I.179).

The pained rapport to the mother is not, however, an Oedipal stereotype, for what Byron fears in relation to his "accursed progenitor" is his becoming a repetition of his father. Captain Byron had married Catherine Gordon for her money. He profligately exhausted it, thereby repeating what he had done to his first wife.

Byron, in other words, fears reincarnating the Wicked Lord, his paternal grandfather's brother—the pere-version/ version of the father or Lord Byron (v) he ambivalently wants to be—yet this reincarnation would repeat the shameful behaviour of his false, biological or biographical father, "false" because he lacks the patronym Lord Byron bears in his absence. Fortunately, the poet's grandfather, Vice-Admiral Byron—who circumnavigated the world in 1764—provides an alternative identification, another sovereign figuration of the nation, a deterritorializing wandertrieb.

Byron's mother also incited his ire by her flattering attention to Lord Grey, a bon vivant who repeated (literally!) the trauma marked "May Grey" by making homosexual advances toward the resistant young Lord. His mother's wish that Byron be reconciled with Grey therefore placed her on the side of the sexual abuse encrypted by the "M" that made young George Gordon suffer before—and this is crucial—he received the Byronic appellation of a minor Lord.

The literal overdetermination of the maternal figure—once supplemented by Byron's fear that he would abuse any prospective wife as his father (a false embodiment of the abusio, catachresis or not-quite "name of the father" embodied by the Wicked Lord) had abused his mother—creates a salt, estranging sea between Catherine Gordon [Byron] of Gight and her son:

But she flies into a fit of phrenzy upbraids me as if I was the most undutiful wretch in existence, rakes up the ashes of my father, abuses him, says I shall be a true Byrrone. Which is the worst epithet she can invent? Am I to call this woman mother? Byron's melancholy situation is evident on the level of the letter. M. and G. encrypt abuse (May Grey/Grey, Gordon/Gight), an abuse unconsciously associated with being G. G. or a George Gordon who suffered abduction by the Greys.

Leslie Marchand thinks it likely that the abuse began in 1797—that is, in the interim between being a young Lord-in-waiting (1794) and becoming a minor Lord-to-be (1798). Byron's limbo state of being between names—not only George Gordon Byron, or at least not for long, yet not yet Lord Byron—can speculatively be linked to the "malaise" and "motor uncoordination" that prevents the child from walking—that is, from mimicking the figure he momentarily recognizes in the mirror image that reflects the upright stature of the adult he wants to be.

The child fills flat on his face and will spend, according to Lacan, the rest of his life failing to identify with the mirror image, or with what Geoffrey Hartman's eloquent analysis of "the adventure" of "having been named" [Sartre on Genet] refers to as the "imago du nom propre" [imago of the proper name/noun/no-of-the-father].

Lacan, with typical melodrama, identifies this pseudo-tragic situation with the "veritable specific prematurity of birth". One need not, however, accept the authority of a psychoanalytic voice that speaks from on high, for Freudian psychoanalysis, as Harold Bloom has noted, is decisively indebted to romanticism in particular, and the literary canon (i.e., Shakespeare) in general.

A more apt formulation, tailored to the circumstances I am dealing with here, is to suggest that Byron is forever prematurely born, inadequate and untimely rapt, or—dare I say it—lame, in relation to the aristocratic patronym he wants to be, a sense of Being he conflates with becoming a metonym for sovereignty or "The grand Napoleon of the realms of rhyme" he will make himself out to be (Don Juan XI.440).

To be the king once and for all, however, one must be dead: no longer longing to coincide with the "posthumous existence" promised by posterity, and no longer desiring to "assume" a "kingless sphere" of one's own in "the abode where the Eternals are" canonized for Love.

George Gordon wants to be the Wicked Lord, to incarnate the burden of the name—"the wicked George Ld. B."—even if this is impossible due to the paradox exemplified by the King's two Bodies.

He gets the chance to fail in this quest, after all, thanks to the fact that the "proper" heir, the Wicked Lord's grandson, was killed by a cannonball while participating in the geopolitical wrangling of the British Empire in Corsica.

Lord George Byron Is Dead, Long Live Lord George [Anson] Byron. Byron's desire to be Byron is a mad desire, a desire that drives one mad, since to incarnate (I use this word to call attention to the Christology underwriting both European theories of kingship and the proper logic of the name) Lord Byron is to do so all-too-literally, to be besmeared with "blood's unbleaching stain," or, if choice were involved here, an Imperialistic slaughter of the innocents.

History, for the hungry post-Volney generations, ruins empires: "We can all feel, or imagine, the regret with which the ruins of cities, once the capitals of empires, are beheld; the reflections suggested by such objects are too trite to require recapitulation". History has "but one page [...] in one red burial blent!" Byron's desire for the non-noxious figure of a Marian ingenue conceived without stain (neither placenta, nor menses, nor bloodied hymen) is a desire for what will overcome all the "evil deeds" and "crime[s]" that soil his "blazon".

And things get worse, for his desire will become, once it is actualized by his relationship to Augusta, socially stigmatized as incestuous. The stigmata of impropriety can only increase the bloodstain that was supposed to be bleached clean. Byron thereby effectuates a double bind that cannot be walked out on, a complex that cannot be worked through.

Byron, in the meanwhile, having nowhere to go, flees, like Harold, "Albion's isle" (I.10), even as he is drawn back to his preferential figuration of desire—an encrypted name for the incestuous ingenu:

Had sigh'd to many though he lov'd but one, And that lov'd one, alas! could ne'er be his. Ah, happy she! to 'scape from him whose kiss Had been pollution unto aug[-usta]ht so chaste; Who soon had left her charms for vulgar bliss, And spoil'd her goodly lands to gild his waste, Nor calm domestic peace had ever deign'd to taste. (I.39-45; my emphasis)

The allusion to wasting "her goodly lands to gild his waste" refers to his fear of becoming the Wicked Lord he wants to be. The "one" is not, of course, Augusta per se. "[A]ug[usta]" is a cryptonym for Byron's doubly bound desire for "peace"—that is, for the perfectly encrypted signifying fragment (a piece or a textualized partial or part-object: object a in Lacan's vocabulary) that promises to free him from his "prodigal ancestry," while perpetually setting him adrift in a fragmentary flow of signifying fragments: "aug" "ht" "usta" "ht" "h'd" "v'd" "l'd" "n'd."...

Byron's desire for the ingenue fantasm—his desire, on the level of the letter, for a desire elusively encrypted from social stigmatization—is evident in his dedication of the poem "To Ianthe" to the eleven-year old daughter of Lady Oxford—a woman Byron had a liaison with in 1812-1814 (thereby recirculating in the real, via displacement, his desire for the incestuous ingenue that he was simultaneously enjoying via Augusta) —and in his falling in chaste love with Teresa Macri, the twelve-year old daughter of the woman who ran the pensione where he stayed in Athens (famously fetishized as the "Maid of Athens," and as "To Inez" in Childe Harold) (B II.6-8, 39-40).

Inez, Ianthe, Ingenue, I I I: "abstract selfness in extremis is that grinding of the teeth which says nothing but I I I." Or, as Hegel's Unhappy Consciousness cries out from the depths, "death is the painful feeling... the return of consciousness into the depths of night in which `I' = `I,' a night which no longer distinguishes or knows anything outside of it."

The desire not to fall out of a perfectly transparent (I = I) encryption—a mirror stage where the letters add up to each other, but where their meaning is illegible to the public gaze—is what the drive for a concealed crypt or burial place can never accomplish.

This ideal crypt serves as a regulatory principle of literary desire, an Idealich, "ideal ego" or fantasy "I" that can only be accessed by anticipating Death as the entryway into this unencumbered scene of encryption-recognition.

Death figures a perfected self-relation since the contingency of my embodied being-in-time will no longer be there to impede the letters from continuing to mean—that is, from resisting the imposition of a stereotypical meaning: a futural resistance that demands that the poet die into a life beyond his Days of Fame.

The prospect of putting oneself to death or, less melodramatically, of literally dying, remains, for obvious reasons, a "painful feeling." Death and all it implies—commodification, canonization, criticism—remains, however, the ultimate court of appeal or the public place (topos) "from where" the poet imagines an other looking—and recognizing in his place—what his fantasmic machinery of "I I I" means.

The historical differential between Hegel and Adorno is marked by Freud, the death-rattle (Ich) stuck in the throat of the ego: an unconscious death drive for an egotistical sublime. Death, another name for Fame, becomes Byron's elegant solution to his shipwreck in a sea of shame, yet commodified fame is only another name for an alienated "Ich = Ich."

Or, as Adorno writes, "Authenticity is death... an Ur-image of defiance in self-abnegation" (tres Byrronne, n'est pas?), while also being death in another sense: "Insofar as death is absolutely alien to the subject, it is the model of all reification. Only ideology praises it as the cure for exchange":

But all unconscious of the coming doom, The feast, the song, the revel here abounds; Strange modes of merriment the hours consume. (Childe Harold's Pilgrimage I.486-88) SIN LESS SIN [To Be Endlessly Inventive... Elsewhere]

If I stopped here I would be reiterating the "metaphorical secret" that deforms the study of Byron into old swell-foot the tyrant. A way out of this double bind is the encrypted intersection between: 1) the desire for the ingenue (figured by the Virgin Mother trope so prevalent in the alleys and art galleries of Italy and Southern Europe, and so encrypted via denial ["Popery!"] and/or denegation ["beautiful but..."]

By Protestants who protest too much against the Catholic aesthetic they continue to frequent), as well as for the ingenue figures of Richardson and Sade (Byron was a reader of Justine [M 211], and the Marquis loved Richardson); 2) the desire for ingenium or rhetorical inventiveness; 3) the desire to be a Lord Byron who is not a Wicked Lord: "Mad, bad and dangerous to know" as Lady Caroline Lamb famously stereotyped it.

The third situation—Byron's desire to be in-noxious—is represented by the figure the young Lord cuts in Albania when he complains of the homosexual advances of a powerful Pasha—yet another repetition of the abusive persecutions perpetuated by his fantasmic parental couple May Grey and Lord Grey—by rhetorically dressing himself up as an "`ingenuous youth'" (Letter to Hobhouse, August 16, 1810; BLJ II.10).

Byronic invention is a following of one's inclination overdriven by a Falstaffian wish-fulfillment to be innocent of the social trans(ag)gression vehiculated by an excessive speech: "'tis no sin for a man to labour in his vocation." To invent in flight from the fantasm of a traumatic, evil, sinful or wicked past.

The root meaning of "ingenuous" in the Roman history Byron read extensively deepens the problematic, for it means born of noble and free parents. "Ingenuous" also means, according to the OED once again, "frank, open, guileless, straightforward, candid, artless, innocent." To be inventive is to be the untainted Lord Byron wants to be, to possess the fluid sprezzatura that seems not to be a style: Sin less sin.

Yet to be endlessly inventive is also to deterritorialize, for the topics of invention central to the rhetorical pedagogy that informed Byron's education refer to topoi—that is, to places.

Travelling places Byron in places that spur his invention ever onwards and keep him one step ahead of the trauma he is fleeing: "Pass we the long, unvarying course, the track / Oft trod, that never leaves a trace behind" (Childe Harold, II.244-45). Yes, to abandon the past, a past that will write no wrinkle in the vicarious literary body of the Childe Byron labors to beget without sin:

'Tis to create, and in creating live A being more intense, that we endow With form our fancy, gaining as we give The life we image, even as I do now. What am I? Nothing; but not so art thou, Soul of my thought! with whom I traverse earth, Invisible but gazing... (III.46-52; my emphasis)

Byron's "Muse," a key figuration of invention, "despises," as Don Juan reemphasizes, "reference," and desires, like Harold, initially called Childe Burun, an ancient version of Byron, to flee the traumatic public/private past encoded by his entitled name:

"Onward he flies, nor fix'd as yet the goal / Where he shall rest him on his pilgrimage; / And o'er him many changing scenes must roll / Ere toil his thirst for travel can assuage, / Or he shall calm his breast, or learn experience sage" (XIV.430; Childe Harold I.328-31). The problem, however, is that the further one flies, the more one is condemned to return: Thus bending o'er the vessel's laving side, To gaze on Dian's wave-reflected sphere; The soul forgets her schemes of Hope and Pride, And flies unconscious o'er each backward year. None are so desolate but something dear, Dearer than self, possesses or possess'd A thought, and claims the homage of a tear; A flashing pang! of which the weary breast Would still, albeit in vain, the heavy heart divest (Childe Harold II.208-16; my emphasis)

"Scheme" is a rhetorical term for the form, figure or arrangement of words, hence to forget the "schemes" of rhetoric is to fall away from "Hope and Pride" or the belief that one can continually re-invent oneself via the tropic tropes instanced by geographical topics of invention.

To forget rhetoric is to return, as is inevitable, to the traumatic past one is fleeing, to the incestuous figurations of desire that re-inscribe one in this past: "And flies unconscious o'er each backward year." The scriptor continues to feel the "painful feeling" of the repressed, for the letter cannot coincide with the vicarious spirit it rhetorically inflates, as it is famed to do, deceiving self.

Byron's "fancy" begets himself in the "form" of a "being more intense," yet the birth of the Childe remains premature despite the distance he has traversed. The poet remains adrift "'twixt life and death". Byron subsists on what Antonin Artaud called L'Ombilic des Limbes, the state of not yet being dead, yet continuing to write one's canonical death, and—somehow—living in it, yet not yet living the "life we image" with no strings attached:

"Invisible but gazing, as I glow / Mix'd with thy spirit, blended with thy birth, / And feeling still with thee in my crush'd feeling's dearth". The young Lord's feelings remain crushed, repressed and buried under painful feelings feelingly painted for the benefit of fame's immortal futurity: another name for death's sunless sun.

He can only feel these affects vicariously, "as second order signs of the presence of a poetical discourse," a crypto-quarry of words, words, words: "If his art is folly and madness, it is folly and madness at second hand." High irony this, the fiction that promised escape from "my crush'd feeling's dearth," becomes this Life-in-Death, a "dea[r]th" of sense, sentiment and sensibility overburdened by superfluous letters that remain the only place [topos] where the "I" can continue to find a semblance of the "Soul of my thought"—that is, a life catalogued in the Library at the End of Time.

All would be well if rhetorical spontaneity or ingenium could divest the heavy heart of its secret—that is, if Childe Byron could incarnate the "ingenuous youth"—"open," "artless," etc.—he wants to be:

Yet oft-times in his maddest mirthful mood Strange pangs would flash along Childe Harold's brow, As if the memory of some deadly feud, Or disappointed passion lurk'd below: But this none knew, nor haply car'd to know; For his was not that open, artless soul That feels relief by bidding sorrow flow, Nor sought he friend to counsel or condole, Whate'er his grief mote be, which he could not control (I.64-72; my emphasis)

On the other hand, the problem may not lie in the Childe's inability to coincide with himself, but in the absence of his estranged confidante Augusta: "A sister whom he lov'd, but saw her not / Before his weary pilgrimage begun" (I.84-85). Byron writes Childe Harold for what she means to him, both consciously and unconsciously, for the ingenue figure he wants and wants to be, respectively, yet the ingenium only assumes material form in the stuttering, metonymic matter of the signifier: "aug" "ht" "usta" "ht."

Augusta's name not only encrypts a desire for the Idealich Byron wants (to be), but, as will be detailed in the third section of this essay, an abysmal relation to empire that deterritorializes the "I" that organizes the figurative experience of reading in terms of the biographical subject.

The secret makes the text and Byron go by remaining in abeyance: "I never will live in England if I can avoid it, why must remain a secret, but the farther I proceed the less I regret leaving it". And so it remains, even as the encryptions, etymologies and inventions endlessly accumulate: "He goes back, weary of the creation he has piled up to hide him from himself, an old dog licking an old sore."Before he left the English territory he was fond of calling this "`tight little island'" (M 100),

Byron had not only seized his political seat or topos for oratorical invention in the style of civic humanism (sedes or seat was occasionally used in Latin rhetorical theory in place of the word loci, the usual translation for topoi), but had cut a figure in the publishing world with his English Bards and Scotch Reviewers (1809), an offensive attack against the reviewers who had castigated his first book of poems published in "the public eye," Hours of Idleness (1807).

Since Byron desired to remain uncorrupted by the interests of either political party, he attacked both Tory and Whig reviewers (as well as Earl Carlile, thereby estranging himself from his sister in the social register) in "this miserable record of misplaced anger and indiscriminate acrimony" (as he reframed it in 1816), a "record" he had once regarded as his coming into his majority or, according to his Imperialistic 1809 "PREFACE," as his crossing of "`the Rubicon'".

The "Second Edition" of this satire, no longer anonymous, stresses that Byron leaves England to assert his literary authority: "The noble author had left this country previous to the publication of that Edition". The significance of this strategic maneuver is emphasized by his paean to Parnassus, "the Muses' seat [sedes]" in Canto One, and to the enabling and ennobling afflatus this classical geographical topos provides:

"Happier in this than mightiest bards have been, / Whose fate to distant homes confin'd their lot". Byron employs his privileged economic class- position (appropriately mystified as the happy fall of an antique Moira or "fate") to assert his rightful place in the print market, yet all is not as seamless as it seems: "And now I view thee, 'tis, alas! with shame".

Byron began Canto One burdened by the same shame: "Oh, thou! in Hellas deem'd ofheav'nly birth". The text opens with a familiar topographic trope—alienation from the geographical source, a resource that remains, as Byron's travels made him intimately aware, unassimilable, alien or estranged:

"Muse! form'd or fabled at the minstrel's will! / Since sham'd full oft by later lyres on earth, / Mine ["this lowly lay of mine"] dares not call thee from thy sacred hill" (I.1-4, 9).

The Byronic Muse's Grecian hill is, as is suggested by anatomy lessons (mons pubis, labia pudendi, pudere: to be ashamed), the Latin nomenclature for hill (mons), or Spenser's Garden of Adonis ("Right in the middest of that Paradise, There stood a stately Mount...", a "fair Mount!" adds Childe Byron, for he was reading Spenser's The Faerie Queene during his travels), a feminine figuration of the innate virtue (ingenuitas: ingenuity) Byron desires to be (Childe Harold I.648).

Instead, he can only write his claim to this foreign topos, a claim he accesses by writing—and being-written by—auto-encrypting topics of psychic invention that deterritorialize a hermeneutics of the self and the mastery implied by a knowing self-encryption.

Ingenuitas encrypts a resistance to Byron's desire to be elsewhere, for it also signifies native or not of foreign birth. There is, then, an acute contradiction between the native inventiveness the English Bard wants to assert as a member of the landed nobility grounded in English soil and his dependence on a foreign topos to gain the authority safeguarded by an other territory.

This strong contradiction is inscribed in the title of the self-authorizing satire, since the Bard in English Bards marks a resistant and repressed Scotch/Celtic periphery outside the English pale, thereby renewing the incongruity between the "Lordly I" of the English Bard and his Scottish maternal blood (yet another soilure accruing to a hybrid identity he ambivalently resists). Byron's shamelessly innocent invention solves these contradictions by a deft step to the side.

He endlessly, ingeniously and ingenuously re-invents the history of his case, yet he cannot come to be, if the reader can forgive a bit of derridiana, l'ingenu(e) queje suis ["The fe/male ingenue that I follow/that I am"], for it is an infinitely contradictory libidinal complex he has construed out of his desire to be an "enfant terrible"—that is, to fall away from a rhetoric of posterity, a ruse of reference or a theatrical appurtenance to a socially defined stance (in-fans = speech-less), while remaining, nonetheless, an innately innocent writer of an invasive, socially transgressive speech:

You know, or don't know, that great Bacon saith, 'Fling up a straw, 'twill show the way the wind blows;' And such a straw, borne on by human breath, Is Poesy, according as the mind glows; A paper kite, which flies 'twixt life and death, A shadow which the onward soul behind throws: And mine's a bubble not blown up for praise, But just to play with, as an infant plays. Don Juan Muet muet entre les ronds Sylphe dans la pourpre d'empire Mallarme.

Byron's side-step is not as successful when he steps beyond his contradictory Anglo-Scottish I-land, for he remains overdetermined by the global reach of British Imperialism. His transcription of his Iberian tour evinces a decided hatred for the British Empire's ignoble efforts to outfox its Napoleonic double. Hate for his own country is, as the epigraph to Childe Harold, Canto One and Two (from the French text "LE cosmopolite") insists, the affect that drove him to deterritorialize: "I hated my country" so as to be "reconciled with her".

Byron reaffirms his belief in native virtue in Canto One by celebrating "this the Spanish Maid," or the Maid of Zaragoza, a heroine who replaced her slain menfolk at the cannons during the Napoleonic wars, yet he omits any mention of her popular name, "Augustina," thereby avoiding another encrypted figuration of the incestuous ingenue. "August-in-a" also encrypts a desire to see England in-nocent of the bloodstains of Empire, for "yon eng-in-e's roar" is an etymological cryptonym of the "distorted" inventive power that drives the Imperial art of war: an English perversion of in-genium Byron despises.

Western Europe is already a lost cause for Byron. He looks, instead, to Greece, once he has transplanted Spanish warrior women into a Grecian landscape: "Yet are Spain's maids no race of Amazons.... Ah! that to these were given such peaceful shades / As Greece can still bestow, though Glory fly her glades" (I.585; 655-57). The last phrase indicates that Greece—the mythic birthplace of Western Liberty—is suffering under empire, in this case, Ottoman. Byron is relatively free of ethnocentrism in his take on an Ottoman Empire of relative toleration.

He reserves all his hate for England's betrayal of the Greek territory that rhetorically originated—via a retroactive rhetoric of origins—the ideal of civic humanism the English fail to propagate (i.e., the notes to ChiNe Harold populate the Classical Greek past with "the struggles of orators"; B II.189).

Byron condemns the political contest between France, Russia and England vis-a-vis the Sublime Porte as a policy that hangs the Greeks out to dry, and unrealistically proposes that the Greeks save themselves: "know ye not / Who would be free themselves must strike the blow?"

Byron's notes are, however, less grandiloquent. The note-form, as Nigel Leask has argued, marks literature as a proto-anthropological simulation of objective knowledge. The notes are another determinant of Byron's runaway success, for his text allowed infantile desire unlimited "play," while also simulating, like Beckford's Vathek, hard factual knowledge:

The Greeks will never be independent; they will never be sovereigns as heretofore, and God forbid they ever should! but they may be subjects with-out being slaves. Our colonies are not independent, but they are free and industrious, and such may Greece be hereafter.... To talk, as the Greeks themselves do, of their rising again to their pristine superiority, would be ridiculous... but there seems to be no very great obstacle, except in the apathy of the Franks [i.e.: Western European powers], to their becoming a useful dependency, or even a free state with a proper guarantee.

Byron reiterates the Imperial sublime I am fond of calling bene-violence: the subjugation of others to a liberty of one's own devising. The oxymoronic mystique of Imperial benev(i)olence violently re-inserts the "I" in "benevolence." It exposes an ego, "I" or Ich subjected to an aggressive drive (Bemachtigungstreib, a drive for emprise, power, possession, or the violent exercise thereof—Bewaltigung—in Freud, "the pleasure of knowing and dominating with jouissance" in Lacan), a drive to exert power over the chaos that I am, a drive that projects this violence outwards in order to assure his Imperial Majesty the Ego of my integrity.

This Bemachtigungstreib ensures that both the English Island (a misnomer thanks to the Scottish alterity encysted within Byron's "Islandish" Britain) and the British "Impire" (to re-cite John Dee) remain, in spite of rampant deterritorialization, an integral, insula-ted, isola-ted (fortified, for instance, for the circulatory virulence of colonial disease) ego or "Iland," as an archaic spelling (King James Bible, Milton, Donne, etc.) still circulating in the romantic era inscribes it. I-LAND elegantly encrypts what is at stake here: A desire to territorialize or ground the fragmentary ego or "I" in the imaginary, ideological and Imperial "unity" of Englished British Isles.

The de-sublimated corruption of English politics voids civic humanism of a fighting chance on its own ground. Byron's political idealism is thereby driven to make the 'source' of this civil ideology mirror it back in order to compensate for what is lacking at home:

What wonder that we esteem heroism grand, when, in order to imagine it, we suppose a mighty conqueror, in opposition to the most formidable dangers, acquiring power over multitudes of nations, subjecting [my emphasis] to his dominion wide extended countries, and purchasing renown, which reaches to the extremities of the word, and shall continue through all the ages of futurity? What can be more truly great than the object of that benevolence, which, unconfined by the narrow limits of vicinity or relation, comprehends multitudes, grasps whole large societies and even extends from pole to pole?

Yet Byron continues to believe he is not being a sloganeer for Empire, for his notes castigate ideologues who oppose British support of the Grecian cause by accusing them of the "distorted" inventiveness he associates with the bloody engines of Imperialism: "One very ingenious person... another, no less ingenious" (B II.203).

His opposition to British Imperialism emerges in his rants against the Scottish Lord Elgin, whose artistic rape of Greece repeats, for Byron, the English apathy that violates the Greeks by not helping them free themselves from the Ottoman Empire.

Yet the vessel that Byron—born and bred, up to a point, in Scotland—returned to England on carried marbles pilfered by Elgin, his co-nationalist in the hybrid Anglo-Scottish sense his Lordship is at pains to deny.

Byron refuses to confront his immersion in an imperium pelagi, despite his reliance on this Empire of the Sea for his self-ennobling deterri-torialization. I will offer a semblance of closure by offering an analysis of how Byron manages to keep his conscience so clean.

My seemingly moralistic way of addressing the problem named Byron is, as I previously mentioned, an attempt to engage Byron's self-inscription in a public marketplace rhythmed by a "culture of culpability."

Historicism, old and new, has negatively or positively reiterated this moralistic culture that, in turn, reestablishes the critical fiction of the biographical subject. I am, instead, tracing the emergence of this subject and the resistances this figure suffers at the hands of the text endlessly invented by an encrypted drift that is inseparable from the act of reading that re-institutes the invention named Byron.

How, then, does Byron construct, in the moralistic account-keeping form of a "conscience," a configuration that compensates for the lack of political agency at home, while also serving as a defense-formation against being immersed in an unidealizable imperialism or a sea of deterritorialized spatial relations that is isomorphic with the unconscious drift of letters traced by this essay?

He inserts himself, as canonical readings have shown, into the "figure of Byron the Pilgrim of Eternity"—as Childe Harold, writer and author, were canonized, for example, by Shelley's Adonais—"who does not show his agony but whose sense of radical sin is suffocating."

The extensive distribution by print capitalism, over the course of the 18th-century, of sentimental transcriptions of "radical sin" drives Byron into a desire to rise above his guilt-ridden immersion in unmasterable letters by arresting the encrypted fetish these letters leave behind, a desire for fixity that is consequently repeated by the reader his desire has interpellated into existence.

Byron's resistance to his writing is legible in his invocation of Muse Athena at the opening of Canto Two: "Ancient of days! august Athena!". Athena is Goddess of both Wisdom and War, or, "of Wisdom and of Wit," where wit conflates, due to the nostalgia for "[t]he warrior's weapon and the sophist's stole," rhetoric and martial virtue, inventive strength and moralized political action.

Athena is said to embody the "beautiful" or beneviolent "idealisms" of civic humanism, or, another way of saying the same thing, the Athens invented by Byron's epideictical rhetoric in the notes:

This theatre of contentions between mighty factions, of the straggles of orators, the exultation and deposition of tyrants, the triumph and punishment of generals, is now become a scene of petty intrigue and perpetual disturbance, between the bickering agents of certain British nobility and gentry (B II.189; my emphasis)

Byron, by figuring his beloved Athens as "august Athena!" invests Athena—traditionally said to be chaste, if not almost wholly masculine—as his ingenue figuration of desire.

She could therefore be called a homosexual figure of desire, since the ego desires reassurance of its phallic self-sameness or maleness: "I" = "I." This hermaphroditic fantasm is, in any case, an interior paramour Byron will soon sexually realize with his half-sister—the lost half of his ego—on his return to England. By calling Athena August, our lordly writer reinscribes the Graeco-Iberian ideal of martial virtue he encrypted as .

"Augustina," while redeploying the inventive authority of the Grecian Muse in order to reaffirm his faith in a native English politics encrypted by Augusta, another name for London: a post-Interregnum name for the Imperial Centre in the Roman tradition of Augustus—sacred, grand, the name adopted by the first Roman emperor Octavian—a name associated with a Golden Age of English literature founded on an Imperial Order, and variously identified, as reference to the OED entry for "Augustan" notes, with the Caroline Restoration and the Reign of Anne. London, endo-colonizing centre of the British Isles, is encrypted as the Augustan Rome of a beneviolent empire: these fragmented I-lands I have shored against my ruins.

This detour through the other (Greece, Rome and Spain) is necessary, since English civic humanism was always disturbed by the lack of an aristocratic virtue that was not to be found on the battlefield, let alone in party factionalism, a lack of theatrically affirmed political agency that could only appear more obvious in contrast to a bellicose classical ideal of rhetorical virtue:

"[t]he warrior's weapon and the sophist's stole." The progressively rationalized business of war during the Napoleonic period—a flagrant consummation of the "sacrificial logic" of Imperialism—deprived civic humanism of the august association between war, virtue and rhetoric.

Byron's adherence to this lost cause led, of course, to his death in the struggle for Greek Liberty. Byron also strives to re-idealize Albion's Empire in Childe Harold, for he encrypts British Imperialism in his encomium to "Land of Albania! [Alb] let me [i] bend mine eyes / On thee, thou rugged nurse of savage men!" (II.338-39; my emphasis).

Albionia functions, like Pallas Athena or the warlike man-woman Augustina, as a cryptogram for native English virtu (Vir = Man), tried and true, and ingenuously innocent of the blood this war engine sheds in the name of Liberty: "Goddess of Wisdom!... Ancient of days! august Athena! where, / Where are thy ["savage" adds "Albania"] men of might?" (II.3, 10-11).

Byron sought, on his return to this "tight little island," to incarnate his highly singular and/or monotonously Imperial republicanism by speaking out against a proposed death-sentence for the crime of frame-breaking in the House of Lords. Yet he felt his speech—which he wrote down and memorized as in his school days so as to counter his fear that "he might," as Marchand writes, "not be able to control his feelings"—to be "'perhaps a little theatrical'" (quoted in M 114). Byron's attempt to replicate the civic ideal of Athens—"This theatre of contentions between mighty... orators" (B II.189)—failed to satisfy because he repressed the ingenium that remains his writerly strength: an uncontrollable flux of affect-laden letters.

The writer had given away, at this time, the copyright to Childe Harold to assure himself of his noble transcendence of the print market, but his disgust with the unsublime interestedness of political rhetoric—partisan, as opposed to "Patrician"—drove him back into the business of writing that he had wanted to keep subservient to his in-rant dream of becoming a statesman or orator—that is, of theatrically incarnating a synthetic state of union: a territorial transplant of "[t]he warrior's weapon and the sophist's stole" retroactively (dis)placed in Greece. "Strong" contradictions abound, proliferate, drift.

Byron soon awoke to find himself famous for Childe Harold. He abandoned all pretense to an aristocratic disdain for inky blots, and bargained for the highest price like any other producer of parchment bonds for public credit, consumption and coin.

He may have been born for Empire, but he is bound to writing—that is, to the struggle to conceive himself. Extra letters continue to extradite him from his Immaculate parthenogenetic fantasy of being a self-begetting Virgin Athena (parthenos, virgin). He is "borne on by human breath"—the far-flung distribution of his publicly circulated letters—"borne darkly, fearfully, afar". And so, B., in reaction to this situation, a reaction that re-enacts the deterritorialization encoded by t[r]opics of invention, writes, encrypts, drifts.

Byron's investment of the ingenue figure, given flesh and form by his incestuous sexual relation to Augusta—Virgin Mother of an Augustan Empire (ingignere, the root of ingenuus—Latin root of "ingenuous"—also means to beget, implant, engender, while augustus encrypts augere, to increase, and "august" englishes, according to the OED, as this proliferant verb) was, I posit, what allowed him to keep his conscience innocent—that is, to find a fetishized resting place amid wild and whirling words.

To wit, the first letter of reconciliation—dated August 18, 1811, as if to prove that the superficial confluence of coincidental letters is far from innocuous—"I hear you have been increasing [i.e., augusting] his Majesty's Subjects, which in these times of War & tribulation is really patriotic....

I think we have latterly had a redundance of these national benefits, & therefore I give you all credit for your matronly behaviour" (BLJ II.74). Is "Ld. B." being ironic, a theatrical pose that would absolve him and his reader from a redundant adherence to the Imperial distribution of his name? mm``

Perhaps, yet irony requires a solid spirit without which the letters would carry the scriptor off into madness, a word-less madness that is figured by the trace-less sea ambivalently invoked by Childe Harold's text as a salve for a debilitating realization: the sheer ruin of "empires, changed in all save thee—" that accumulate along "[t]hy shores...

Assyria, Greece, Rome, Carthage, what are they?" (IV.1630-31). To be free of the British Empire's frailty—which means, in this case, the concomitant frailty of the published figurations Byron relies on to resist public disfigurement—is also to be free of the traumatic fragmentariness that Byron's errant itinerary desires to erase:

"Pass we the long, unvarying course, the track / Oft trod, that never leaves a trace behind" (Childe Harold II.244-45). The question posed in the opening stanzas to Canto Two returns to haunt the Imperial "I" of the Beneviolent Briton: "What am I? Nothing; but not so art thou" (III.50). The answer here, however, is decidedly different. The "Hope and Pride" Byron placed in the posthumous existence of "art"—the posterity assured by aesthetic presentations (Darstellungen)—slips out of his signifying chain:

Thy waters washed them power while they were free, And many a tyrant since; their shores obey The stranger, slave, or savage; their decay Has dried up realms to des[art]s:—not so [] thou, Unchangeable save to thy wild waves' play Time writes no wrinkle on thine azure brow— (IV.1632-37) The "trackless" sea promises a freedom from a traumatic past that is distorted in the act that enacts this freedom: the action of writing a vicarious figure where the "I" can encrypt itself from itself (II.221).

To be untraceable in the public personae that personify one's text is to be transcendentally ironic. To make one's relation to the geopolitical world-system abysmally traceless is to be even more ironically above it all.

A world-historical irony is, however, identical to its subjectivist upgrade, for it pretends to provide the same thing—a transcendence, however momentary, of trauma, interminable analysis, and the "blood, blood, blood!" of Empire—the very thing that is not possible for he who lives on or survives in the limbo of writing. To write, as Byron's endlessly digressive style suggests, and as Christensen's "strong" text re-enacts, is an endless, unquenchable endeavor, for when the words stop, there re-reading begins.

Augusta encrypts the unspeakably private and the unrepresentably public by never enabling the reader to decide which is which, an undecidability that is no more than the precarious positioning of the literary subject within the perpetually distracted process of emergent globalization this essay has assayed to address.

Byron's invention of his death by writing remains endlessly alive by remaining interminably readable in terms of this traumatic pastness—a biographic, sociohistorical and geopolitical dimension that serves as an ingress into Byronic errancy—even if the text eschews a final tally. Irony, version 1.0 and 2.0, is, like the promise of a trauma-less existence, declined.

Byron writes his pain. The only other option is an absolute irony, which, if it is not insanity, is certainly Death-in-Life. Heidegger's "Being-towards-death" is another name for worldly fame or Life-in-Death—that is, for the impossible drive to master the madness of words or the wor(l)ding of the marketplace in the shadow of an imminent death that has already taken place: "—and what is writ, is writ" (IV.1661).

Since "Time writes no wrinkle on thine azure brow" the sea is not an option or a final solution, for it neither writes, nor remains to record the strain. Byron can find no fetishized arrest amidst the "trackless" sea: a figuration of his desire for a trauma-excised surface.

Byron's de-sublimation of "old Ocean" (Paradise Lost IV.165) does not prevent the sea—an Ur-Romantic topographic trope—from encoding the consumption of melancholy as an affective fix for Byronically-interpellated readers eager to deny the blood on their hands by enjoying it as a re-presentation: "Look on the hands with female slaughter red...

Flows there a tear of pity for the dead?" (I.902, 900). Of course, by sentimentally melting in the face of horror, one continues to enjoy it. The ever-popular marine image of Imperial striving that closes Childe Harold interpellates this melancholy enjoyment—"and if the freshening sea Made" the "Ocean['s]" "breakers.... a terror—'twas a pleasing fear"—a maritime image that was cynically, and hence all the more effectively, recoded for public consumption by Tennyson & Co. in the Victorian era (II.1648, 1651-53).

Since Byron is inexorably situated by the specificities of his space-time, he can never forget that the boundless violence of naval Imperialism is responsible for George Gordon's stepping into the empty place left by the violent death of the Wicked Lord's "proper" son in Corsica: "Arm! Ann! and out—it is—the cannon's opening roar!" / "Ann arm, my name!

A puny subject strikes / At thy great glory" (III.198). If post-feudal filiation stands in need of a theatrical "facta ficta," then Byron's attempt to supplement his assigned place in the signifying order—the publicly legitimated role of an aristocrat, an excessive, transgressive or libertine practice resisted by the middle classes that imaginatively consume it—can only reiterate the "strong" double binds decrypted in this essay.

Childe Harold pulses on unsubdued, one step ahead of its reification by a fiction marketplace continually expanding into the peripheries. Childe Harold insouciantly reinscribes Byron's support—"& therefore I give you all credit"—of socialized subjectification of the multitudo—"his Majesty's

Subjects" in the August name of the State Byron-tannia in his sororal letter (August 18, 1811) as "Subjection's woes" (BLJ II.74; I.359). Interminable encryptions continue to displace Byron from his theatrical stance of appurtenance to territorially-situated subject-groups—that is, to the class-fractions who (the brackets schematize to simulate an ending) entitled him (aristocratic), stereotyped him (middle class), and canonized (cultural workers) his errancy.

This overdetermined process of recuperation is stereotypically exemplified by the bringing of his dead body back from Greece to bury it near his ancestral seat (sedes)—"Then loath'd he in his native land to dwell, / Which seem'd to him more lone than Eremite's sad cell" (I.35-36)—a topographic containment of the literary eccentricity enabled by geographical topics of invention.

The unconscious materiality of the corpus, in the meantime, encrypts the crypt by reflexively staging Byron's all-too-mortal desire for a final fixity, a consummate encryption and a fetishized Immortality: "She is me," "Byronne" = "Byron," "I" = "I." The crypt continues to haunt "yet rife / With airy images, and shapes which dwell / Still unimpair'd, though old, in the soul's haunted cell" (III.43-45). Topos also seems to signify—"burial place."

[O]verdetermination" signifies the "multiple" significations of a signifying function in a dream-text (Sigmund Freud, The Interpretation of Dreams (First Part) [1900], The Standard Edition of the Complete Psychological Works IV, trans. James Strachey [London: Hogarth, 1953] 307; Cf. 282-84; Jean Laplanche and J. B. Pontalis, Vocabulaire de la Psychanalyse [Paris: PUF, 1967] 467-69). Althusser trans-coded Freudian undecidability to undermine a vulgar base/superstructure determinism, and to stress, instead, the heterogeneous levels ("political, economic, ideological, aesthetic, philosophic, scientific," etc.)

That determine the "global structure of a mode of production," a situation of "sur-determination" where the economic is one determinant among others (Louis Althusser, Lire: Le Capital I [Paris: Maspero, 1968] 123-31; Pour Marx

[Paris: Maspero, 1965] 99, 101; Lire: Le Capital II [Paris: Maspero, 1968] 57 [abbreviated as LC I, LC II hereafter]; Cf. Gregory Elliot, Althusser: The Detour of Theory [New York: Verso, 1987]; Robert J. C. Young, White Mythologies: Writing History and the West [New York: Routledge, 1990]; and The Althusserian Legacy, ed. Michael Sprinker [New York: Verso, 1994]).

For Freud, overdetermination indicates the "unknow[able] navel" of the dream-text (III). For Althusser, the omphalos or "the absence of the cause" (the "absence" of the "concept" of "the efficacity of a structure over its elements" [LC I.30]) of 'my' psychic problems (the normative or egological level of Freud's concern) is simultaneously a "'metonymic causality'" (a "formulation of J. A.

Miller to characterize a form of structural causality demarcated by J. Lacan in Freud," [LC II.65]) overdetermined by the libidinal economy of global capitalism continually building & continually decaying desolate.

The "Strong Determinations" in my title signify the interminable co-implication of "public/private" (Cf. Slavoj Zizek, "The Specter of Ideology," Mapping Ideology, ed. Slavoj Zizek [New York: Verso, 1994] 1-33), an abysmal causality that cannot be mastered by a deterministic or hermeneutic Marxism, yet remains readable on the level of the letter, the singular "evasions of as" marked by the signature, in this case, Lord B.—.

Jerome Christensen, Lord Byron's Strength: Romantic Writing and Commercial Society (Baltimore: Johns Hopkins UP, 1993) on Byron's public reproduction by the commercial marketplace and on his relationship to the economic world-system (abbreviated as CH hereafter). Cf. Daniel P. Watkins, Social Relations in Byron's Eastern Tales (Cranbury, NJ: Fairleigh Dickinson UP, 1987); Eric Meyer, "'I Know Thee not, I Loathe Thy Race':

Romantic Orientalism in the Eye of the Other," English Literary History 58.3 (Autumn 1991): 657-99; Nigel Leask, British Romantic Writers and the East: Anxieties of Empire (Cambridge: Cambridge UP, 1992); and Saree Makdisi,

Romantic Imperialism: Universal Empire and the Culture of Modernity (New York: Cambridge UP, 1998).

A Thousand Plateaus: Capitalism and Schizophrenia [1980], trans. Brian Massumi (Minneapolis: U of Minnesota P, 1987) 312 (abbreviated as TP hereafter). Anti-Oedipus: Capitalism and Schizophrenia [1972], trans. Robert Hurley, Mark Seem and Helen R. Lane (Minneapolis: U of Minnesota P, 1983) 213-14 (abbreviated as AO hereafter). The Tragedy of Hamlet, Prince of Denmark, I.v.97, 103; IV.ii.27-30 (William Shakespeare, The Riverside Shakespeare, ed. G. Blackmore Evans [Boston:

Houghton Mifflin, 1970]; my emphasis). All Shakespearean citations will be taken from this edition. For example, Jonathan Goldberg, "Fatherly Authority: The Politics of Stuart Family Images," Rewriting the Renaissance: The Discourses of Sexual Difference in Early Modern Europe, eds. Margaret Ferguson, Maureen Quilligan and Nancy Vickers (Chicago: U of Chicago P, 1986) 3-32.

For a convincing argument that the cosmos is a deterritorializing machine, see Brian Massumi's explication of the chaos theory structuring the thought-experiments of Deleuze and Guattari (The User's Guide to Capitalism and Schizophrenia: Deviations from Deleuze and Guattari [Cambridge:

MIT Press, 1992]). Massumi is also helpful on deterritorialization, but see D&G (AO; TP). Kafka: Toward A Minor Literature [1975], trans. Dana Polan (Minneapolis: U of Minnesota P, 1986) 83-84. Gayatri Chakravorty Spivak on the differance between representation (Vertretung, to speak for others by "proxy") and presentation (Darstellung) (A Critique of Post-Colonial Reason: Towards a History of the Vanishing Present [Cambridge: Harvard UP, 1999] 256-64).

Gilles Deleuze, Difference and Repetition [1968], trans. Paul Patton (New York: Columbia UP, 1994) for a properly philosophical elaboration of a transcendental empiricism of immanence (abbreviated as D hereafter). Jacques Lacan, Ecrits I (Paris: Seuil, 1966) 271, 33 (abbreviated as J hereafter). For Julia Kristeva, the "not-yet-meaningfull" flux of the "semiotic" is opposed to the patriarchal dominance of the "symbolic," a reified reiteration of meaning, or, more complexly, "the introduction of the object of jouissance into the `social norm'" (Revolution in Poetic Language [1974], trans. Margaret Waller [New York: Columbia UP, 1984] 75).

The "symbolic" relies on castration or on a "sacrificial logic" (CH xxi): "Far from unleashing violence, sacrifice shows how representing that violence is enough to stop it and to concatenate an order... based on representation: what is violent is the irruption of the symbol, killing substance to make it signify" (Kristeva 75). Sacrificial logic is Imperial logic: the "sacrifice" of English,

British, "subaltern [i.e., Scottish] and colonial populations" to disease in the name of Empire (Alan Bewell, Romanticism and Colonial Disease [Baltimore: Johns Hopkins UP, 1999] 85; Cf. 38, 248, 283). Imperial... "sacrifice confines violence to a single place [i.e., the abstract topos of Empire violently over-codes or endo-/exo-colonizes the peripheries within/ without the centre], making it a signifier," while "castration... perpetuat[es] the well-ordered signifier... positing it as sacred and unalterable within the enclosure of the Other" (Kristeva 75, 51).

The unconscious reason for empire is, I hazard, desire as the desire of the Other, a "vanguard Protestant" desire to serve the Other (simultaneously a hidden God-subject and the Other as object of beneviolence), to sacrifice whatever is demanded to Empire and all that name displaces: Nation, Race, Canon. All for a chance to "consume" the "Strange modes of merriment" produced by a global space organized under the aegis of this name (Childe Harold I.488; G. G. Byron, The Complete Poetical Works. Volumes I-VII [II], ed. Jerome J. McGann; abbreviated as B hereafter).

For Christensen, the "semiotic" writer in Byron resists the "sacrificial logic" of the British Empire—that is, the Imperial production of space qua the distribution of multiple sacrifices (soldiers, sailors, maharajahs, radicals, rioters, coolies): "Yet oft-times in his maddest mirthful mood Strange pangs would flash along Childe Harold's brow" (I.64-65). Bruce McLeod,

The Geography of Empire in English Literature: 1580-1745, for an explication of "vanguard Protestantism": a socio-symbolic integration of the peripheries plotted in longue duree terms as a desire to serve the abstract topos of "Imperial Britain" (John Dee's "IMPERIAL SHIP," "this Island Empire," or "Islandish Impire," General and Rare Memorials pertayning to the Perfecte Arte of Navigation [1577], quoted in McLeod)—a desire preformatting the actual emergence of the "British Empire" (2, 37, 41). Cf. Henri Lefebvre, The Production of Space [1974], trans. Donald Nicholson Smith.

In regard to encryption, see Nicholas Abraham and Maria Torok for the fundamentals (The Wolf Man's Magic Word: A Cryptonymy [1976], trans. Nicholas Rand [Minneapolis: U of Minnesota P, 1986]; Jacques Derrida for a theoretical explication ("Fors," trans.

Barbara Johnson, foreword to Abraham and Torok, xi-xlviii); Esther Rashkin (Family Secrets and the Psychoanalysis of Narrative [Princeton: Princeton UP, 1992]) and Anselm Haverkamp (Leaves of Mourning: Holderlin's Late Work, With an Essay on Keats and Melancholy, trans. Vernon Chadwick [Albany: SUNY, 1995]) for literary applications.

"A large chest-of-drawers crammed with accounts, Verses, love notes, legal proceedings, romances, With heavy locks of hair rolled in receipts, Hides fewer secrets than my sad brain. It is a pyramid, an immense sepulchre, Which contains more corpses than a mass grave" (The Flowers of Evil, [Spleen and the Ideal], "Spleen," Charles Baudelaire, Oeuvres Completes, eds.

Y.-G. Le Dantec and Claude Pichois, rev. ed. [Paris: Plieade, 1961] 69). "step beyond/no-step beyond/no beyond," "step of the no-step" (La Carte Postale: de Socrate a Freud et au-dela [Paris: Flammarion, 1980] 359, 377 [abbreviated as CP hereafter]. See notes 13 and 37 for Derrida and de Man on Abraham and Torok. Michel Foucault, The History of Sexuality: An Introduction, Volume I [1976], trans. Robert Hurley (New York: Pantheon, 1980).

Clifford Siskin, The Historicity of Romantic Discourse (New York: Oxford UP, 1988): a vivisection of the vie morte of lyric subjectivity. Ann Laura Stoler has situated the "cultivation of personality" analyzed by Foucault and critiqued by Siskin in an agonistic global force field overdetermined by race, class, gender, sexuality, etc. (Race and the Education of Desire: Foucault's History of Sexuality and the Colonial Order of Things [Durham, Duke UP, 1995] 191). Fredric Jameson, "Beyond the Cave: Demystifying the Ideology of Modernism" [1975] The Ideology of Theory: Essays 1971-1986, Volume II: The Syntax of History 115-32.

Walter Benjamin, Charles Baudelaire: A Lyric Poet in the Era of High Capitalism, trans. Harry Zohn (London: Verso, 1973). Benjamin's commentary on Baudelaire's "asocial" or fundamentally ambivalent "drive-structure" is cited by Derrida in a context that productively relates the stereotype of Byronic Satanism to Byron's ingenious practice of an encrypted writing:

"Or dans une note > Baudelaire definit le satanisme par l'ingenuite, l'incons-cience, l'ignorance ou la meconnaissance de soi, a moins que le > ou le > ne soit un supplement de simulacre diabolique ou l'exces de zele d'une pewersite sans fons" (For in a note "On Dangerous Liaisons," Baudelaire [who regards de Laclos's work as a "prepar[ation]" for "The age [temps] of Byron,"

(Oeuvres Completes 640)] defines satanism by ingenuity, unconsciousness, the ignorance or the misunderstanding of self, unless "to make oneself into an ingenue" or "to become an ingenue" is the supplement of a diabolical simulacrum or the excessive zeal of an abysmal perversity [Donner le Temps: 1. La Fausse Monnaie (Paris: Galilee, 1991) 210-11]). I cannot resist citing, slightly out of context, another bit of Baudelaire: "Satan s'est fait ingenu" (Satan has made himself into an ingenue [Oeuvres Completes 640]).

For Derrida, it is, from early on—that is, from the Poe-Baudelaire epigraph onwards—the problematic of a literary writing-towards-death that is at stake: "Ma mort est structurellement necessaire au prononce du Je" (My death is structurally necessary to saying 'I' [La Voix et le Phenomene: introduction au probleme du signe dans la phenomenologie de Husserl (Paris: PUF, 1967) 108]). David Simpson's critique of "historically uniform expressions of culpability" ("Is Literary History the History of Everything? The Case for 'Antiquarian' History," Sub-Stance: A Review of Theory and Literary Criticism 28.1 [1999]: 5-16 [11]), yet see John Barrell, The Infection of Thomas De Quincey:

A Psychopathology of Imperialism (New Haven: Yale UP, 1991), and Robert M. Maniquis, "Lonely Empires: Personal and Public Visions of Thomas De Quincey," Literary Monographs: Mid-Nineteenth Century Writers: Eliot, De Quincey, Emerson, eds. E. Rothstein and J. A.

Wittreich (Madison: U of Wisconsin P, 1976) in regard to how the "culture of culpability" is a romantic response to the dis-orienting transcription of social ills in terms of a religious rhetoric: "Nineteenth-century writers ceaselessly constructed analogies between self and society, and their works abound with secular transformations of sin and guilt" (Maniquis 52).

A bio-graphic unconscious informs reading "since biography is not something from which we can swerve," rather it "identifie[s] the arena of dispute" (Stanley Fish, "Biography and Intention," Contesting the Subject: Essays in the Postmodern Theory and Practice of Biography and Biographical Criticism, ed. William H. Epstein [West Lafayette, Indiana:

Purdue UP, 1991] 9-15 [15]). Biographical determination takes the form of a "triple analogy between poetic, personal and national identities" (Jerome Christensen, "Ecce Homo: Biographical Acknowledgement, the End of the French Revolution, and the Romantic Reinvention of English Verse" 53-84 [60]; abbreviated as EH hereafter).

After-Barthes refers (via the birth of the writerly text in S/Z [1970], trans. Richard Miller [Hill and Wang, 1974]), to my transcoding of Barthes in terms of the bio-geo-graphic overdetermination of an encrypted style of reading "this distracted globe."

For an analysis of this opposition from a praxis-oriented perspective, see Thomas P. Miller, The Formation of College English: Rhetoric and Belles Lettres in the British Cultural

Provinces (Pittsburgh: U of Pittsburgh P, 1997); for a theoretico-historical overview, see John Guillory, Cultural Capital: The Problem of Literary Canon Formation. Harold Bloom, The Anxiety of Influence 8-9; and, for an encyclopedic codification of earlier insights, The Western Canon: The Books and School of the Ages (New York:

Harcourt Brace, 1994). The characterization of Lacanian psychoanalysis as a voice that speaks from a "bouche" or an "hauteur" of arrogant self-certainty can be found in Derrida's fundamentally misguided "resistance to psychoanalysis" ("La Facteur de la Verite" [1975], CP 441-524 [510]). Derrida is echoing Deleuze-Guattari's troping of "despotic" social production as "the eminent voice" (AO [1972] 211). Mikkel Borsch-Jacobsen in regard to how Lacan does not neglect the "defiles of the signifier" in favour of a phonocentric "full speech" (Lacan: The Absolute Master, trans. Douglas Brick [Stanford: Stanford UP, 1991] 273).

Adonais 411, 495; Percy Bysshe Shelley, Poetry and Prose, eds. Donald H. Reiman and Sharon B. Powers (New York: Norton, 1977). Andrew Bennett's lucid analysis of the romantic habitus of placing one's "Hope and Pride" in the epitaphic inscription the "I" hopes to become in Romantic Poets and the Culture of Posterity (Cambridge:

Cambridge UP, 1999) neglects to relate the mattering "madness of words" (i.e.: the letters of encryption Christensen relentlessly decrypts) to the question of the signature, a tactic some of his auctores—a Jacques Derrida or a Maurice Blanchot—have made de rigueur. How, then, is one to deal with the drive for the desired name offered by Fame—that is, for this singular name borne in opposition to the exchangeable emptiness of a mass-produced name: a death drive that lives on the posthumous inscription that canonizes the writer above and beyond commercial contingencies?

A historicist focus on encryption is perhaps a way out of the dead end of de Man's Derrida or American deconstruction: "No degree of knowledge can ever stop this madness, for it is the madness of words" ("Shelley Disfigured," The Rhetoric of Romanticism [New York:

Columbia UP, 1984] 122). Crypto-analysis, on the other hand, "succeeds because of its very specific lexical interpretations coupled with a demonstration of how a genuine link between psychoanalysis and literary analysis can be established" ("Paul de Man, 1983," quoted on the back cover of Abraham and Torok's The Wolf Man's Magic Word).

Geoffrey Hartman has delineated the drive for the "imago du nom propre" that defines literature as an anagrammatic quest for a "hidden—spectral or specular name" he opposes to the "signature or proper name" (Hartman 93, 109). This opposition seems to apply to Shelley (i.e., Shell-Lyre; Timothy Morton, Shelley and the Revolution in Taste:

The Body and the Natural World [Cambridge, Cambridge UP, 1994] 79; Gary Farnell, "Rereading Shelley," English Literary History 60.3 [Autumn 1993]: 625-50) and John Keats ("Junkets," his "having been named" by Hunt), whereas for Lord Byron the aristocratic signature or (im)proper name is itself the specular or spectral name, since what Lordship or Sovereignty means to George Gordon is not what it means for a political economy of the sign. The inscription "Lord Byron" remains encrypted, mirrored, fractured, buried..

He was, of course, enjoying "the desire to be One"—"le desir d'etre Un," i.e., "he lov'd but one... that lov'd one"—and not the object-cause(s) of this fantasmic desire for desire: "... c'est que ce a quoi il a a faire, c'est a l'objet a, et que toute sa realisation au rapport sexuel aboutit au fantasme" (... it is because that which he has to deal with in his affairs is the objet a, and that his entire realization of the sexual relation results in the fantasm [Jacques Lacan, Le Seminaire de Jacques Lacan: Livre XX Encore, ed. Jacques-Alain Miller (Paris: Seuil, 1975) 12, 80]). Theodor W. Adorno.

The Jargon of Authenticity [1964], trans. Knut Tarnowski and Frederic Will (Evanston, Illinois: Northwestern UP, 1973) 152 (abbreviated as A hereafter). Georg Wilhelm Hegel, Phenomenology of Spirit [1807], trans. A. V. Miller (Oxford: Oxford UP, 1977) 476.

Zizek for the difference "between `constituted' identification ["ideal ego" or Idealich] and `constituting identification' ["ego-ideal" or Ich-Ideal]," the "ideal ego" Being "the image representing `what we would like to be,'" and the Other being "identification with the very place from where we are being observed, from where we look at ourselves so that we appear to ourselves likable, worthy of love" (The Sublime Object of Ideology [New York: Verso, 1989] 105).

The unconscious archiving is complex here since Byron appears to be quoting his own English Bards and Scotch Reviewers, where "ingenuous youth" is used (footnote to line 56) to refer to George Lamb, a dramatist Byron deigns to savage: "This LAMB must own, since his Patrician name Failed to preserve the spurious Farce from shame.

No matter, GEORGE continues still to write, Tho' now the name is veiled from public sight" (55-57; B I.400). George Gordon continues to write, since he must also assure himself of the "Patrician name" said to "preserve" his ovine innocence against the "shame[ful]" failure that afflicts a proper name when it circulates in "the public eye" of a print marketplace. He must veil, encrypt, drift.

The First Part of Henry the Fourth I.ii.104-5. Studies of the Byron-incest mis-relation note that the ingenue becomes Byron's way of figuring his "outlaw[ed]" desire to be "One": A "wandering" I-land "of his own dark mind" (Childe Harold III.19-20): "It is not a very long step from the assertion that the mind is its own place to the awful feeling that perhaps it is the only place" (Peter Thorslev Jr.,

"Incest as Romantic Symbol" Comparative Literature Studies 2 [1965]: 41-58 [55]): "the external view quickly dissolves as it becomes an image of his [Byron's] own mind" (Joanna E. Rapf, "The Byronic Heroine: Incest and the Creative Process" SEL: Studies in English Literature, 1500-1900 21.4 [Autumn 1981]: 637-45 [644]). Antonin Artaud, L'Ombilic des Limbes (Paris: Gallimard, 1968).

Jerome J. McGann, The Poetics of Sensibility (Oxford: Clarendon, 1996). William Hazlitt, "On Poetry in General" [1818/1819], Selected Writings, ed. Jon Cook. James Joyce, Ulysses (Harmondsworth: Penguin, 1992). Byron's travels force him to confront incommensurable "synchronic histories" situated in "distinct" and "differential loci of space and time," thereby enforcing the impossibility of a universal mode of cultural explanation (Makdisi 124, 13). Byron is unreconciled between his nostalgia for pre-/anti-modern "'states'" and his entanglement in Imperialism. If Byron "conveys a strong sense of the copresence of the 'states' ["'of society'"] through which he passes in the contemporary world order" (James Chandler, England in 1819:

The Politics of Literary Culture and the Case of Romantic Historicism [Chicago: U of Chicago P, 1998] 381; my emphasis), and if the sense of "strong" is taken in the sense of Lord Byron's Strength or Althusser's Freudian "sur-determination" of "different times" (LC I.130), it then becomes possible to outwork Chandler's questioning of the possibility of a "historicist" mode of cultural explanation via an interrogation of the "case form" ("Altering the Case: The Invention of the Historical Situation" 203-64): the "eccentric and inexorable itinerary" of "Romantic biography" (CH xxii).

The "Lordly eye" of Paradise Lost (III.578; John Milton, Complete Poems and Major Prose, ed. Merritt Hughes [New Jersey: Prentice Hall, 1957]) pre-curses Byron's Satanic desire to "traverse earth, / Invisible but gazing... / To climb the trackless mountain all unseen," for he is unable to achieve the panoptic God's eye-view Milton attained via his unproblematic subscription to the Protestant Idea of an English Nation—unproblematic, that is, in comparison to writers closer to Byron's sensibility, i.e.,

Spenser, Dryden or Pope (III.51-52; II.221). Bruce McLeod, "The 'Lordly Eye': Milton and the Strategic Geography of Empire," Milton and the Imperial Vision, ed. Balachandra Rajan and Elizabeth Sauer [Pittsburgh: Duquesne UP, 1999] 48-66).

Byron the Wanderer cannot incarnate Milton the Geographer because the latter's transcendental re-source has become a "source" located out there in the geopolitical world: "Oh, thou Parnassus! whom I now survey... soaring snow-clad through thy native sky" (I.612, 615; emphasis added). In regard to the resistance encoded by the word "Bard" contra "imperial nominalism" ("scientific" reifications of endo-colonial territories; i.e., the "census" or the "survey"), and to English attempts to domesticate the bardic figure in the name of Imperial nationalism, see Katie Trumpener, Bardic Nationalism: The Romantic Novel and the British Empire (Princeton: Princeton UP, 1997) 3-34.

Derrida's speculations on Freud (CP 431 & 275-437), Laplanche and Pontalis (364-67) and Lacan. The sentiment of universal benevolence enables, as Howard Caygill has argued in The Art of Judgment (New York: Blackwell, 1989), the apparent resolution of epistemological, aesthetic and temporal dilemmas by affectively soldering the putatively providential proportioning of sentiment and intellect, sensibility and reason, etc.

Bewell on the British Empire's anxiety, in relation to the fantasmic desire to be "This fortress built for Nature for herself/ Against infection and the hand of war," The Tragedy of King Richard the Second II.i.43-44. Alexander Gerard, An Essay on Taste [1759]; excerpted in The Sublime:

A Reader in Eighteenth-Century Aesthetic Theory, eds. Andrew Ashfield and Peter de Bolla (Cambridge: Cambridge UP, 1996). Harold Bloom, The Visionary Company: A Reading of English Romantic Poetry, rev. ed. (Ithaca: Cornell UP, 1971) 247.

The complex relations marked by the signifiers "Byron" and "Irony" cannot be pursued here, where the dominant literary problematic remains encryption, yet it is hard to see how irony's "incorrigible reflexivity"—"when," in the words of Friedrich Schlegel, "irony runs wild and simply wont let itself be governed at all" ("On Incomprehensibility" [1800], Theory as Practice:

A Critical Anthology of Early German Romantic Writings, ed. Jochen Schulter-Sasse, trans. Elizabeth Mittman and Mary R. Strand [Minneapolis: U of Minnesota P, 1997] 118-28 [125])—is available to Byron except as what it is to his later readers: "the ironies of a poetic self-criticism" that prevents the factical in-mixing of the subject in the world-system from producing self-disgust, self-hatred or self-contempt by providing a semblance of "self-identity" (Paul Hamilton, "Keats and Critique," Rethinking Historicism: Critical Readings in Romantic History, ed. Marjorie Levinson [Oxford: Blackwell, 1989] 108-42 [135]). Byrony?

The becoming-theatrical of English politics in the Renaissance is a New Historicist truism (i.e., Jonathan Goldberg, James I and the Politics o[Literature: Jonson, Shakespeare, Donne and Their Contemporaries [Baltimore: Johns Hopkins UP, 1983]).

Christensen argues that the theatricality of the French Revolution—"a theatrical state, where all—actors and spectators—must speak and, speaking, struggle"—and of the Burkean counterrevolution were both revised by English romanticism's "biographic inventiveness," or, in my case, an encrypted invention dis-places theatrical reterritorialization without reserve (EH 55-56).

In regard to the "yron" in Lord B—. I refer the reader to Spenser's "Talus," Imperial strong man par excellence. Childe Burun was subliminally enjoying The Faerie— >—Queene during his seeking abroad:

But when she parted hence, she left her groome An] yron man, which did on her attend Alwayes, to execute her stedfast doome, And willed him with Artegall to wend, And doe what euer thing he did intend. His name was Talus, made of yron mould, Immoueable, resistlesse, without end. Who in his hand an yron flale did hould, With which he thresht out falshood, and did truth vnfould. (The Faerie Queene v.i.12: 1-9; my emphasis) joshua david gonsalves is a recipient of the Halsband Fellowship for Eighteenth-Century Studies at New York University. He has published reviews in postcolonial and romanticist journals and is currently completing a book-length study entitled "Keats Goes Global: The Geopolitics of Poetic Production."

MAZEPPA (BYRON)

Mazeppa is a Romantic narrative poem written by Lord Byron in 1819, based on a popular legend about the early life of Ivan Mazepa (1639-1709), a Ukrainian gentleman who later became Hetman of the Ukrainian Cossacks. According to the poem, the young Mazeppa, while serving as a page at the Court of King John Casimir II, has a love affair with a Countess named Theresa, who was married to a much older man.

The Count, on discovering the affair, punishes Mazeppa by tying him naked to a wild horse and setting the horse loose. The bulk of the poem describes the traumatic journey of the hero strapped to the horse. The poem has been praised for its "vigor of style and its sharp realization of the feelings of suffering and endurance". This poem also inspired Alexander Pushkin to write his poem *Poltava* as an answer to Byron's poem.

The poem opens with a framing device: Mazeppa and the Swedish King Charles XII, together with their armies, are retreating from the Battle of Poltava, where they were defeated by the Russians. Exhausted and war-weary, the two men set up camp for the night. (Stanzas 1-2) The King admires Mazeppa's horsemanship, and Mazeppa offers to tell him how he learnt this skill (Stanza 4).The poem then switches to the first person.

Mazeppa describes his youth and his service as a page to King John Casimir II in Poland. (Stanza 4). He becomes acquainted with Theresa, an beautiful Orientalized woman who "had the Asiatic eye" (l. 208). She is married to a Count who is thirty years her senior (l. 155). Mazeppa falls passionately in love with her (l. 266-7), is unable to control his passions (l. 290-295), and they meet at night and consummate their love. (l. 298-300)

However, the Count's men catch them together (l. 325-6) and bring him to the Count. The Count orders an unusually cruel punishment: Mazeppa is to be tied naked to a steed, which is then to be taunted and set loose. (Stanza 9) Stanzas 10 to 18 recount the steed's flight across Eastern Europe, emphasizing the pain, suffering and confusion that Mazeppa feels.

However, the horse has seemingly limitless energy. Mazeppa nearly dies twice. In Stanza 13, he describes himself "full in death's face" (l. 557), but is restored when the horse swims through a river. Stanza 18 concludes with a description of "an icy sickness" and his vision of a raven flying overheard, ready to feast on his corpse. However, in Stanza 19, Mazeppa awakes to find himself in bed, with his wounds being tended by a "Cossack Maid" (l. 817). In the final stanza, Mazeppa's narrative ends. The poet-narrator describes Mazeppa preparing his bed for the evening. The King is already asleep (l. 867 - 880)

There are historical sources which verify that Ivan Mazepa served in the Polish Court to John Casimir I. However, it is unclear why he left Poland in 1663 and returned to his homeland in what is now the Ukraine. There is no historical evidence to support that Mazepa was exiled from Poland because of a love affair, or that he was punished by being strapped to a wild horse.

However, this colorful legend was in circulation before Byron published his poem. Voltaire repeats it in *History of Charles XII, King of Sweden* (1731). This appears to have been Byron's main source for his poem: his 'Advertisement' to the poem includes three long quotations from this work. Several critics have also speculated that Byron was familiar with the novel *Memoires d'Azema* (1764) by the French writer André Dorville, as there are significant similarities between the plot of this novel and of Byron's poem. Byron's references to Mazepa's participation, in the Great Northern War alongside Charles XII, and their eventual defeat, are historically accurate.

ANALYSIS

Many critics see *Mazeppa* as a transitional work in Byron's oeuvre. Its dates of composition (1818-1819) place it between the earlier Eastern tales such as *The Prisoner of Chillon* (1817), which describe agonized, maudlin Byronic heroes and the later satirical, ironic *Don Juan* (1818-9). Leslie Marchand argues that *Mazeppa* is a partly unsuccessful work, as it is torn between high emotion and lighter irony. Mark Phillipson also sees *Mazeppa* as a transitional work of a "mongrel genre, the historical verse-romance".

He argues that the poem is characterized by "moral

ambivalence", and it remains unclear whether Mazeppa is a sympathetic hero or not.

The question of whether the audience is expected to sympathize with Mazeppa has long been a subject for critical discussion. W.H. Marshall (1961) argues that Mazeppa is entirely unsympathetic: a "garrulous and egoistic old man" who never atones for his crime and whose hackneyed description of his passion for Teresa "becomes tedious at once". Jerome McGann (1968) takes the opposite view, arguing that Mazeppa's "wild ride" acts an initiation process which makes him into a mature hero who is able to restrain his passions, unlike King Charles. He compares Mazeppa to Meursault, the existentialist hero of Albert Camus' novel *The Stranger* (1942).

Hubert Babinski (1974) also offers a sympathetic reading of the character Mazeppa, pointing out his kindness to Charles and the horses in the opening and closing chapter. Babinski suggests that the hero Mazeppa is "one of Byron's most realistic creations, heroic within the bounds of human potential" and that he is a "fine specimen of a man". He further argues that Mazeppa's death-in-life experiences during his "wild ride" are central to the poem's meaning and symbolic of the possibilities of human transformation and rebirth. He argues that the French painters who took up the Mazeppa theme further developed this idea.

More recent interpretations have attempted to apply the insights of critical theory to the poem. Zbigniew Bialas (1999) offers a Saidian postcolonial reading, suggesting that Byron orientalizes Eastern Europe and attempts to stamp an identity on Mazeppa, who nonetheless evades fixed national and political identities. Jane Stabler (2004) reads the poem through the prism of postmodern theory, suggesting that uses Byron's *Mazeppa* as an example of a poem which "draws attention to the fictive contours of history".

Literary significance and reception

Babinski points out that although *Mazeppa* received a flurry of reviews upon publication, later critics of Byron have rarely addressed the poem. Certainly there is less scholarship on *Mazeppa* than many of Byron's other narrative poems, and *Mazeppa* does not appear in Byron anthologies such as the 1978 Norton Critical Anthology.

However, Byron's poem was popular among his contemporaries and provoked the rise of a 'Mazeppa Cult' among his contemporaries. Several French artists produced paintings depicting Mazeppa's "wild ride" including Théodore Géricault, Eugène Delacroix, and Claude-Joseph Vernet. Currier and Ives published an illustrated edition of Byron's poem in 1846.

In Russia, Aleksandr Pushkin's narrative poem *Poltava* (1828-29) deals with a later stage of Ivan Mazepa's life, his switching of allegiance from the Russians to the Swedes and his defeat in the Battle of Poltava. In the theatre, a show called "Mazeppa, or the Tartar Horse" premiered at the Cirque olympique in Paris in 1825. This was copied in both the USA and England In the USA version of this act, Mazeppa was played a female, Adah Isaacs Menken, who was scandalously clad only in tights.

Mazeppa became the most widely performed drama in the American west from the 1860s until the turn of the century, and was also popular in London. In 1877, Albert Aiken wrote a dime novel called *The Indian Mazeppa or The Madman of the Plains*, where the Mazeppa myth is transposed to the Wild West. In the early twentieth century, a film *Mazeppa or the Wild horse of Tartary*, based on the stage play derived from the Byron poem, dir. Francis Boggs, (1910) was produced in the USA.

Bibliography

Lord Byron. Harold Bloom, Karen Wills & Duke Pesta. Chelsea House Publishing, 2003).

Lord Byron's Religion: A Journey into Despair. Paul D. Barton. (Edwin Mellen Press, 2003).

George Gordon, Lord Byron. Martin Garrett. (Oxford Univ Press, 2001).

The Literary Relationship of Lord Byron and Thomas Moore. Jeffery W. Vail. (Johns Hopkins Univ Press, 2000).

Lord Byron and Madame De Stael: Born for Opposition. Joanne Wilkes. (Ashgate Publishing, 1999).

Lord Byron. Peter W. Graham. (Twayne Publishing, 1998).

Lord Byron's Strength: Romantic Writing and Commercial Society. Jerome Christensen. (Johns Hopkins Univ Press, 1995).

George Gordon, Lord Byron. Ed. Harold Bloom. (Chelsea House Publishing, 1990).

Lord Byron and His Contemporaries. Charles E. Robinson. (Univ of Delaware Press, 1982).

Lord Byron As a Satirist in Verse. Claude M. Fuess. (Haskell House Publishing, 1973).

Lord Byron & His Circle. William S. Pratt. (Haskell House Publishing, 1970).

The Dra+mas of Lord Byron: A Critical Study. Samuel Claggett Chew. (Scholarly Press, 1970).

The Pilgrim Poet, Lord Byron of Newstead. A. Brecknock. (1911).

The Love Affairs of Lord Byron. F. H. Gribble. (1910).

Byron: The Last Phase. Richard Edgcumbe. (1909).

Lord Byron and his Detractors. J. Murray. (1906).

Astarte: A Fragment of Truth concerning George Gordon Byron. Milbanke, Ralph. (1905).

Last Links with Byron, Shelley and Keats. W. Graham. (1898).

The Life, Letters and Journals of Lord Byron. Thomas Moore (John Murray, 1892).

Life of Byron. Roden Noel. (1890).

Byron re-studied in his Dramas. W. Gerard. (1886).

Lord Byron and his Works. C. Cantù. (1883).

The Real Lord Byron. John Cordy Jeaffreson. (1883).

Lord Byron Vindicated. E. W. Preston. (1876).

Byron: Essays and Studies. A. C. Swinburne. (1875).

Lady Byron Vindicated: A History of the Byron Controversy. Harriet Beecher Stowe. (1870).

A Vindication of Lord Byron. Alfred Austin. (1869).

Conversations with Lord Byron. Lady Blessington. (1834).

The Life of Lord Byron. John Galt. (1830).

Conversations on Religion, with Lord Byron and Others ... Previous to His Lordship's Death. James Kennedy. (1830).

Lord Byron and Some of His Contemporaries; with Recollections of the Author's Life, and of His Visit to Italy. Leigh Hunt. (1828).

Narrative of a second visit to Greece: The Last Days of Lord Byron. E. Blaquiere. (1825).

The Last Days of Lord Byron. W. Parry. (1825).

A Narrative of Lord Byron's Last Journey to Greece. P. Gamba. (1825).

Lord Byron. Louisa S. Belloc. (1824).

Letters on the Character and Poetical Genius of Lord Byron. Sir Samuel E. Brydges. (1824).

The Life and Genius of Lord Byron. Sir Cosmo Gordon. (1824).

Recollections of the Life of Lord Byron. Ed. A. R. C. Dallas. (1824).

Journal of the Conversations of Lord Byron. T. Medwin. (1824)

Remarks, Critical and Moral, on the Talents of Byron. C. C. Colton. (1819).